*Conditions of Rational Inquiry*

# CONDITIONS OF
# RATIONAL INQUIRY

## A STUDY IN THE PHILOSOPHY OF VALUE

BY

## DAVID POLE

UNIVERSITY OF LONDON
THE ATHLONE PRESS
1961

*Published by*
THE ATHLONE PRESS
UNIVERSITY OF LONDON
*at 2 Gower Street London* WC1
*Distributed by Constable & Co. Ltd*
*12 Orange Street London* WC2

*Canada*
*University of Toronto Press*
*Toronto* 5

*U.S.A.*
*Oxford University Press Inc*
*New York*

*Printed in Great Britain by*
WESTERN PRINTING SERVICES LTD
BRISTOL

# Contents

# Introduction

A READER on opening a book may expect an indication, at least in general terms, of the themes to be discussed in it; but in the present case I find myself in some difficulty. Among the older logicians 'judgement' was a recognized topic—judgement viewed in one way at least. And the phrase 'value judgement' has also a fairly wide currency. But little need seems to have been felt of bringing the two notions together, nor again of linking them with a third, which I can hardly even find a plain or simple name for: let me call it merely thought, conceived as a process or growth, or progressive inquiry. It will be, perhaps, the best statement of my general aim to say that I hope to establish connexions holding between these several concepts which may serve to make all of them more intelligible.

To say that one cannot even express one's project in any existing language may sound too like a huge claim to originality. But after all we can name one set of humps rather than another as a single hill or ridge of hills, and not alter the landscape; the change nonetheless has its significance. It is, I fear, bibliographically inconvenient; for such a plan must overrun the departments of logic and ethics, and perhaps of epistemology too. But I have to confess that I am not convinced that the breaking-down of bibliographical departments, tiresome as it may be, is always entirely reprehensible in one who sets out to be a philosopher. One cannot but follow where the argument seems to lead, but I admit that if I have followed it rightly it leads over very various ground. Along with 'value judgement' we have another, older notion, also much discussed, that of 'moral judgement'; indeed, though the two cannot be strictly coextensive, they are often taken as introducing much the same topics. And together they are treated as largely self-contained. My contention shall be, on the contrary, that a proper prolegomena to moral philosophy, at least to the issues generally dealt with under the heading of moral philosophy, must be a study of inquiry in general. The converse holds too: judgement itself is hardly intelligible apart from all notion of evaluation.

Moral judgement, I said, has been much discussed. Certainly the phrase appears on the title-page of some half-dozen accessible books; it would be thought no more than a paradox to suggest that in reality it has hardly been discussed at all. Yet the point perhaps may be arguable; at least in Britain one may pick out—among the many shifts and movements in the history of thought—two main schools or tendencies. And on one side the whole notion of moral judgement has been deliberately repudiated, sentiments, attitudes or moral decisions being put in its place: while on the other, where we might look for its exponents, we shortly find that the term that we are being offered is no longer 'judgement' but 'intuition'. That is not obviously the same thing: it is the next best, perhaps, or even better. The notion of judgement may prove on closer inspection to have no right to separate existence; but if so it is a point to be proved, not passed over. The two notions look very different; no doubt this appearance may be illusory, but the illusion, at least, needs to be accounted for.

Besides, this alternative notion, intuition, has been made the target of much hostile criticism, which might have missed judgement or passed it by. Consequently other alternative concepts have been set up in its place. These competing claims are what meet anyone approaching the subject; so that it seems that to reach our objective we must first cut a way through a battle already in progress. But this course may have at least one advantage, that if we get through these preliminaries we shall ultimately be surer of our own ground and know where we stand in the end. My first chapter will therefore be devoted to objections urged against the notion of intuition, which, I fear, must involve much recapitulation of familiar arguments. But these need sorting-out. Next I shall turn to its proposed replacements; and with this ground covered, I shall be free to proceed to my main theme: broadly, the place of evaluation in the process of rational inquiry. Lastly, by way of concrete application of the views developed here, I shall add a more detailed discussion of moral judgement itself—ending with some special problems falling within the content of morals, which even a conscientious reader may omit if he wishes.

# I

## A Critique of Intuition

FROM the eighteenth century to the present the appeal to the notion of intuition has figured largely in British moral philosophy; it is the natural expedient for those to use whose wish is to vindicate the rationality of morals without recourse to ambitious speculation. For the concept lies ready to hand: without intuitions we can know nothing—such is the contention. All our knowledge ultimately comes back to them. And, that being so, it seems that a great part of our ordinary moral beliefs can be saved for us at the least possible theoretical expense. Here we have the intuitionist's proposal, and what, he will naturally ask, could be more advantageous or attractive?

So it might seem, but its attraction has not been felt equally strongly on all sides. Indeed, for a purely theoretical issue, it would be hard to name any concept that has provoked a deeper or more stubborn antipathy. And its opponents represent what remains, with all allowance for changing modes and the splits and re-groupings of schools, the dominant tradition in the broader movement of British thought. The feeling is pretty deeply fixed. To naturalistic or empirically minded philosophers the name 'intuition' represents, not merely one fallacy among others, such as one meets in the normal business of inquiry, but something altogether more sinister: the last heirs of the Enlightenment recognize the badge of their old enemy and close their ranks against the power of Unreason itself. Whole systems of philosophy have been built less on any positive basis than on the hope of dispensing with intuition: any expedient has proved acceptable—the reduction of reasoning to tautology or convention, the founding of science on voluntary definition or arbitrary postulates and the total extrusion of ethics from the province of significant discourse—rather than return to the old basis. At the same time in the human sciences, which have sprung largely

B

from the same philosophical tradition, the term has been long since under ban: no psychologist without risking his scientific status—a matter of some importance to psychologists—could allow the term 'intuition' in his vocabulary.

Attitudes as deep and vigorous as these, even prejudices, if you prefer to think them so, are not planted and do not flourish for nothing: but this hostility to the notion of intuition cannot be traced to any single root, for the term has been used vaguely as well as variously. John Stuart Mill in his essay on Coleridge, a semi-popular work, distinguished two great historical schools, the one being that of Locke and his followers who seek to found all knowledge on experience, and the other—apparently grouping under one head the rationalists, Kant and the German idealists—who claim to attain by intuition to a knowledge of truths not otherwise accessible. This large indiscriminate embrace could hardly forward the interests of intuitionism or recommend the concept to cautious minds. But the many diverse uses of the term do not concern us here. Metaphysicians, before Mill's time and since, have certainly laid claim to a kind of acquaintance with Reality truer or more intimate than anything that science or sense-perception can give us. Legitimate or otherwise, however, these claims need not detain us; this is not the form of the concept that moral philosophers have relied on. Nor need I dwell at much greater length on intuition as the non-philosophical understand it: on those confident assertions, not about 'Reality' but about very ordinary things—say, the weather or the success of a marriage—which prove justified in the event, although on the basis of no communicable evidence. It is, however, likely enough that this common use of the term, no doubt first derived from its philosophical use, may have contributed to its falling into disrepute. Claims such as those I have spoken of are generally testable in the long run; but by hypothesis they are not testable, nor even arguable, here and now. For broadly what we mean by 'intuition', in this sense, is knowledge or true belief that the believer cannot support with any *logos*. And that alone is exasperating to businesslike minds. Since this faculty, too, is a little mysterious at first glance, whatever account we may give of it on reflection, those who are themselves unintuitive may be slightly on edge already. Whether in fact tough-minded philosophers, Benthamites, positivists and the like, have more often than not been unintuitive people, or largely so, I do not know; but to speak the truth I sometimes suspect it. Nor is it safe to assume that a man's professional and non-professional attitudes or reactions can never coalesce in philosophy, even though the common centre that they turn on, the hub of the wheel, so to speak, is no more than the form of a word. This term 'intuition' has certainly been widely suspected of being a title arbitrarily assumed by any prejudice or dogma that sought to escape trial by rational argument.

But however far the confusion of popular with technical usage, and of romantic metaphysics with rationalist epistemology, may have contributed to the formation of a prejudice, it alone can hardly suffice to account for the deliberate stand taken by thoughtful philosophers: yet we find that the philosophical notion of intuition formulated with all Cartesian rigor has proved hardly more acceptable than the other. We must pause at this point, then, to consider more accurately what it involves.

Intuition has often been defined as direct knowledge. It seems that if any truths are to be known discursively, that is by inference, there must be some, at least, that are non-discursively or directly known. For otherwise the inference will lack a premiss and never begin. Such direct knowledge is intuition. Knowledge, it further seems, would indeed not be knowledge if it still allowed the possibility of error; and in any case what we have to do with here is supposed to be directly presented to us—in its own shape, so to speak—so that there is no room for error to creep in. So most intuitionists have argued, though with one or two notable exceptions. For in speaking of knowledge, it seems, we are referring to a particular state of mind; knowledge is something mental, not physical. And here, in a state of mind, nothing can be hidden or obscure, for the reason that there is nowhere to hide it. (We may leave aside the account given of unconscious mental states, which, even if we accept the notion at its face-value, will represent in effect a different and additional concept, rather than a modification of the old one.) Any particular conscious state will be distinguished from another by nothing but its own internal character, hence knowledge must announce itself for what it is. If we know something, we also know that we know it; a true intuition is infallible.

Let us suppose that some object such as a Berkelean idea or a sense-impression is before the mind. A sensible idea can conceal nothing; its face is its fortune, like the milkmaid's. And philosophers seem to have been surprisingly ready to be squared on such terms; for, they seem to reason, at least the dowry cannot come short here or give grounds for wrangling later on. But suppose now, instead of a sense-impression, that certain simple concepts are similarly present to the mind; it would appear that whatever relations may hold between such concepts must be present too. The relations directly depend on the visible character of the concepts themselves. A statement, then, asserting these relations will appear as self-evidently true: we need no more than to have the concepts before our minds and to know the conventional meaning of the marks that serve to express them.

Here, in outline, we have the traditional view, or at least a reasonably representative version of it. Those truths for which such knowledge is claimed are, however, nothing recondite or unfamiliar, they involve no insight into the heart of Reality. Fair samples are the proposition that two things equal to the same thing are also equal to one another, or that no part is ever greater than the whole of which it is part; and to these we must add, on behalf of the ethical writers whom I have mentioned, the basic principles of practical morality. Most intuitionists, though not all, have taken mathematical and logical truths as their paradigm; so that principles of morals— that one ought to keep one's promises, for example—were seen as the same sort of propositions as those that I have cited. And most though not all of them, too, have thought of true intuition as infallible.

Such is the view, then, and it lacks neither authority nor

antiquity to maintain it. For we may follow it back from the British realists of the present century to Descartes and Locke, and again from them back to Aristotle. Yet after all we might discover a different parentage, might trace it to rather humbler origins, supposing its great patrons will let us. For those who lack the advantages of philosophy rarely appeal to intuition in support of their views, except, perhaps, in the more popular sense; yet they claim often enough to see or to be able to see that something that has been asserted is true—to see that one thing must follow from another or that one action is right and another wrong. Now seeing in the primary or literal sense of the word involves the use of one's eyes; hence the present sense, in which it does not, requires to be distinguished at least for philosophical purposes. Our use of the verb 'to see' when we speak of 'seeing that one proposition follows from another' can hardly be called metaphorical, though plainly it was so once. At all events the one usage derives from the other, and the philosophical term 'intuition' seems to reflect this well-established, secondary use. Intuition is thought of as a sort of seeing. Indeed one may suspect rather more; these doctrines would never have made such headway, have proved so readily acceptable, if the ground had not been prepared for them already, a path was worn by our earlier habits of speech. For our old ways draw us insensibly and lead us back with a kind of gravitation.

This being so, there is at least one complaint sometimes made against the notion of intuition which may be summarily dismissed: that what we have here is no more than a gratuitous resort to jargon, a show of vocabulary—to cover, perhaps, a shortage of ideas. Where ordinary language has one word for two things a technical terminology distinguishes them: it is required to do so. There are, however, more serious objections to be taken notice of: though, indeed, the first that we must deal with is still not far from that popular movement of thought that I have already referred to. The appeal to intuition is avowedly an appeal to some sort of subjective certainty, to the internal character of certain distinctive states of mind, which bring with them an assurance beyond dispute. That to its critics represents a mere bar or veto on thought, a dogmatic, unarguable claim; the appeal to intuition that serves to back whatever belief its adherents may choose to withdraw from the arena of rational disputation. That is a telling accusation, the more so for the ghosts that it raises. For it stirs echoes of old battlefields and ancient champions; the freedom of speculative inquiry is a cause that we have reason to feel deeply.

But let us not too easily be borne away; the defenders of intuition, in the sense in which we are concerned with it, will certainly not admit the charge of irrationalism. And before we line up Pritchard and Sir David Ross with Meletus and Galileo's inquisitors it will be well to look closer. Intuitionism, we have seen, is advanced on rational grounds and no other support claimed for it than those reasons that are explicitly given. It has indeed been maintained that truths known intuitively need no further argument; for we find the notion expressly introduced to supply a need for such ultimate truths, which in their very nature are unarguable. If this, then, is to be made an objection, those who make it—to avoid an infinite process of demonstration—leave themselves with the large task of finding an alternative theory of first principles. Now a theory which shall leave principles of this sort open to argument is not something easily to be found. As to the philosophical critics of intuition, an intuitionist might observe that their own rationalism is not much more in evidence than that of the philosophers whom they criticize —at least if the great mark of rationality is to leave everything for argument to settle. For the expedient which they have generally resorted to has been the use of purely volitional definitions or of edicts in one form or another which they themselves decide on or lay down. These, as a basis for principles, are evidently no more arguable than the intuitions that they supersede; (though so long as the issue remains inside ethics plain irrationalism may offer an alternative; so long, that is to say, as ethics itself can be isolated as a separate and self-contained department and the barrier holds).

But with all this the objection retains its force. Let us grant on general grounds that premisses of some sort must be known indubitably: even so when once particular candidates are put forward difficulties will surely arise. The history of thought tells us of too many 'self-evident truths', propositions based confidently on intuition, which the progress of science has swept aside. The scientifically minded may have other objections to raise as well; the matter, it seems, has yet another side to it. For suppose that we admit that logic has no further account to give of such ultimate principles, it does not follow, surely, that psychology can do no better. One might answer, no doubt, that the business of psychology is not with propositions or truths—apart, of course, from those that are themselves psychological truths—but rather with states of mind: but just here is the difficulty. It seems that certain states of mind, which we can at least distinguish as being states of strong conviction, are to be described or installed as 'intuitions'—and so put beyond further investigation. But how are we to know, we may be asked, that these interesting states might not repay study and admit of psychological explanation? Here, then, from a somewhat different approach, we meet the same complaint as before; in effect the appeal to intuition puts a closure on rational inquiry.

To resort to this appeal, after all, is not to proceed with an argument but rather to put a stop to it. For there are times at which we are prompted to say, perhaps in face of obstinate questioning, that we merely see that such and such is true. Sometimes we may be right to say so: there may be points reached in arguments at which it is logically proper to refuse further reasons for what one says. But if so, it would still remain true that the refusal ought not to be seen as a further informative answer. The rôle of the term intuition is the same here as that of the verb 'to see', it functions as a logical silencer. It tells our hearers, perhaps, that we assert something 'because it's obvious': and that, except in a negative way, tells them nothing more than that we assert it.

At the same time the difficulty as to which particular propositions are to be assigned to intuition remains; for one man's intuitions are presumably as good as another's. Intuitions are said to be unquestionable, and truth cannot conflict with itself: where two would-be

intuitions are found in conflict we need guidance as to how to proceed. And the very theory of intuitions seems to make such guidance
impossible, for the appeal to intuition is an ultimate one. This
difficulty, indeed, may not be acutely felt so long as our discussion
of first principles is confined to the province of logic, perhaps even
of natural science. Here, before one starts to quarrel over first
principles one needs to be pretty well advanced in the subject. But
in morals the case is different. Ordinary people may not question
the so-called laws of thought or argue as to whether the same body
can be in two places simultaneously, but they certainly come into
collision over the questions of right or wrong conduct, which,
ultimate or not, not infrequently seem pretty intractable. And this
is an argument which has weighed, perhaps with scholars, certainly,
I think, in the popular mind, more than any other.

Indeed the popular view may not be wholly clear. Moral disagreement might be taken to cast doubt simply on the reality or
trustworthiness of moral intuitions, or again on the notion of intuition generally. If the latter—and that is our present concern—we
shall once again be faced with the problem of finding an alternative
that will serve us in fields other than ethics; (for while we confine the
issue to ethics we can fall back on simple scepticism, we can, that is,
deny the reality of moral knowledge). But the issue now gets lost
amidst complexities. After all there are numerous familiar alternatives already in the field; we might imagine, then, that the problem
of first principles can be split up and a head-on encounter avoided.
Thus, for example, apparently indubitable principles, those that it
makes no sense to speak of doubting short of supposing a Cartesian
demon—and these were always the intuitionist's first examples—can
plausibly be recategorized as 'analytic'. And for the rest, if the first
principles of our substantial or factual thinking still give trouble,
there are other objections to basing them on intuition: the axiom of
causality, for instance, the intuitionist's likeliest candidate here, can
at least be shown to be a different sort of thing from the laws of
thought or the principle of excluded middle. The problem of induction may after all remain intractable; but one can hope for better

progress in time—or in the last resort fall back on simple postulates like Russell, or on volitional definitions.

Besides, the force of the difficulty remains; however hard it may be to provide a comprehensive alternative, we can scarcely retain the same faith in moral intuition if we find that our strongest convictions clash. And such clashes are audible enough. Indeed it may be that even within morals we should distinguish between scholarly and popular views; for it has also been denied that the moral views of different societies conflict, or conflict at all widely, on those few fundamental matters for which the authority of intuition is invoked. As to this we must leave the experts to decide. The general impression is, certainly, that modern anthropology has opened the eyes of reflective people to the variousness of moral codes. Each country has its laws, as Chaucer says,

'In sondry ages
And sondry londes, sondry ben usages.'

The mere fact of such differences makes intuition an uncomfortable notion to rely on, whatever counter-attacks the intuitionist may launch on his critics. And for the rest, the sense of the difficulties that it involves has no doubt been sharpened by the stiffer claims sometimes made on its behalf; by the rigid distinction drawn between what is properly called knowledge on the one hand—a mental state *sui generis*—and any sort of belief, though both true and well-founded, on the other. Here we meet claims that may arouse some stir of scepticism even in the mildest of critics: the claim that knowledge properly so called not only excludes error but carries its own guarantee; that we are both assured of the truth in question and also of our own perfect assurance. But yet, when all is said, for our knowledge that two times two equal four it may be hard to claim less than that; and philosophers who pay a formal tribute to the possibility of error—which the temper of the present age requires, as much as the past required certainty—may be offering a gesture and little more. Nonetheless legitimate doubts remain; for certainly instances could be cited of views that men have naturally taken as self-evident, which after all have had to be revised. And besides there remains the objection to a psychological or phenomenological distinction which apparently is unknown to introspection: intuitionism draws a hard line where, preconceptions apart, what we find is more like a continuum. It is true that not all intuitionists go so far, but the rest will have other problems on their hands; for if these differences are not to be settled by introspection we shall need to know of some other way of settling them—and our concern is with ultimate principles.[1] But here, with these issues, we are led on to different and more technical difficulties and to more recent discussion of intuitionism.

## II

On the face of it the term 'intuition' seems to belong to the vocabulary of psychology. For an intuition must be someone's intuition: and in the stream of John Doe's consciousness, along with percepts, scraps of imagery, physical sensations and the like, each having its own place in the series, his intuitions, if he has any, must find a place. Such a notion has sometimes been ridiculed as if it were very fantastic and artificial, an invention of mystery-mongering philosophers. But, of course, it is nothing of the kind. For it appears that the term 'intuition' was introduced, among other things, to avoid the ambiguity of the verb 'to see'; and it must surely take a very ardent scourer of mentalistic mysteries to deny that at a given time John Doe may truly report, say, that he has just seen the solution of some problem that has been worrying him. New truths dawn on us, no doubt, with more or less vividness, but the fact of such occurrences is beyond question; and moreover we pause from time to time to remind ourselves of truths that we already know.

Such truths, re-examined or newly dawning, may strike us with a

[1] Sidgwick has, indeed, tackled the problem, and—careful as we should expect him to be—laid down a series of tests for distinguishing genuine intuitions from their merely psychological counterpart, states of strongly felt conviction. (See *Methods of Ethics*, 7th edition, pp. 338–42.) For these tests themselves he would, I suppose, have claimed intuitive certainty. In fact they have a strongly Cartesian flavour, and suggest that logical and mathematical truths are still serving as paradigms.

force that excludes doubt. And it is certain that this assurance, infallible or not, is generally justified. Indeed, if our natural conviction in those cases where it seems clearest were to prove illusory more often than not it is hard to see how reflective thinking would be possible at all. It may be worth remarking here that, though exceptions are of importance for philosophy—we do right to take notice of them—there is also some fallacy of vision which philosophers are liable to, a sort of occupational distortion, whereby the exceptional rather than the normal comes to hold the centre of the field. This present commonplace—that what most clearly seems so normally is so—is one that we must not lose sight of: it holds both of thought and perception. Yet it is also undeniable that occasionally even our clearest convictions deceive us; the feeling of certainty, what in a psychological sense we may call 'evidence', is a good guide but not an infallible one. Now the strict intuitionist, wherever it fails, will be bound to deny that what we experienced was in truth an intuition at all; we merely 'seemed to see' such and such a fact, we did not really see it. For things that are not there are not to be seen, either in the primary or the secondary sense.

But this ruling is plainly *ex post facto*, otherwise we should have known it at the time—the intuition making itself plain. There is nothing in a state of consciousness but what we find in it: this was among the intuitionist's own premises. We may now retrospectively deny that our 'seeing', our supposed intuition, was really such; but if so, that cannot be on the strength of anything given internally, belonging to the experience itself—as we might distinguish one somatic sensation, say, from another slightly different. Here, apart from the exigencies of a theory, there seems little reason for thinking that any such differences are to be found. We are thus led to one main accusation that contemporary philosophers have made against intuitionism, that of confusing questions of psychology with those of logic: the truth or falsity of any belief must be one issue while the mental state of its believer is another.

The confusion in question is already present in ordinary language where we find a single verb combining two rôles. For on the fact of it the verb 'to see', in both its primary and its secondary sense, is a psychological one; to tell us of anyone that he has seen something is to record a particular event in his mental history. But philosophers have lately come to see it as playing another rôle at the same time. We must ask in what circumstances or on what grounds one would withdraw any claim to have seen something—saying instead that one only seemed to see it. The two experiences, seeing and seeming to see, may be identical in themselves; but external evidence, say, the united testimony of other people, might subsequently convince a man that his would-be perception had been illusory. And hence it cannot be a merely psychological rôle that the word serves to play. A marriage, similarly, involves the performance of certain cere- monies, and to say of two people that they have been married is to speak of an event occurring at a given time and place; yet a marriage may be declared null on other than ceremonial grounds, in which case the first statement must be withdrawn. So too with the appeal to intuition: philosophers have used it to justify moral and other beliefs, it has served as their certificate of authority. But it appears that the validity of the certificate can never be completely guaranteed by—what need not be doubted—the occurrence on a particular occasion of a certain kind of conscious event.

It may be thought that the critics of intuition are here on strong ground, as strong as any we have so far surveyed. Yet here too the case is not wholly clear; for we must always bear in mind the great function that intuitions were required to fill, namely the provision of premisses. Now given a premiss which is really such, we may be asked how the supposition on which the present argument turns is admissible to all; for what we supposed was that a belief based on intuition should subsequently prove false. But to prove it false its contradictory must be deducible from some other prior principle which we know to be true, intuitively or in some other way still to be shown; and in that case our premiss is this further principle rather than the one to which we appealed before. But here, perhaps, the objection may be renewed. We have to distinguish, it seems, between the claim to know a given proposition intuitively and the use that we make of it in consequence. For it serves as a premiss. But whether what is in question is the truth of a given proposition or rather its logical status, the position that it holds in our system, the same doubt arises: here, as before, it will be said, we have a logical matter confused with a psychological one.

A resolute intuitionist, it seems to me, may still stand his ground; though perhaps to do so among so many doubts and difficulties he will require a pretty high devotion to the *a priori*. But as to this new formulation of the argument, he need only reaffirm his previous position. Some sort of premiss there must be—if there is to be knowledge at all. We may demote one proposition and install another, but the general position is untouched. Those propositions that stand as premisses, once again, cannot be derived from any others, and hence if we are to know them at all, we have nothing but their own intrinsic evidence or certainty to appeal to—and, if we do not know them, we know nothing. This argument undoubtedly claims to show that certain truths must be self-guaranteeing; because they are self-evident they are known to be true, and because they are known to be true they serve as premisses. But to say that is not to confuse their self-evidence with their truth nor yet with their logical status.

It would appear, then, that the anti-intuitionist arguments we have so far looked at, the charge of dogmatism and the charge of confusing psychology and logic, are inconclusive; a die-hard intuitionist need not be shifted—not at least so long as no alternative account of first principles is forthcoming. There are other arguments which I wish to review presently; but it may be useful to explore the present issue a little further, even at the cost of some digression. My aim in the present chapter is primarily critical; but if there exists, as I believe there may, another more promising approach to the problem of first principles, it will be well to glance at it while these issues are before us.

## III

A noteworthy testimony, we may observe, to the strength of the old way of arguing is the fact that so many of our contemporaries, rather than challenge it, have, in effect, quietly adopted its conclusion. For they lay no claim to knowledge of first principles; rather, they make their acceptance a matter of legislation or decision. They do so in spite of the plain consequence that anything that we normally call knowledge cannot really be so: or should we say, to soften it a little, that it is only knowledge—supposing such expressions to make sense, which I doubt—relative to given premisses, or premisses freely laid down? But what concerns me at present is the possibility of a less drastic alternative to thorough-going intuitionism.

The intuitionist tells us first that we need premisses, and here he can hardly be challenged. But he tells us further that our premisses must be indubitable, and plainly this second position is no necessary consequence of the other. Take, then, the first step by itself, and let us ask where that leaves us. Perhaps after all there is little need to strain the resources of logical subtlety: from hypothetical premisses we normally infer hypothetical conclusions, and in the same way, I suppose, from intrinsically probable premisses—supposing such things are to be found—we may infer conclusions to be taken as probable too. A premiss is nonetheless a premiss for not being thought indubitable. And we may proceed with the work of inquiry not on the foundation of any supposed infallible certainties, which we do not need, but making our starting-point merely whatever we naturally find or feel to be acceptable—intuitively in a Pickwickian sense. 'This is simply what I do,' Wittgenstein tells us, of certain basic logical or linguistic procedures—to be expressed in appropriate forms of statement.[1] We may say, then, that he does these things instinctively: and views that he holds in this way, he holds intuitively.

If, then, we follow this principle, adopting whatever it seems natural to adopt, we at least have an intelligible procedure, a basis on which thought can go forward: on these lines it is possible to set to work—as in practice, perhaps, we always do. Indeed it is hard to imagine how we could do otherwise. For what sort of men, one may wonder, would choose just those views or would-be logical practices

[1] *Philosophical Investigations*, i, 217.

that come least naturally to them, the hardest or most repugnant, and base all their thinking on these? The views that we adopt unreflectively will make our inevitable starting-point—though later, of course, they may be modified. For we must not confuse the raw material with the finished product. Ordinary thought is not necessarily self-consistent, and it is certainly not richly inventive or finely discriminating: how far subsequent reflection may lead us to change our initial views even when they seem clearest cannot be known for certain in advance. Perhaps, as I suggested above, certain propositions remain whose rejection we cannot seriously contemplate; we may make formal gestures in deference to our recognition of human fallibility but little more. But so far as the present account goes we are committed to nothing indubitable. We always leave open the possibility that what at one time seems staringly obvious will subsequently seem questionable or false; indeed the history of thought provides examples of it. All that it is necessary to maintain is that at any given point we take our stand on those principles that we then find most naturally acceptable; that they serve us provisionally as premises. But it remains conceivable that we may later modify or go beyond them, or even reject them altogether. We may also, without either rejecting or modifying them, install further premises over their heads, and thus reduce their status to that of theorems.

This, I have said, is not only a possible course, it is actual too. We follow it as a matter of course in all our thinking. But granted that we do, it may still be asked whether we are right to do so, whether this procedure has any rational basis. What we are to consider is a basic rule that we may roughly formulate as follows: to accept views where we find them acceptable, in so far as we find them acceptable; to treat them provisionally as right. Here, possibly, we may have a workable first principle, but how are we to try its claims further? Put to its own test, perhaps it will not seem very secure. Intuitive self-evidence has been claimed for a good variety of beliefs but not, to the best of my knowledge, for this one; nor would the claim be very plausible. Yet we must not reject it out of hand on that account; reflection, we know, has vastly altered the views that men find it natural to accept, their intellectual attitudes have been radically reshaped in the history of thought. To find the basis of inquiry in naturally acceptable views is not to say that progress is to be made merely by consulting our feelings, by staring at propositions in isolation; and in this case the reflective process called for is no very long or elaborate one. We need only insist on what we have already observed, that all thought must work on some foundation, so that unless we start with those views that we find obvious or natural we shall never be able to start at all. It is plain that no inquiry can begin from nothing; here as elsewhere we must use what proclivities we possess. But once this much is granted it seems that we have a general principle that will stand to all other intuitive principles somewhat as the *dictum de omne* has been supposed to stand to the major premisses of particular syllogisms. In fact we could now present these as minor premisses in a type of syllogism in which this principle will serve as the major: 'Propositions felt as evident are to be accepted; $p$ is felt as evident, therefore $p$ is to be accepted' (which is tantamount to simply asserting $p$).

Here, however, another objection may arise. I have spoken of the acceptance of what we find naturally acceptable—or what is self-evident to us—as a principle which in fact we adopt; and I have claimed, further, that we are right to adopt it. But of these two positions, the former, it may be said, is no more than tautological; and the latter, if not strictly tautological, is nonetheless vacuous in its own way. For, it may be asked, by what tests or criteria are we to decide whether or not someone finds it natural to accept any given belief? Presumably our ultimate evidence can be nothing but that he actually accepts it; and if so, to say that he will accept whatever he finds naturally acceptable or evident, is to say nothing. And again if we are told, in accordance with this rule, that as a matter of right and wrong we ought to accept those views and procedures that we find naturally acceptable, we are told to do what we cannot help doing. For suppose we already accept a given view unquestioningly, then, it seems, we are told to accept it. But on the other hand once we begin to question it, it must become questionable in the same measure; and now we are right to doubt it precisely so far as we already do. Here, a critic may remark, we have no beacon-light to guide us among our perplexities.

Of all this there is much that might be said; I cannot attempt here to sift the issues involved to the bottom. Nor shall I have recourse to the ready-made notion of a 'useful tautology'; this epithet 'tautology', I believe, would raise less dust in philosophy if we could keep it to its ordinary and original function as a term of abuse. In so far as what we call a tautology, being applied in a particular situation, proves either useful or illuminating, it has ceased to be simply tautological. It might indeed seem so, presented as a mere applicable schema; but then it is hardly yet a statement at all. Now the present rule, let me recall, has its proposed application too; it is to be applied in connexion with the justification of first principles. The justification of these principles, as the intuitionists' argument demonstrates, would require their derivation from further principles, which would either require justification in turn, or, failing that, would have to be taken as self-justifying: hence it is plain that if the beliefs which we first took as premisses are themselves intuitively evident nothing can be gained by the process; we already have as much as we can ever hope for. I am not aware that this argument, familiar and simple as it is, has ever been met. The only real fault that we may find with it is the too rigid notion of intuitive certainty in terms of which it has commonly been presented; for what we have to do with is really a whole graded scale of self-evidence, not only a single absolute point. Indeed it may even be held that no absolute point is ever reached. If not, we must say that no belief can be wholly secured from the possibility of future correction; but, conversely, any degree of self-evidence however weak will serve to establish a certain claim. The traditional intuitionist account is at this point undoubtedly misconceived; we must not limit ourselves by insisting on too exclusively high demands. Still less should we look for that particular sort of self-evidence that belongs only to the skeleton propositions of pure mathematics or logic—which, if we take

C

them as our paradigm, will exclude any substantial beliefs whatever.

Properly qualified, however, the argument can still stand; and hence, in face of the recurrent demand for some justification of our fundamental principles or procedures, a first perfectly sensible reply will be merely that they present themselves as evident, as naturally acceptable or plausible. There may remain for all that a certain sense in which they are dubitable too; for apart from the quite intelligible empirical hypothesis that they may cease to seem evident in the future, the history of philosophy tells us of doubters. These thinkers, it may be, induced in themselves some psychological state, or perhaps they merely repeated the verbal formula 'I doubt'. At all events, being assured that such doubt was possible, they went on to ask for positive support, rational justification, for these—evidently dubitable—beliefs; and found, often, that none was forthcoming. Now here we find the use of our principle. It tells us to accept what we find it natural to accept; it makes this a condition of all thinking. Indeed these views that have been assailed by sceptical doubt have in general been views so natural, so universally accepted, that even the doubters could hardly take themselves seriously. And that alone is some ground for accepting them.

Here, however, our critic may reaffirm his first objection. Your principle, he may say, amounts to no more than this, that what we accept, we are right to accept; and if so you are committed to saying, too, that whatever we doubt we are right to doubt. Now suppose that we come to doubt our first principles: we doubt them, perhaps, under the false impression that everything might somehow be justified, or again we may have been misled by the difference between logical schemata and substantial assertions. For the latter admit of falsification in a way from which the former are immune; these, then, may seem dubitable in some special way, and hence in need of further support. Now our critic may grant or assert that all these doubts rest on confusions or errors; but that, he will insist, is immaterial. Once led to reason—well or badly—along these lines, we certainly find this doubt natural: and, if the principle before us is to be accepted, wherever it is natural then, at least provisionally, it is also to be taken as right. So after all the proposed principle tells us nothing; it remains, in what we ourselves allow is the properly pejorative sense, merely tautological.

So much for the critic's retort. But let us reconsider the sceptic's case. It rested, we may recall, on no real positive fault to be found in our ordinary beliefs; he was not led to doubt them, for example, because he had found them to conflict with some other established belief which he also found it natural to accept. That would be substantial grounds for doubting, but here we have none. The sceptical case we have considered turns on nothing but the complaint that no sort of rational support can be given for certain classes of belief; and these are admittedly beliefs which it is natural to accept without question. But that fact alone is their support—at least if the proposed principle holds. We are to accept in the first place whatever is naturally acceptable. It is plain, then, that to adopt this sort of sceptical position at the same time as the present principle would be to commit oneself to a contradiction: it follows that the principle itself—here at least, as applied in the present argument—cannot be merely vacuous or tautological. Its acceptance has real consequences, if only negative ones. Besides, supposing it were, we may notice something else that would be strange, namely that it has repeatedly been denied—and denied, I suppose, by philosophers who had no thought of denying a mere tautology. 'The mind never perceives any real connexion between distinct existences';[1] and perhaps the occurrence of a given state of mind and the truth of any given proposition, will fall under the heading 'distinct existences'. At all events we find it made some sort of basic principle that the one can never constitute ground for the other; though if that is so it must be an intelligible supposition that no-one should ever entertain any but false beliefs.[2]

All this, no doubt, invites more inquiry; but I shall return to these

---

[1] Hume, *A Treatise of Human Nature*, Appendix, ed. Selby-Bigge, p. 636.

[2] If I understand him rightly what Professor Popper attacks under the name of psychologism is more or less the position maintained here. Cf. his *The Logic of Scientific Discovery*, p. 105. Such is also Wittgenstein's view throughout the *Tractatus*.

issues at a later stage. At present I must pass on. If, however, the complaint is finally urged that what we have here is after all a form of intuitionism or psychologism, for the mere fact of a belief's actual acceptance is made a positive ground for its acceptance—which must itself be a synthetic *a priori* proposition— what are we to say? I shall not go to war over a word: I can only answer that, if so, 'intuitionism' and 'psychologism' must be names of eminently sensible views. Indeed there are legitimately exceptionable doctrines associated with them: there is the claim that seeks to base knowledge on some distinctive state of our consciousness which ordinary introspection fails to find; and further, on the strength of this supposed mental state, to exclude the very possibility of error. These claims are dogmatic in logic and, I believe, false as psychology; but we ought not to be blinded on that account to those quite simple and yet fundamental truths that intuitionism contains. As to this other great bogey, the synthetic *a priori*, I shall only observe here that there are signs that the all-but-paralytic hold which the mere name seems to have had for so long, casting a sort of spell on whole schools of philosophers, is at last losing part of its force. The two issues, however, are really one: much of this strange attitude derives from the connexion between this concept and the concept of intuition, and is coupled with partly legitimate objections to the traditional form of the latter.

## IV

It is time to return from this digression to our account of the concept of intuition in its traditional form. I have so far spoken of two main items in the indictment commonly urged against it, the charges of dogmatism and psychologism (though of the latter there is still more to be said). As to dogmatism, the case proves on examination much less clear than it might seem at first glance: at least a critic will need to be pretty sure of his own ground before he can safely press it. If we take the issue first at a merely practical level, where intuition has in fact been invoked, we shall find that the principles that it serves to support are not such as seem likely to form any grave impediment to progress either in morals or elsewhere. To claim to know by intuition one's *prima facie* duty not to lie is surely no very rash resort to dogmatism, at least so far as common life is concerned. It is true that the theoretical position is less clear: it may at least plausibly be urged that once we admit this appeal in any one instance we cannot forbid it in others, and there the principles which it is used to justify may prove less inoffensive. For conduct of all sorts may be backed by reported intuitions. But to make any polemical use of this argument a critic must be sure that he himself is better equipped to deal with such unwelcome possibilities should they arise; his own theory must suffice to exclude them. And none that appeals to mere decisions, for instance, or to *de facto* attitudes enjoys that advantage.[1]

Several other lines of criticism remain to be dealt with. I have touched on the delusive explanatory air that may go with the term 'intuition'; we tell someone that we know a given truth, and we seem also to tell him how we come to know it. We know it, we say, 'by intuition'. This second complaint is in fact connected with the previous one: for the appeal to intuition, it is urged, not only cuts short discussion of whatever particular issue is at stake, but at a different level it further prohibits any psychological investigation of the possible sources of our beliefs. It is a view widely held that a logical and a psychological inquiry of this kind can be carried out independently, and neither need compete with the other. For it is one thing for a psychologist to ask why a given individual holds certain views or principles—or even why everybody does so—and another to justify or validate them: this latter will be a task for a specialist in the relevant field, say, a physicist, an art-critic or a mathematician. This claim indeed remains abstract, and it might be more convincing if we were ever actually shown the dual process at work: the notable

[1] As against the picture sometimes drawn of reaction and obscurantism entrenched together behind an intuitionist ethic, it may be worth remarking that the foremost British exponent of intuitionism in the eighteenth century—and perhaps since—was the radical and pro-American Richard Price. The tory Hume was his great opponent, the champion of emotionism.

thing about the physiological account of perception, for example, is that it always falls short of explaining the phenomenon itself, namely the experience or fact of seeing. But that does not concern us here. Our concern is with the concept of intuition, which has this special feature, that it seems to fill both these rôles simultaneously— though in fact, a critic will add, it does not fill either. The concept appears to play this double part inasmuch as intuition is thought of as a kind of mental vision. The claim is simply that we know some- thing because we see it; and we see it because it is there. The in- tuitionist theory tells us on the one side of a direct faculty of knowledge, and on the other of non-sensible objects, of truths, values or the like, which are immediately present to the mind. The relation is one of confrontation; a relation by virtue of which our knowledge is given and guaranteed at the same time.

We need not enter into any general question as to the limits of psychological explanation; in any case the present explanation is not of the sort that professional psychologists would look kindly on. But what has often been urged in recent years is that the intuitionist theory represents at bottom no more than a too literal reading of the visual metaphor that we use in ordinary speech: hence a kind of picture of the mind, half-consciously used, underlies what is offered as doctrine. Further, once the picture is given up the apparent ex- planatory power of the notion of intuition will vanish as well. Sup- pose that we press the metaphor at every point, that we seek in detail to represent the mental situation in terms of the parallel physical one: intuitionism provides us, we shall find, with all the different elements that we need. To correspond to the physical eye we have, on this account, an immaterial subject, the ego or mind, itself a substantial thing; and instead of the tables or chairs or the like, which we might see in the primary or literal sense, we have truths, universals or special non-sensible qualities. And these are said to enjoy as solidly independent an existence as any ordinary material object—as the forests or the hills, for example, which ante- date all emergences of consciousness. Lastly as to the relation be- tween the two, the 'seeing' which is intuition itself: what we are told of here is the direct confrontation of the one by the other. An ordinary physical object being immediately in front of a man's eyes, we assume that he will see it as it is. This is indeed our very image or prototype of obviousness; and if we set out to frame a picture of what is as plain as anything can be, or plainer still—of a kind of cognition from which the very possibility of error is excluded—we shall take it from this sort of original. Yet, though we work on this basis, we must also go beyond it; no sublunary exemplar can be infallible. Our account must be still further idealized if it is to do justice to the realist's notion of knowledge. We shall, as I have said, use the same analogue, the physical organ of vision, but what we are now to imagine is an organ that has left its earthly imperfections behind. The eye of the mind works in no flawed or variable medium, it has no need of the gross instrumentality of nerves and membrane. Shadowless objects stand before it, visible in a non-spatial medium, in pure consciousness clearer than the clearest daylight. We were always told that knowledge of its very nature excludes error, for it would no longer be knowledge if it were wrong; and we may now see how that comes about. In the situation as we have pictured it nothing could be hidden from view, so that no room for misperception remains.

I do not mean to substitute a caricature for an argument. Arguments are to be assessed on their merits, and a critic may reasonably complain that it is no proper method in philosophy to attack a given position by exhibiting or satirizing those pictures or models that its exponents are said to be unconsciously dominated by—while leaving their avowed doctrines unexamined. But that is not my intention; our question was whether the intuitionist theory could support its dual claim, at once to justify given principles and also to explain how it is that we come to know them. Much of what intuitionists assert can certainly be taken in their own theoretical terms, but this last claim appears rather to be founded in the picture which I have sought to uncover. We are not to object to a mode of thought merely because it is partly pictorial, perhaps we shall find little significant philosophical thinking that is not—but that is a question which it will be as well not to embark on. At all events I believe it to be true that some such picture as I have indicated has really been influential; though variously, no doubt, with different philosophers, some subscribing to some and others to other of its features. Its influence is intelligible in the first place because it represents no more than the working out of a metaphor already embodied in common speech. But that is not all: our minds naturally seize on an image that serves to crystallize and hold together any abstract body of thought. There are various theses concerning knowledge, views that might well be based on purely discursive argument, which the picture we have high-lighted serves to interpret—in the sense in which, say, chess or a free market might serve as possible interpretations of some mathematical calculus. What I hope to show, however, is that these arguments themselves retain their force—such force as they legitimately have—independent of these imaginative aids: and further that where critics have objected to the notion of intuition, most of the features that they have taken exception to have followed less from the bare argument than from the pictorial model that goes with it.

The arguments are pretty familiar and most of them have already been dealt with, so a summary statement may suffice. I wish to distinguish three. The first is the main intuitionist argument which we have considered at some length, that to claim any knowledge at all, to infer any conclusions that we may claim to know, we need some knowledge that is non-inferential or direct. Here, then, there can be no mediating process; nothing intervenes between the mind and those objects that it apprehends. And further we have seen that it has often been held that knowledge, to be properly counted as such, must exclude the possibility of error. One cannot both know and be wrong—though in this case there may be reasons for doubting whether what we have brought to light is really more than a function of language. For we require terms in which to express commitment. Certainly it would be nonsense to say 'I know it—but possibly I am wrong.' But that does not prove knowledge to be infallible, if by 'knowledge' we mean a special state of mind. It serves merely to show that we sometimes commit ourselves: thus one cannot set one's signature to a document and at the same time retain the prerogatives of indecision; and yet we can always conceive that with developments, perhaps unforeseeable, the terms in question will prove after all to have been impossible to fulfil. We have ritual acts of logical commitment too, for discourse would be practically impossible without them; but many philosophers have been led to think that the formula 'I know that . . .' must report a unique mode of apprehension internally guaranteed against error.

The third argument presents the cardinal thesis of realism, the thesis, namely, which asserts the independence of any object that may be known from the mind that knows it. If it were not for this independence the whole notion of knowledge would break up: such is the realist's contention. For suppose that in the act of apprehending anything we ourselves partly make or perhaps mar it, as an archaeologist digging carelessly might falsify his own findings: what we are left with will no longer be knowledge—or, at least, it will no longer be knowledge of the object that we first claimed to know. For that object is not longer as it was. At least, we may be told in reply, there is some item of knowledge that we are sure of, if not of that then of some other thing instead. The reply fails, however: once we grant in general that our knowledge acts on its objects or modifies them then, in so far as it does so, this second object, which we now claim to know, must be altered too. And the process will go on indefinitely.

If we now turn back to the picture that we have been looking at we shall soon see its attraction; it provides a model in terms of which we can represent all these doctrines simultaneously. We are to speak, first, of the immediacy of knowledge, next of its consequent infallibility, and thirdly of the independence of known truths from the fact of our knowing them. Let us recall the picture we have drawn in which the mental eye confronts its special object: we shall find all these conditions fulfilled. Knowledge is direct and infallible, for there is nowhere that error might creep in; the mind sees its objects face to face—objects which are naturally independent since

they are conceived on the analogy of those of our ordinary perception. Plainly, then, the picture is a natural one, but we may manage
without it after all. To speak of certain truths as 'known directly' is
only to say after all that they are not derived by inference from
others; and that is a possibility that we can admit without basing it
on any special picture of the mind. And the same will hold of the
independence of what we know. The proposition $p$ is never to be
identified with the proposition that a given person knows $p$, however else they may be related. For the rest, it is true that there still
remains the metaphysical problem of the character of those truths,
values and the like, which we may claim to know intuitively; there
are difficulties here even for a modified form of intuitionism, which
abandons the picture which we have been speaking of. But that must
belong to another argument.

The picture, then, would seem to be superfluous, and perhaps it
is objectionable too. We have seen that it underwrites exorbitant
epistemological claims; and, on the side of psychology, introduces a
discontinuity in mental life which experience does not appear to
warrant. If there is a difference in kind between what we call 'knowledge' and 'true belief', it is not the sort of difference that we can
discover introspectively as belonging to mental states; it belongs
rather to the use-in-their-setting of the two words.

Now, let the visual metaphor be once abandoned and the apparent explanatory power of the concept of intuition goes too. For the
immediate presence of the object of intuition can no longer be
pointed out as the cause of the special mental state that we call our
knowledge. Philosophers sometimes seem to hope to justify particular views by appealing to intuitive knowledge: similarly in ordinary speech, on being asked how we know a thing, we often reply that
we simply see it. But to say this, as we remarked, is not to give an
explanation; rather, it is to refuse one. The refusal may sometimes
be proper; we have not excluded that possibility. But the objection
to the term 'intuition' is that—being in reality non-explanatory,
serving simply to terminate inquiry—it keeps up a deceptive appearance of explaining. One may know truths 'by intuition', we are told,

as we know them by deduction or by experiment; that is to say, as if 'intuition' were a special technique.

I pass to one further argument which enjoys general currency and carries great weight—though it can be stated in a few words. To deal with it adequately, indeed, would involve us in metaphysical issues which I cannot enter into here; but neither can I pass it without a word. In fact its exponents, too, have often been summary with their metaphysics. Intuition, we found, is akin to seeing. Now plainly for the analogy to be carried through, there will have to be objects to be seen—not physical objects such as tables and chairs, nor even submicroscopic objects such as electrons or magnetic fields, but truths or universals or propositions, or non-sensible qualities such as goodness. It is a suggestion that many philosophers jib at; legitimate or otherwise, the objection to such entities as these, treated as independently real, is widespread and deep. Indeed the rooted antipathy to intuitionism of which I spoke at the start belongs to the whole empiricist tradition in epistemology, which is also a tradition of hostility to metaphysical views of this sort—though, no doubt, the influence is mutual, so that the hostility to such objects of knowledge is reinforced by this prior hostility to the intuition which we should need if we were to know them. The issues involved are far-reaching; it must suffice here that these widely unwelcome consequences have played their part, and no small part, in the general discredit of intuition. But I shall speak more of this argument in the sequel.

We have not yet quite done with intuition. I fear that the process has been lengthy and perhaps tedious too; we have had to cover much familiar ground. But the concept itself is as old as the Greeks, and the objections urged against it are not only various; they are also, as we have found, mixed in value. Hence there seemed to be no satisfactory course but to examine the main points one by one. It may be some recompense to end by offering a few considerations that, perhaps, have received too little attention rather than too much. And here I must return once again to the metaphor of vision.

The secondary use of the verb 'to see' has not established itself for nothing; analogies really exist between the perceptual situation and the exercise of judgement: we express a peremptory confidence by simply asserting that we 'see'. At the same time there are differences too. And in fact we have no ordinary noun, only the philosopher's coinage 'intuition', to correspond to the non-technical verb: for 'sight' is not used in this way. In ordinary speech, it would seem, we implicitly claim certainty for the particular acts but not for the faculty itself. And if we use the term I have used here and speak of 'judgement', we have something that is far less naturally compared to vision. Eyesight—unlike virtue, as Aristotle noticed—is an implanted faculty; it may not be perfect at birth but at least it owes little to education. There is such a thing as sharp sight, of course, and also as trained sight; a huntsman will doubtless see much in a landscape that a townsman misses. But these are differences that are rarely felt outside special situations: broadly speaking, what we can see is not thought to reflect our training, our age or experience. In all this these two things, on the one hand literal vision and judgement as a theoretical or practical faculty on the other, are not only different but antithetical. Further, though from time to time visual illusions occur, yet—barring a few rare diseases—we do not meet with permanently distorted or false vision: eyesight, not being derived from education, cannot be warped by it either. But judgement, and especially moral judgement, can be and often is perverted, just as it can remain undeveloped, stunted or crude: and that, too, lies in the nature of the case.

We have looked at many objections to the concept of intuition; but not the least serious, perhaps, especially when we apply it to ethics, is the black-and-white picture that it leaves us with. For there seems to be no middle-way between intuiting and not intuiting a given truth. Yet we know very well that judgement grows slowly; that assertiveness does not always imply insight; that a thousand variable and doubtful factors act on it, influencing its growth. No doubt we may often be right to place in it the confidence that we do, but the background of this confidence is very different from that of our confidence in our eyes. These differences are involved in the concept of judgement as we commonly use it; but philosophers have done little to explore it or to formulate explicitly what it involves. That must be our main task in the sequel, but I cannot proceed to it directly; for there is another account of first principles to be examined first.

# II

## The Concept of Decision

THE rejection of intuition leaves a gap that has been filled in different ways. Some other rational basis has to be found at least for our deductive and empirical beliefs; within morals, so long as we can draw a line and keep the frontier closed, the alternative of irrationalism remains. Thus the Scottish philosophers of the eighteenth century used the notions of sense or sentiment to provide a new basis for ethical theory. On their view what we normally call judgements in morals, as against those of mathematics or science, are not properly judgements at all. What we must examine to explain these things are the emotions that certain objects arouse in us; these philosophers undertook to explain moral sentiments, pursuing this line of thought, in terms of the mechanism of the mind. And more recent irrationalists have set out from the same general position, though re-interpreting it in terms of their own linguistic preoccupations. Morality is referred to the emotions as before, or else—a useful new word that the eighteenth century understood only in its physical sense—to attitudes of a particular sort: these, then, are what moral utterances serve to influence, or else merely to express. Another notion, more recently introduced, which has proved of infinite service to the opponents of intuition, and of the synthetic *a priori* in whatever form, is that of decision: and it is with this that the present chapter will be chiefly concerned.

The concept of attitudes is doubtless important too. I omit further discussion of it partly because I hope that if I can make my general position clear it will be found to have been superfluous; and also for this reason, that I am far from clear that the theory of judgement which I mean to develop need bring me into conflict with it. My concern is with the conditions of rational judgement, with the logical setting that serves to make it possible. Now there are, presumably, both rational and non-rational attitudes, both which we express; and the former may well include judgements. Professor Nowell-Smith, for instance, distinguishes between what he calls 'pro-attitudes' and 'con-attitudes', which he introduces with two lists of such words as 'liking', 'admiration', 'approval' and 'desire' on the one hand, and 'hatred', 'disapproval' and 'hostility' on the other.[1] A moral utterance commending a good action, on his view, expresses a pro-attitude; but then, it would seem, so must a philosophical or scientific judgement commending a good theory or a good piece of reasoning. These predicates 'rational' and 'irrational' are applicable to certain sorts of attitude and not to others; if Hume and his followers are to be believed moral attitudes fall into the latter class—but what concerns us is the ground of the distinction. Since, however, it cannot be within the concept of an attitude itself that that is to be found, I shall confine myself to a discussion of decision.

As far as I know the term played no prominent part in ethical writings before the appearance of Professor Popper's *The Open Society and its Enemies* in 1944; though both he and others had used it freely in the discussion of methodology. His exposition, moreover, though quite brief, is clear and forcible and we shall be well advised to take it as a starting-point.[2] Popper distinguishes between norms which, he says, are man-made and conventional, and facts that are not made but discovered. Normative laws, he writes, are 'rules that forbid or demand certain modes of conduct; examples are the Athenian Constitution or the rules pertaining to the election of M.P.s, or the Ten Commandments'.[3] And among these various normative edicts, moral laws presumably form a particular class, distinguished from facts like the rest. Popper, along with many other modern philosophers, endorses Hume's view that the logical gap between these two things is not to be bridged: we cannot legitimately

---

[1] P. Nowell-Smith, *Ethics*, Penguin, pp. 112–13.

[2] I am told, and partly gather, that Popper's views on these matters have since somewhat changed. I do not know how far these changes would affect the following discussion; anyway it is plain that the position maintained in *The Open Society* deserves to be examined on its own account.

[3] Op. cit., i, p. 52.

get our norms out of any scientific inquiry or infer them from any statements of fact. As a psychological matter it may well be that a given person's adoption of particular norms admits of some causal explanation; but, if so, we are not to see this as anything like a logical passage from one to the other—from an account, say, of an individual's psychological constitution and biography to the normative laws that he accepts. Let him take some decision: that at any given time he adopts a particular norm is itself a fact, in principle explicable perhaps; but what he adopts is a norm and not a fact, nor is it deducible from facts but only from other normative statements.

This adoption of a norm is a matter of what Popper calls decision. We may reject existing norms in favour of others which 'we have decided are worthy to be realized', and in this we commit ourselves to these latter. 'But even these standards are of our own making in the sense that our decision in favour of them is our own decision and we alone are responsible for adopting them. The standards are not to be found in nature.'[1]

Here, then, we have the introduction of the notion; and Popper's account of decision seems to be substantially preserved among other philosophers who have employed the term. But *The Open Society* is primarily a political work; a later and fuller treatment, in a book wholly concerned with morals, is that of Mr. Hare. It is his views, chiefly, that I mean to examine in the present chapter. What we are to decide on in Hare's terminology are not 'norms' but 'principles'; but like Popper he associates the expression of these principles with imperatives or commands (Popper's illustrations were mostly of rules or commandments); and like him he emphasizes the impassable logical gap between these utterances and those that state matters of fact. Hare calls the latter 'descriptive'. Lastly he agrees with Popper in distinguishing between the fact of the adoption of a given principle by a particular individual—which, granted suitable data, may be theoretically deducible from psychological laws—and the principle itself, which is never so.

[1] Loc. cit.

The term 'decide' in Hare's treatment is put in opposition to the term 'perceive'; and this latter is a near relative of 'see'—and of the technical term that has engaged us for so long 'intuit'. What we perceive, in this terminology, are facts, but on questions of moral principle we can only decide. And as for those moral philosophers who search for, or who claim to have found, a way of deducing ethical utterances from descriptive ones, they, Hare writes, 'leave out of their reasoning about conduct a factor which is of the very essence of morals', namely decision.[1] The considerations at work in Hare's thinking are evidently closely similar to those stated by Popper: since there are no standards in nature it is impossible that we should find or perceive them. It only remains, therefore, that we ourselves institute them; we decide.

All this, broadly, is clear enough; but Hare's whole account involves a more elaborate conceptual structure, and it is important to see more precisely at what point the notion of decision is brought in. In general its function is to provide a source or basis for ultimate principles, those, namely, that are not to be deduced from others of greater generality: but there are, it seems, two different ways in which this question may be raised, or two approaches to these ultimate principles. First, we may proceed in argument from the more particular to the more general. We justify a particular moral judgement by pointing on the one hand to the facts of the case and, on the other, to the principle or principles that cover situations of this sort. On being challenged we might justify these principles by appealing in turn to the others more general; but clearly this process must have an end. So long as both parties to the discussion agree in accepting the further principles invoked, then, so far as concerns the resolution of present differences, this appeal itself will suffice; we need only show the lower principles as deducible from the higher. But after all the possibility remains that even here, on the last appeal, our differences will remain unresolved. These, then, are principles, ultimate principles, that admit of no further support. A full statement of such principles, Hare writes—though we hardly

[1] R. M. Hare, *The Language of Morals*, pp. 54-5.

D

arrive at such a thing in practice—would amount to a specification of a whole way of life; yet even this specification, supposing that we could give it, might still fail to gain our hearer's acceptance. And in that case nothing remains but to tell him 'to make up his own mind which way he ought to live'.[1]

Hare's other approach shows us decisions, perhaps in the same logical rôle—I shall speak of this shortly—but as playing a somewhat different part in the business of our lives. It may happen, he observes, that we come on a situation of a sort that we have not met with before; that some new experience or encounter leads us to modify our principles. A simple example will be that of a child who has been taught merely that it is wrong to tell lies but, meeting a new situation, decides for himself that a lie told to save a friend from punishment is not wrong. Now Hare cannot say of this, what most people might find it natural to say, that this child now, for the first time, is brought to recognize the claims of loyalty—which may prove to conflict with those of truthfulness. In any situation such as this we merely 'decide' on a new or, rather, a modified principle.[2]

Here, then, we have the notion of a decision; it is in these terms that its exponents present it. Hare, we see, explicitly opposes 'to perceive' and 'to decide', and broadly it is clear enough that the concept is filling the same place that intuition filled in earlier theories. To provide propositions from which others may be deduced but which are not themselves deducible from others; to explain how we come to be in possession of such principles in the first place— these two needs, at least on the face of it, are met by both concepts alike. But the notion of decision, it will be claimed, escapes those criticisms which its rival proved to be exposed to. Fault was found with intuitionism on various grounds. First, to recapitulate the case, the notion appeared incompatible with certain apparent facts, that is to say, with the actual relativity of moral views; and further charges were that of dogmatism in the shutting-down of free inquiry; of the confusion of logical questions with psychological ones; of pseudo-explanation; and lastly of a sort of mythology, in the intro-

---

[1] Op. cit., p. 69.        [2] Op. cit., pp. 51–3.

duction, which follows, of a class of metaphysical entities to serve as objects of intuitive knowledge. (I confine myself here to the common run of polemic.) Now certainly as regards the last two of these, decision does better than the concept that it replaces; and possibly, though this is less clear, with the others. The last, indeed, seems to have weighed most. In introducing the notion Popper, we saw, asserts explicitly that there are no standards existing in nature, and Hare is almost equally clear on the point. His treatment of moral utterance as 'prescriptive' as a sort of command, has for him this twofold advantage: first that it serves to make sense of its practical character, its effective or preventive rôle in our lives, and secondly that it excludes any self-subsistent moral facts, or rather, enables us to dispense with them.

The command 'Do such and such', on this view, is similar in character to the moral prescription 'You ought to do such and such.' Popper's norms, too, were 'rules that forbid or command modes of conduct'. Hare goes on, however, to distinguish moral imperatives from imperatives in the ordinary sense; they differ he maintains, following Kant, in their implicit universality. It is as if they were addressed to 'whomever it may concern': they will apply to anyone appropriately placed. So far as ordinary imperatives are concerned a man may well give one order on Monday and another different one on Tuesday, though the two situations are in all other respects exactly the same. If so he will be thought odd or erratic and perhaps unsuitable for a position of command; but whatever these judgements may bear on they do not raise any question of logic. Now suppose, however, that he tells us on Monday 'You ought to do that', and on Tuesday 'You ought not to', where no other differences appear—I leave out of consideration communities where one or other day is a sabbath or a feast, or any question of a weekly routine. We shall now have reason to accuse him of contradicting himself —but this truth for Hare, unlike Kant, is a merely analytic one, language alone requires it. It seems that in a moral judgement on a case before us we commit ourselves to a similar judgement on any other case where no relevant differences can be found: this, if not quite Hare's own statement of the point, is, I think, substantially similar, and possibly the safest and most satisfactory. (The term 'relevant' may perhaps give rise to trouble; but as to this, Hare will of course deal with his own critics, while my views on the matter will appear in the sequel.)

It is plain that any theory such as this can have no place for the perception of moral truths; one can give a command or decide to give it, but in no sense can one see or discover it. It is nothing to be found or even looked for. It was much the same difficulty that led logical positivists to a downright denial of the meaningfulness of moral utterances; meaning for them was defined empirically—apart from that of analytic statements. And these moral statements, or seeming statements, are such that no observations can serve to verify them. And the eighteenth-century school of moral sentiment was influenced by similar considerations; they referred morality to the sentiments of an observer because it seemed impossible to refer it to anything that he might be said to observe. Take any act of unprovoked violence: describe it in what detail you will, scrutinize with eyes and with ears, measure it, magnify it or the like: in all data that you gather by such means you will find not a trace of its wrongness. The moral, however, that both Popper and Hare draw from these facts is not that ethical utterances are meaningless but merely that, unlike certain others, they do not state facts or describe situations. They still have a proper place of their own; and these two philosophers join again in insisting that there are more forms of meaning than are reckoned with in the positivist's vocabulary.

It is clear then, that decisionism has no need to furnish the world with special non-sensible entities, such as seemed requisite to provide objects for ethical intuition; so far the new notion avoids what were felt to be difficulties in the old one. When we turn next to the charge of dogmatism—which in practice has told so heavily against the appeal to intuition, making it look barely respectable—the position, we find, is less clear. Decision is called on to fill the same place that intuition had filled, namely to provide ultimate principles, premisses that are to stand beyond argument. If, therefore, we call it dogmatism to lay down any such starting-point, to rest one's assertions in the end on principles which are not further justified or further argued for, the one view is as dogmatic as the other. But the difference, we may be told, is this, that the appeal to intuition not only puts a closure on argument but closes it with a definitive claim to knowledge; whereas merely to announce a decision is not to claim to know anything at all. And undogmatic humility, it might be urged, could hardly go further.

Let us do all justice to this Socratic reserve. Yet for one who knows nothing, and admits and avows that he knows nothing, it is somewhat singular to address imperatives to all the world. At least it is nothing odd or extraordinary for a man to announce his beliefs, to assert what most plainly seems true to him. Even our best certainly is fallible, as indeed he himself may recognize; it is still all that we have to act on. And sometimes we are bound to commit ourselves. I remarked earlier that once we suppose that our surest apparent perceptions might prove false not only occasionally but generally— that they might mislead us more often than not—the very notions of truth and falsity will lose their meaning. Intuition, then, though not infallible, will give us some intelligible basis for moral utter-ances; it is hard to see how decisions can provide any at all. There is, I fear, some force in the complaint that Hare brushes brusquely aside, that his account of ethical utterances will leave our final choice of principles wholly arbitrary. It sounds plausible to say that on any view we must come back to ultimate principles, for which, in the nature of the case, no further reason can be given. And of the voluntarist view that is indeed true enough. Rather, it is more than the truth: for surely we are hardly 'giving reasons' where we support one unfounded principle by appeal to another which is no better. 'No further justification' is a phrase we hear too often in this con-nexion, as though at least some sort, or some measure of justification had already been found. What ought to be said on this account is 'no justification whatever'. You support a particular action by appealing to a principle $p$, and you support the principle by appeal-ing to another $p_1$; but plainly where you have no ground whatever for accepting $p_1$ you have not as yet given any ground for accepting $p$; nor any support, therefore, for the original action. The intuitionist position, however, is very different. It is strictly false to say of the intuitionist, even on this last appeal, that he has no further reasons to give, for he gives philosophical reasons. He argues, first, that the particular principles in question are intuitively plain; and secondly that unless we accept such principles as these, unless we make our starting-point the plainest beliefs that we possess, we can never begin to think at all. And this argument is so far from being contemptible that we find that our contemporary champions of rationality tacitly agreeing, accepting the consequence and abandoning the claim to any real knowledge—or for that matter any reasonable belief.

The issue can be put in another way. The decisionist is modest epistemologically; and for the rest, it may be said, anyone can conduct his own life as he chooses. But the question is one of issuing moral imperatives, of entering other people's lives on this basis, and here, plainly, one's rights may be challenged. It is a matter, then, of right or wrong conduct. We are to consider a particular principle; one which, as far as meta-ethical issues go, an intuitionist and a decisionist alike might equally well accept or repudiate. My own intuitions, I may report for myself, speak unequivocally against it. Or alternatively if I am invited to decide, I shall decide against it —supposing for argument's sake that I fell in with that way of thinking. I would further venture the prediction, as a factual matter, that other people in some numbers would do the same. It now seems that imperativism has odd consequences: we have an account of the function of moral language whose very workability presupposes a particular decision which many moral agents, and perhaps most of them, will in fact reject. Conceivably everyone might reject it. If the aim of Hare's inquiry is to make the language of morals intelligible, to explain in terms of the function that it is to fulfil, namely the guidance of conduct, this point may give him some difficulty; for the function will apparently be self-stultifying as soon as the theory is accepted.

But here, I may remark by the way of anticipation, we touch on a central weakness of voluntarism (to give the general doctrine its older name): a weakness which is nothing obscure or recondite, but which voluntarists for the most part, when larger issues outside the field of ethics come in question, seem to leave in the background, keeping us occupied elsewhere. The trouble is, as far as I can discover, that no one will ever take voluntarism at its word—perhaps not even the voluntarist himself. I fear that otherwise, if we dared be naïve, the outcome would seem too grossly absurd. Particular arguments go forward well enough, with all the customary battle-noises of philosophical disputation, and only when fundamental questions are urged, only when the whole theoretical structure is called in question, is the thesis brought into the open. Here, on the ultimate questions, we are told—since all the reasons or arguments that may possibly be invoked have already played their part and done their best—nothing but a decision can remain: or perhaps a 'volitional definition' or the like. And here, no doubt, the answer is plausible; indeed the outcome may not be all that we might wish, but at this stage, it would seem, with the best will in the world rationalism can go no further. For unless we are to resort to the discredited theory of intuition no other alternative is to be had.

It is notable that in standard expositions of analytic philosophy this voluntarist thesis, which after all turns out to be fundamental, is rarely given the place of honour that it deserves: it makes its appearance at last, but rarely at the front of the argument. And when it comes we let it slip through. The truth is that the voluntarist has in effect won his battle in advance once you give him his own choice of pitch. But turn back from these ultimate principles to the ordinary mêlée of controversy: here we find him urging his own views against others quite as if he really believed them—believed, like the rest of us, in simply discoverable truths, in right answers that sound thinking might bring to light. But what we must notice is this, that the process can be stopped at any point; we can choose the limit as well as he. What he virtually relies on, it seems, is that his opponent, not being a voluntarist presumably, will never take advantage of those privileges that he claims and makes use of for himself. Let us once take him at his word and we are as free as he is to lay down what principles we please. And these will be ultimate principles too: the question what principles we are to treat as ultimate will itself be a matter for decision, like any other question of principle. For this so-called decision, let us recall, is not anything that the term would ordinarily be used for; what we have here is in effect a way of re-naming the point—wherever that point may be—at which an argument finally sticks. Here, we say, are ultimate decisions. Now where people, perhaps of strong views, but limited intellect, engage in philosophical argument, then plainly they may stick pretty soon; and moreover theirs are the 'decisions', decisions which as far as logic goes must be as good as the next man's, that prove really immovable. One sometimes can argue with error, but with sheer muddle-headedness one can do nothing; a fool with fixed ideas is invincible. So that the voluntarist now, on his own ground and with all his fine logistic weapons in his hands—for he is often a splendid dialectician—may find himself outmatched by the greater obtuseness of his opponent; and rational inquiry will be far more abruptly terminated than it ever was by an appeal to intuition.[1]

[1] It should be remarked that Professor Popper in his *Logic of Scientific Discovery* uses the appeal to decision not only frequently but explicitly. Yet for all the superior candour and mental clarity to which this course witnesses, it must surely serve to force the main question only more plainly on our attention. Suppose that we decide differently from Professor Popper: it appears as a mere matter of fact that various philosophers have adopted views that conflict with his. Normally we argue with our critics and attribute their rejection of our own views—what else can we do?—to some failure of grasp or insight on their part. But one whose views rest explicitly on his own decisions is worse placed; for him there seems no course but to acknowledge that they have decided differently from him—for we see that even a stupid critic's decision must count too—or else we shake hands with conventionalism. We learn from Popper, for instance, that the causal principle represents nothing but 'the scientist's decision never to abandon the search for laws' (op. cit., p. 248). The truth is, if we are to understand the words in their ordinary sense, that there never was any such decision: scientists, and indeed non-scientists too, instinctively search for explanations; at a late stage, led to reflect on their own previous and present procedures, some, much perplexed, might find no better account to give of it than this. The term 'decision' must itself be defined in terms of a system of usage that Popper in effect is proposing; the adoption of the system will be a matter for decision in turn—so that its author in effect deprives himself of any possibility of disputing or reasoning with those who reject it.

But let us return from this digression: my main aim at present is to reckon up those grounds on which the notion of decision may recommend itself as against the theory it seeks to replace. The issue of dogmatism, we see, must remain in some doubt; but at least the decisionist need not claim to possess any special source of knowledge, and further he escapes the difficulty of the conflict of would-be intuitions. And this difficulty would seem to be insoluble so long as intuitive knowledge is defined and identified internally; so long as a single state of consciousness is supposed to bear its own mark of its special status. For intuitions cannot conflict: to intuit something is to see it to be true. Yet what we take for intuitions evidently do so. The logical paradox disappears both on the earlier emotivist theory and again on the theory of decisions; for there is no difficulty in supposing that different people's feelings differ, or again that they issue contrary commands or have committed themselves to conflicting decisions. Yet generally in popular discussion what we find exploited is the contrast between the supposed uniformity, say, of our scientific views and the frequent conflicts that are met with in morals. That argument, however, is one that no consistent voluntarist can make use of; for him first principles in all these fields alike will reflect nothing more than our decisions, and will all be equally rational or irrational.

Another objection which the new theory can fairly claim to avoid is that of using a psychological pseudo-explanation. 'Intuition', we remarked, sounds like a special form of knowledge, and the appeal to intuition might be thought to answer the question 'How do you know?' But where there is no claim to knowledge there can be no question of spurious techniques from which knowledge may be thought to be derived. I shall not say that the notion of a decision is wholly free from similar difficulties—its precise psychological status certainly invites further inquiry. To explore that would take us too far afield. But thoroughly tough-minded thinkers, one may notice, have a preference for feelings or attitudes.

Whatever its difficulties, it is easy to see why the notion of decision has been thought a great improvement on its predecessor.

In the section immediately to follow I shall ask what sort of case may be made by its opponents on the other side; but before leaving the present ground it may be useful to enlarge on what has been said by considering something of its wider philosophical context. I have spoken already of the general denial of real, independently existing standards or values: these things are not there of themselves and hence cannot be found or perceived. This sort of negative thesis is part of any naturalistic metaphysic; and it follows from positivist doctrines more plainly still. It seems that the problem—not, I suppose, for Professor Popper himself, but for many philosophers favourably disposed to views similar to his—has been to find some plausible account of morals compatible with a positivist theory of meaning. I do not hesitate to use the term 'positivist', for the thing is certainly still with us however carefully the name may be avoided. The traditional doctrine is, I suggest, visibly present in Hare's exposition; for he sets out the two main forms of discourse to which, he says, moral utterance might—though wrongly—be thought to belong. He tells us first that 'all deductive inference is analytic in character', and secondly that no statement other than an analytic one can be meaningful unless 'there is something that would be the case if it were true'.[1] This latter claim, as it stands, certainly leaves everything open; and a critic may ask how it can be taken as implying any positivist commitment or special view of meaning. But as it stands, one may answer, it implies nothing at all, it is merely an empty tautology. It 'is the case', for instance, that three times three equal nine, since the statement that 'three times three equal nine' is true—and so, too, with the statement that a breach of trust is wrong. If the statement is true we can say that that, too, is the case. But this plainly cannot be Hare's intention; for, on his view, there is nothing to be called 'the state of affairs that breach of trust is wrong'. I conclude, then, that though he has expressed himself in this passage—not precisely carelessly—rather over-cautiously, what he means by 'something would be the case' must be something observable. I hope this is no great forcing of his

[1] Op. cit., p. 32 and p. 8.

text, for otherwise it can hardly mean anything. And if so, the initial problem is plain; it is simply to find room for ethics between the fork of the analytic-synthetic dichotomy: and the solution comes with the doctrine of imperatives. The main positivist edifice is left to stand; the project is rather to find a way of accommodating morals without seriously disturbing it. We have additions, but no structural alterations. And Hare's theory of inference, we shall find, has a place of some importance in his system. All deductive inference is analytic, and therefore can yield nothing substantial. And where Professor Toulmin claimed to employ a mode of inference which might lead to substantial conclusions, might cross from the factual to the ethical, Hare denies that this is inference at all. He prefers to rewrite it instead, in terms of his Aristotelian paradigm, so that what for Toulmin is a principle of inference becomes for him simply a new major premiss; and on this premiss, as on all others, he can only invite us to decide.[1] But what is of special interest here is not only what he asserts but what he denies. Bad reasoning, he emphatically tells us, is not to be attributed to what he characterizes as 'logical purblindness'[2]—the same visual metaphor, we may notice, found objectionable as ever—but rather, what may seem strange, to simple ignorance. This paradox, of course, is not peculiar to Hare; it is no less paradoxical. For suppose that someone grants the premisses but rejects the conclusion of an ordinary syllogism: he must, we would say, have failed to see that it followed. But Hare denies 'logical purblindness' and hence too, I suppose, logical seeing. His view is that the reasoner, or would-be reasoner, must be ignorant of the meaning of those words which the inference turns on; and here of the meaning of the word 'all'. For such knowledge consists, among other things, in the ability to make such deductions. And since this account is given generally of analytic reasoning—and presumably all the reasoning in Hare's own work, for instance, is to be taken as analytic—it follows that wherever two reasoners disagree at least one of them must suffer from this kind of ignorance. The inability to reason, then, or to follow reasoning, is not something that could ever

[1] Op. cit., pp. 45 ff.     [2] Op. cit., p. 33.

be expressed as the failure to grasp logical relationships; indeed it hardly seems to be an intellectual matter at all. For ignorance is not want of intelligence.

The theory of moral imperatives, first put forward by Viennese positivists, and later much developed and recast, has answered what is sometimes called a felt need; what it gives us is a plausible account of ethics compatible with the main categories of Positivism, and its acceptability is not to be wondered at. But in truth to say this is only to make more explicit what we have seen already; for what lies behind positivist epistemology is the same as what lies behind imperativism. The old bogey is the synthetic *a priori* and the great object to provide for all essentials in accordance with this negative covenant—without bringing back intuition.

## II

In the light of the arguments we have surveyed the acceptability of the notion of decision may seem intelligible enough; at least a large part of the difficulties that have been found in intuitionism disappear with the new approach. But it is time to ask whether it does not involve others of its own; we subjected intuition to some critical scrutiny, and we must now do the same by decision.

Let us ask first what it is that we are to decide on; to what more precisely, on this view, do these decisions relate? Popper writes that we are morally responsible for the norms that we adopt; it is, he says, our business to improve them. And indeed we have already seen in what terms he sets the question: we are to ask ourselves what norms 'are worthy to be adopted'.[1] Hare's language is similar: a man faced with a moral decision must 'make up his own mind on the way he ought to live'.[2] The responsibility is his and no one else's; and in this connexion he speaks, too, of 'the oldest and most ineradicable vice of moralists—the unwillingness to take moral decisions'.[3]

The objection to the position, thus stated, is not far to seek—

---

[1] Op. cit., p. 52.         [2] Op. cit., p. 69.
[3] 'Universalizability', *Proceedings of the Aristotelian Society*, lv (1955), p. 302.

though so far, perhaps, it may not be hard to find some modified form of statement, a degree less plausible no doubt, but still defensible. But we must take it in the form which it has deliberately been given. Moral decisions, on this view, themselves serve to establish or institute norms; hence it is hard to make sense of this proposed decision as to what norms 'are worthy to be adopted'—or again in what way 'we ought to live'. Clearly talk of worthiness and questions of obligation are only intelligible against a background of already existing norms. Hence it is theoretically impossible that the question, at least as it relates to our system of norms in general and not merely to particular norms, should present itself in this way; and the case with particular norms, which we are called on to 'improve', is not much clearer. Unless we evaluate our improved norms by reference to themselves, which would be vacuous, we must appeal to those that already exist; now those old ones may be just the norms that we propose to change, so on these terms our proposal, perhaps, will appear not as an improvement but rather the reverse.

Nor do I find the notion of responsibility much easier to make sense of—though it seems to be a favourite, not only with those writers I have cited but with others, too; who apparently feel something akin to exhilaration in the thought that their moral code rests upon themselves alone. The attribution of responsibility requires not only the minimal condition fulfilled here, that a man's own act is in question; it requires a further background, some code of conduct or system of principles that the action falls under, so that we can speak of it as right or wrong. Let us suppose a weighty moral issue to be decided: the agent may ask whether to make the decision —or whether he ought to make it—with careful thought and long scrutiny of the issues involved or, perhaps, with the toss of a coin. The latter suggestion may seem absurd; such conduct would be a pattern of irresponsibility. So it would; I do not mean to deny it. Yet until, on the basis of decisions already taken, we recognize norms to appeal to, we cannot say so. Perhaps another man with his choice already made may fix his eye on the agent, now choosing, and hold him responsible; he will call the choice a good or a bad one.

But the chooser himself cannot do so, except on the basis of previous choices, now perhaps thrown back into the balance. There is no responsibility in a moral vacuum. Indeed one may recall that Descartes avowedly retained his orthodox beliefs for ordinary purposes, even while he put everything through the ordeal of systematic doubt. Perhaps philosophers, hardened to such imaginative exercises —professionally accustomed to straining the hypothetical faculty— may let themselves fancy that one might in some sense decide or re-decide on one's own principles while in effect retaining them all the while; one might put them only into a kind of theoretical suspense. But then, plainly, what we have to do with is no longer a moral decision taken in earnest.

I shall not dwell on this point further. Suppose that the objection is allowed: a voluntarist may meet it by merely reducing his claim and formulating a more cautious position—one that may be somewhat less attractive but is no doubt still plausible enough. Hare's statement of his view is, however, exposed to other objections as well, which it will need much more drastic overhauling to avoid. It will be recalled that in that imaginary argument which pressed moral differences back to first principles we were finally invited, or required, to make up our own minds as to how we ought to live. And elsewhere we find that Hare tells us in his own person—a morally unexceptionable utterance, no doubt, only puzzling in its logical setting—that he himself thinks that torture is wrong.[1] Now an ethical utterance, we must remember, is to be cast into the imperative mood. Let us suppose that we are to make up our minds on some particular practical question; the indicative 'I ought to do such and such' has the interrogative 'ought I to do such and such?' But the imperative has no interrogative counterpart at all. One might ask 'Shall I go?' and get the answer 'Go'; but if 'I ought to go' is tantamount to 'Go' or 'Let me go' (addressed to oneself), there is no such form as 'Ought I to go?' The ethical imperatives differ, of course, as being implicitly universal, but that does not affect the present issue. We find again that neither the sentence 'He has made

---

[1] 'Universalizability', *Proceedings of the Aristotelian Society*, lv, 304.

up his mind (on the way in which he ought to live)' nor 'I think that (torture is wrong)' could, as a matter of grammar, have been completed in the imperative mood.

Now questioning is regarded by some people as a part, nor the least important part, of moral life; so the loss of all strictly moral questions—as distinct from factual or logical questions that may have a bearing on conduct—is, perhaps, one that will be felt. That is the first consequence of voluntarism; but now let us return to a more direct examination of this notion of a moral decision.

First, perhaps captiously, I shall quarrel with the name. Names, as we know, are important, and there is many a flourishing philosophical doctrine that has not smelt nearly so sweet once a different label has been affixed. These so-called decisions, we must observe, are required to meet needs that are quite general, their office is to furnish us with first principles—which may or may not relate to morals. We shall need principles of this sort no less in logic, science and so forth, but we do not hear of 'logical' or 'scientific' decisions. Now it would surely be better either to use the expression systematically or not at all; and if one were told of 'scientific decision', I for my own part would be surprised to learn that what was meant was, say, the decision to use the principle of induction or any other fundamental procedure—on this view, we must remember, a mere decision, that cannot itself be right or wrong. And similarly the phrase 'moral decision' surely suggests a decision that falls not outside but within morality, for which we are and may see ourselves as being morally responsible; whereas these, we have seen, establish or institute moral systems and must, so to speak, stand above them. They are not moral in their own nature then, but only in the subject-matter that they relate to; other decisions, having the same logical status, will legislate in the same way for other fields.

But there is no need to insist on this point, and more serious matters claim our attention. Let us first, taking a more general view, concern ourselves for the time being not with the particular content of Hare's doctrines but rather with their character or status; let us ask what sort of statements these are. What Hare has said of moral principles, we must recall, is not and cannot be confined to those principles; it must hold good, if it holds at all, of evaluation in general. And we evaluate objects of every sort. There are good cars, good peaches and good reasons for beliefs, no less than good actions and good men. Nor is this accidental to a system that explains ethics in terms of the function of such words as 'good'; which insists on the distinction between the rôle that evaluative words play, which is constant in all fields, and the variable criteria for their application. In theory objects of any description may be commended, and logic, we are told, can recognize no step from the one type of linguistic task to the other: no description can entail an evaluation. Indeed, if moral utterances are in the nature of commands this consequence follows naturally enough: for presumably nothing in logic can prevent us from commanding any action or sort of action whatever.

Hare's avowed theme is the evaluative use of language. True, he calls his book more specifically *The Language of Morals*, but it would seem that only a single section—Part II, section nine, to be precise—is concerned directly with moral concepts as such: and even there it is his chief object to insist that this moral use of the word 'good' does not need a special logic of its own.[1] Objects of all sorts, we have found, are equally candidates for evaluation, and among those listed above one especially interesting class was included, namely our reasons for our beliefs. Their inclusion is not merely an inference from the general account that Hare gives, though indeed the inference would be plain enough; but in point of fact he tells us himself that 'probably' is usually a value-word: for to call a thing probable, generally speaking, is to say that we have reasons—good reasons—for thinking it true.[2]

Now having got so far a critic might take a short cut and ask straightaway whether Hare's analysis is a good analysis—and, supposing that it is, what can make it so, or what such a claim would involve. But let us proceed by more orderly degrees. In any case to

---

[1] Op. cit., p. 140.

[2] Op. cit., p. 60. An alternative course would be to omit from this definition the adjective 'good', and treat 'reason' itself as a value-word. On this point see below, pp. 69–70.

decide whether or not it is a good analysis we shall need to know
first what standards or criteria to apply, and that in turn depends on
our interpretation of his work. Let us sum up the thesis that we
have been concerned with so far, namely that 'there can be no perception of moral truths'. These are not Hare's own words but they
are, I trust, a tolerably fair statement of a position which he is concerned to maintain. If so, what sort of statement would he be
defending? I suppose it will be what is called an 'analytic' one; there
is, at least, no obvious alternative. It is not at least overtly evaluative,
and we can leave out of account the possibility that it might be
empirical. Now an analytic statement is normally conceived as one
exhibiting or illustrating procedures that belong to some given
system of linguistic usage; and unless we are warned to the contrary
we shall suppose the system to be ordinary English. The unpre-
pared reader will surely understand Hare in this sense, and could
hardly be expected to do otherwise; yet, unless this is to misunder-
stand him, what he is asserting is plainly false. We have already
found that this account of moral language conflicts sharply with
almost all our ordinary ways of speaking. 'I think that this course is
the right one . . . I ask myself whether it would be . . . I realize, I see
plainly that it would . . .': an account that disallows such expressions
as these, whatever other merits it may claim, can hardly represent
existing usage. Indeed the statement in which I sought to sum-
marize Hare's view expresses the very opposite of the fact: that 'one
cannot be said in English to perceive moral truths'—anyone who
speaks the language knows that that is false.

But the theory before us is not so easily to be disposed of. It is
true that Hare himself has given no hint of the matter; but apparently we must see his real purpose as the introduction of some new
system of usage—and one within which, no doubt, the proposition
in question will indeed be strictly analytic. Now any system of
usage, new or old, will always admit of evaluation, though our normal
tendency may be to take existing things for granted. But where a
pretty radical innovation is proposed the issue is virtually forced on
us; here we can hardly help but ask ourselves whether the change is

E

for the better or the worse. But if so how are we to settle the issue, how can we decide? Let us refer again to Hare's work. Any evaluative utterance has two sides to it: there is the function of prescription or commendation, and there are particular criteria in virtue of which we prescribe or commend the object in question. We commend things of a given description; the criteria will be specified features of objects of the relevant sort. They vary from one case to another, but whenever an object is called 'good' it must be proper to ask what makes it good: to ask, that is to say, what particular standards are we appealing to, what criteria we see fit (or have 'chosen') to apply. What makes a good apple good, for instance, will perhaps be that it is large, sweet and juicy, and what makes a motor-car good that it is comfortable, fast and manœuvrable; lastly as to the goodness of people—which, we remarked, does not need a special logic of its own—they too are commended for the virtues proper to them, such as honesty or humility or kindness. These last-mentioned terms themselves may still be evaluatively coloured, but at bottom it must be possible to get down to a merely neutral description of certain qualities: of qualities which we shall be equally free, in logic, either to commend or to condemn. There is no inference from description to commendation; the missing step is supplied by that crucial element in Hare's system, namely decision.[1] Further we may notice in this connexion that in setting out the facts of the case Hare tells us that we should be as factual as possible.[2]

Now the issue before us concerns two alternative systems of linguistic usage; for we find that if Hare's work is to be taken as analytic the language to which his statements belong—whose usage they reflect as analytic statements are supposed to—differs markedly from ordinary English. To evaluate different linguistic systems, we shall need criteria; that is to say, we shall need to specify certain features—strictly describable features—in virtue of which we shall choose one or the other. It is natural to ask, then, what criteria Hare himself has decided on; but as far as I can find we are never told; and hence it is hard for another person to say whether he would

[1] Op. cit., pp. 111 ff.            [2] Op. cit., p. 57.

decide likewise or not. Perhaps, other things being equal, we ought to prefer the *status quo* rather than follow innovation. It may, indeed, sound somewhat anomalous to talk of choosing criteria for linguistic systems—if what we mean in effect is choosing between different systems of philosophy. For then many philosophers might tell us that they prefer one way of speaking to another simply for this reason, that they believe that it gets us nearer to the truth: in ethics they may be concerned to understand the concept of 'right' or of 'good'. They believe in some right way of talking, which will also be a right way of thinking, which it is a philosopher's business to discover. That, I fear, cannot be Hare's aim—though I do not say that it is not the real effect of his achievement. Whatever is valid in his work, whatever ethical truth we may learn from it—and that in my own view is not a little—may happily be understood in terms that make it something more significant than the expression of individual choices or decisions. Nonetheless his own statements are unequivocal. We have not only his account of those decisions of principle on which evaluation of objects of all sorts is ultimately based, but his further assertion that failure to follow valid arguments does not derive, to use his own phrase, from 'logical purblindness': there is no perception or recognition of logical truths. It follows that we cannot recognize or fail to recognize the rightness of a given way of speaking in moral philosophy either. In the last resort we can only decide: Hare, too, has decided then, but what criteria he has used we are not told.

But surely, it may be said, we should be able to set out for ourselves critieria that would be generally accepted. The matter may be partly controversial, but we can give some broad indication of the sort of qualities that we look for in anything that we commend as a satisfactory philosophical system. As a rough sketch one may say, perhaps, that we require that it should be tolerably economical and systematic, and, further, do fair justice to our ordinary feelings or intuitions. Now here we might enter on lengthy issues, which I prefer to postpone. At least we have already found reason to question how far our ordinary feelings, embodied in ordinary language, get a fair hearing in Hare's system. But the deeper puzzle here is the old one: how we can think or philosophize at all if we treat the standards by which theories are to be judged as matters on which we merely decide—decide without asking, without allowing that it makes sense to ask, whether or not their acceptance is likely to bring us nearer to the truth. Considered in this way, for example, I cannot see why ordinary intuition, which I spoke of in the previous chapter, should be taken account of at all, or again why economy should be thought a virtue. A simple and economical linguistic system is doubtless quicker and more convenient to work with; but it would surely be strange to suggest that the merits of philosophical doctrines should be assessed on such principles. Philosophers are not usually pressed for time; the greatest economy of words would be to give up the subject altogether.

Let us suppose that we were given features, descriptive criteria: one step would still remain—their commendation. Hare may commend to us his new system, he may speak of it as good. In other circumstances one might be impressed, but unhappily we now know what 'good' means: the word has the force of an imperative, it is tantamount to saying 'Choose this'. There are people to be found I believe, at least among the foolish and feeble-minded, who merely on being spoken to in the imperative will do whatever you tell them to do. You say to them 'Sit down' and they sit; you say 'Stand up again' and they stand; but that, I imagine, is not the sort of ascendancy an analytic philosopher would wish to exercise over his readers. For the rest, we shall naturally ask why we should let it affect our conduct that Mr. Hare, or that anyone else, having made certain decisions of his own, chooses to address us in the imperative mood. For my own part I find myself quite unmoved. Hare's intended exposition of the function of ethical words has operated more like an exposure: we were promised some account of this sort of language that would serve to make its meaning intelligible in terms of the function that it fulfils, namely the direction of conduct. But, alas, once its principle is made plain, *eo ipso* its function disappears: we know now how the trick works and it is too late.

When we are told that something is good we shall no longer imagine that we have been given anything like a reason for choosing it.

As to all this there is one more word to add. I may be told that it is perverse and unnecessary to offer counter-arguments to conjectural developments of Hare's views, to speculate on their logical status, when he himself is at pains to make purpose clear. For, in the final chapter of his book he constructs what he calls an 'analytic model'; a sketch, that is to say, of a possible language in which all evaluative expression should answer exactly to his own previous account. In existing language he does not claim that they do so. It would seem rather that ordinary language-forms, much like household instruments, tend to get used for several purposes. But we can distinguish the functions from the tools, and often it will be possible to say what particular function a given tool is best adapted for. It may be that we have only one tool that will serve for a particular job, although it has acquired auxiliary functions that might equally be handed back to others. And that special job may be one that we cannot leave undone if we are to live on any reasonable terms. In this way we may give some sort of non-metaphysical account that will serve instead of a theory of essence; and one might take Hare to be saying after his own fashion that the guidance of conduct is the essence of moral discourse. Moral utterances are, in the present sense, essentially universal imperatives; and in the model language which Hare sketches at the end of his work certain language-forms confined strictly to this rôle are to replace the moral terms that we have at present. Then we may see by comparing them how much or little we lose on the exchange; for no doubt the doubling of rôles, whereby one word does work that might be redistributed among others, is more a matter of convenience than of logic.[1]

---

[1] Op. cit., pp. 180 ff. I take the opportunity of adding in proof that Hare has just published an interesting further account of the work of philosophy (v. 'Philosophical Discoveries', *Mind*, 274, 1960, pp. 145–62). His position, I think, has affinities to that developed below (v. pp. 130 ff.), for I shall speak of reflective thought as eliciting rules from previous practice. Hare maintains that logic, as he calls it, identifies and describes, and sometimes names, 'various sorts of things that people say . . . It has to rely on our knowledge, as yet unformulated, of how to do these things.' (Loc. cit., p. 159.) This

I shall not go into the detail of Hare's model, nor follow out the other interesting questions that it raises. After all if the question is to be the comparison between the new and the old way of speaking, the main difference leaps to the eye: I have dwelt on it sufficiently already. All moral questioning, all talk of bringing men to see or realize what is right, is excluded from the language of the model. Hence, whatever advantages the new system can claim, supposing the only alternative is the traditional theory of intuition, the choice will be no foregone conclusion. Besides, while it remains a mere choice, nothing much can be made of it: we shall want a more significant account than Hare's theory of inference seems to allow of the merits and demerits of philosophical theories. If we say 'decision' and mean it—if we mean a bare option for one system or the other —philosophical argument as we usually understand it, a rational attempt to resolve differences, will have come to an end already.

But here further consequences ensue, consequences which I have already touched on in speaking of the wider implication of voluntarism, but which will perhaps bear repetition. For the point is a central one. We might drop our hypothetical language when we speak of this decision which concerns us—the putative decision to adopt Hare's new usage—and set down the historical fact: many philosophers have actually rejected it. And that can only mean, in Hare's language, that they have decided against it. Indeed the step may not have presented itself to them in those terms, in the form of a decision of principle. His critics in deciding against him may not have known what they were doing, and might even have emphatically rejected such an account of it. But it is one plain consequence of the present treatment of evaluative language, if we suppose for

seems to me in essence entirely right; yet we are hardly likely to name and formulate implicit rules without occasionally feeling some slight need to modify or at least to tighten them. Hare himself, we have found, both modifies and tightens them pretty drastically. How that should be possible—how we should evaluate innovations in usage, or choose on any rational basis between them and conservatism—is, I fear, no clearer than before. Or if philosophy, either by the philosophers' choice or by Hare's definition, confines itself to identifying and describing, that once again can only reflect a personal preference.

argument's sake that we accept it, that many things must be labelled 'decisions' which, in common parlance, are nothing of the sort. Here everything comes back to decision; and yet if we should set out to experiment, should ask people generally where or when they took their 'ultimate moral decisions' or whether they were conscious of doing so, I fancy that we should meet a pretty blank response.[1]

The fact is, then, that numerous philosophers, taking an ultimate logical decision—the decision, perhaps, to reject proposed linguistic innovations that do excessive violence to common intuitions or common sense—have chosen against the theory before us. And further, issuing imperatives, they have told or ordered other people to do the same: for that is what it means to call it 'wrong'. You may attribute this decision to any sort of imaginable source, to muddle-headedness, restricted views or what you will; none of this can bear on the argument. It may derive, indeed, from mere contra-suggestibility, a thing not unknown in philosophical discussion. Logic can take no notice of that; psychology might explain it perhaps, but philosophy, we know, has left that epoch behind when it noticed psychological matters. It remains that a man's ultimate principles, those on which he merely decides, are those that he himself treats as ultimate; and logically such decisions are on a level. The difference between mature judgement, judgement which rightly commands respect, and ignorance, perversity or the like, does not exist for the theory before us. For suppose you go beyond those given principles on which a man actually argues, prejudiced or stupid as he may be, to find other, better principles no doubt, which, as you say, he would adopt if he clearly saw what he was doing. Once we speak like

[1] It seems clear in the passages that I have cited above (cf. pp. 33–4) that decisions are taken to be indispensable in Hare's general theory of moral discourse—as the sole source of ultimate principles. They are 'of the very essence of morals'. Yet I am not wholly sure where he stands on the issue; for elsewhere (op. cit., pp. 72–4) he seems to distinguish between moral conservatives and moral innovators, those who merely inherit and those who decide for themselves on their moral principles. Supposing that in all of us there is something of both, it would yet seem that only where we have chosen to modify our inherited principles—or perhaps consciously reaffirmed them—can we properly be said to have decided. And in that case a man might in theory go through life using moral words intelligibly and yet never take a decision at all.

this we part company with voluntarism: it is plain that the whole position has been given up. For we have now passed from the notion of decidable principles to something very different, to that of discoverable truths; we have reintroduced evaluative terms, appealing to right principles that a clearer reasoner would accept, into our meta-ethical superstructure. If these in turn rest on decisions nothing is gained; we shall be liable, here as before, to be brought to a halt by the intractable stupidity of moral philosophers who take different meta-ethical decisions from ourselves. These decisions, too, must be allowed to stand; they have with no different logical status from that of the decisions that they oppose. And the decisionist is left with no sense in which he can call his critics' views wrong—except the supremely empty sense in which he may issue imperatives to them that they will surely not feel moved to obey.

## III

These difficulties suggest others that, perhaps, deserve some brief notice, before we finally take leave of this concept of a decision of principle. A decision must, no less than an intuition, be some individual's decision. He will take it, presumably, at some particular time and place—pausing, it may be, for a moment, with a raised teacup in his hand, or looking out over a London street, with a terrace of stuccoed houses in the rain. It does not concern us, however, to ask in what romantic or unromantic circumstances decisions of principle are taken; logic cannot interest itself in *them*. And yet why, if not, we may ask, should it interest itself in these details at all—biographical particulars, as they seem to be, incidents in individual lives? In surveying the objections to intuitionism we noticed among them the charge of psychologism, of mixing psychological material in what is properly a logical discussion. Something like the same complaint seems called for here.

The authors whose work we have been studying are interested in the logic of ethical discourse or of inquiry generally; we should expect from them something in the nature of a setting out of the pattern of moral argument—not indeed of particular arguments, but rather an ideal reconstruction that will bring out the logical relations involved. What is given us instead, when we get to the core of the matter, is rather a psychological concept which seems to have no place here at all. I have spoken hitherto somewhat vaguely of the common rôle of these two concepts of intuition and decision; they both claim to provide us with first principles. Yet surely it will need no deep training in the methods of contemporary linguistic philosophy to distinguish two different questions here: we may ask for the logical ground or the justification of these principles—in which case the decisionist's real answer, given the courage of his convictions, is simply that they have none—or we may ask how one person or another first came to possess or adopt them. And to that we should expect the reply that it is a question of no concern to philosophy. They may, for instance, have been passed on by his teachers so that he accepted them unquestioningly or derived from unconscious emotional needs: the person in question may be a voluntarist himself, and deliberately have asked himself at some moment on what ultimate principles he should decide; or again he may be an ethical naturalist and believe himself—wrongly, if you like—to have inferred moral principles from factual grounds. It makes no difference; no doubt there are many ways of acquiring principles, and for the purposes of voluntarist logic they must all be on a level. The objection to the notion of a decision is that it muddles the issue by trying to answer both these questions in one.

But here we meet a rather deeper doubt: we might ask—at the risk of seeming foolish—how it is that these philosophers come to know that we all possess such ultimate principles at all. The answer seems too obvious, we must possess them. The argument will no doubt resemble Spinoza's, that since everything is either a mode grounded in a substance or itself a substance, some substance, which is its own ground, must exist. You may ask of any principle that a man holds whether it is an ultimate principle or derived from others; if the latter, these in turn may be either ultimate or derivative, so that unless the process is infinite certain ultimate principles must be there to be found. To be sure the man who holds them may not know which they are; he may never properly formulate his principles or may shift confusedly from one to another. But once a competent logician intervenes, overhauling the body of his beliefs and presenting them in systematic form, all that will soon be put in order. Those few most general principles whose deductive power is the greatest will be formulated and set at the top, and the rest will be derived in successive steps. Thus we shall restore to every street-corner moralist the true system of his own ethical beliefs—perhaps in a form in which he himself no longer recognizes them, but one, at least, much nearer to the preference or ideal of mathematicians and symbolic logicians.

Let us, then, ask once again what the contention amounts to that we all must, in the nature of the case, possess some such ultimate principles. Apparently this: that we have each our own system of beliefs—or want of system, but at least we have beliefs. And secondly that any set of beliefs admits in principle of recasting in accordance with a certain preferred model: let us call it the linear or Euclidean model. Now lastly, once it is so recast, we are left with a sort of pyramid of propositions, some among them being chosen to stand at the top, for that is the very pattern of the schema or plan that we have adopted. And those at the top are called 'ultimate'. Hence it follows that anyone having principles at all must have ultimate principles among them; and these beliefs, thus extracted and exalted, are those associated by the philosophers whose work we have been looking at with choice or decision.

This association is generally fictitious: let us suppose that a man testifies that he witnessed a particular event a year ago, and further —what would normally seem superfluous—that he is called on to justify his testimony. He may claim that he vividly remembers. Now Lewis Carroll's Achilles, and, I suppose, Mr. Hare,[1] would have us write in some superfluous major premiss, say, that one's clear memory of an event is ground for asserting that it took place—for I have said that an argument will always admit of recasting in accordance with the one favoured model. (And premiss in turn may

[1] Cf. above, p. 43.

be based on some mythical decision taken at no specified time.) The triumphs of modern physics persuaded scientists that all true science in any field, whether it deals with particles of matter, with microbes or with human behaviour, ought properly to be mathematical in form; and so too, since the time of the Greeks, some sort of Euclidean ideal has fixed and fascinated the minds of philosophers. They have longed to do with the heterogeneous manifold of common reasoning what calculation and measurement have done with the volume and movement of bodies; and Aristotle himself, who was the first to protest against the use of inappropriate standards in ethics, against the demand for mathematical precision where it serves no purpose, nonetheless largely contributed to the general acceptance of this one paradigm.

Our business here, however, is not a critique of formal logic. The truth is, perhaps, that what logicians offer us is something in the nature of ideal type, analogous to the notion of economic man, arrived at first by isolating certain features of the concrete process— and then carrying them, in this ideal isolation, as far as they will go. For the rest, the value of these procedures, their justification and limits, are topics for some other inquiry. But the approach, applied to ethics, is certainly plausible; it seems that there are certain moral principles that are not to be derived from anything more fundamental: the principles of honesty, perhaps, or at all events of rational benevolence, do not seem to admit of further justification. Now suppose that we reject the Euclidean model in favour of some other; it is not clear that much will be gained or lost. We might appeal to the common course of actual argument, which seems the right place to look for logical patterns: there we find, for instance, the wrongness of a given act directly inferred from the suffering that it causes. That may be treated as a rule, and here we have a mode of presentation, a possible logical schema, on the face of it no worse than any other. But as regards the justification of principles we stand pretty much where we stood previously. Whether we call the prevention of suffering a principle of morals or a rule of inference we still may be called on to justify it, and here we are no better off than before.

Now there are certainly further doubts that might be raised here. As to the Euclidean model itself, it may be said in general that it always allows us alternatives: that what appears as a premiss in one sort of systematization may appear as a theorem in another and *vice versa*: and we might ask again, when we are told that some principles must be ultimate, how we know in advance that we may not find new reasons for beliefs that we have hitherto accepted unquestioningly. Philosophers have often enough found reasons, good or bad, for things that they believed previously on instinct. Yet to all this there is a reasonable reply, that these are merely general possibilities; and after all when some principle such as the principle of benevolence is in question, no other plausible course seems to be open than to accept it as ultimate.

As to the status of the notion of decision, the outcome would seem to be this, that the bare logical structure of the imperativist and voluntarist theory can stand intact, provided it remains within its strictly non-psychological ground. The thesis will then be simply this, that moral utterances are in effect universal imperatives, any one of which may in principle be derived from some other more general; that in the linear setting out of any system of moral beliefs some such principles must appear first, at the top: from these, then, other principles may be inferred but they themselves cannot be inferred from others. For the rest, any question as to how individuals arrive at their moral principles, ultimate or otherwise, will be left out of the argument. Such a re-statement would meet the difficulty, and so far this more contracted position would perhaps be a tenable one, though Hare himself, I believe, would not welcome the change; for he tells us in a passage already quoted that decision is 'of the very essence of morals'.[1] On what ground he can say so is less plain, unless on the basis of a particular moral choice of his own. He may have decided to recommend principles originating in decisions as better than other sorts—or those who adopt them as better. That, indeed, would accord well enough with his general emphasis

[1] Cf. above, p. 33.

on individual responsibility, which is something that he evidently sets great store by.

There is one other point that may deserve notice before we leave the notion of moral decision. On behalf of his own account of ethics Hare makes the further claim that, as against earlier emotivist theories, it serves to vindicate the rationality of moral discourse. He makes much of the contention that moral utterances do not beg or bully, they do not operate persuasively or use pressure on those who hear them; rather they are addressed to them as rational beings. One has still to make up one's mind and act as 'a free responsible agent'.[1] But how much this thesis amounts to is less clear. There are, for instance, many philosophers who hold that all mental phenomena, including true and reasonable beliefs, must in principle be psychologically explicable; if so, a man's belief that he ought, say, to make or not to make some false statement, will also be psychologically explicable. And perhaps part of the explanation will be that someone has addressed him in the imperative, has told him what he ought or ought not to do. If imperatives act on us at all, as they must if they are to serve to guide conduct, they presumably act on us psychologically—and perhaps no emotivist ever meant to claim more. To insist that their action is rational, let us agree, is to rule out any influence working on the mere emotions of the hearer; but precisely what that involves is less obvious. Indeed the whole topic badly needs analysis. Broadly, at least, it seems that to call a reaction 'emotional', where this does not simply mean 'violent', is to imply first that it is contrary to 'reason', that is, to some system of standards which the agent was in a position to know; and secondly that explanations of the deviation are available, at any rate in principle. We shall refer to jealousy, panic or the like. Now none of this seems to arise where moral imperatives are concerned. Hare calls moral utterance rational, so he tells us, to contrast it with propaganda, advertising and the like, and no doubt the difference is real. But what account he might give of it remains obscure. If both moral

[1] Op. cit., p. 15.

imperatives and advertiser's slogans act on their hearers, it is hard
to see how we can distinguish them as irrational and rational respec-
tively, unless we are first to presuppose some sort of normal or
right response—from which deviations, *qua* deviations, need to be
accounted for. And Hare's voluntarist system hardly allows that.

Perhaps the point Hare means to insist on is that an ethical utterance still leaves its hearers free to choose; after all they must decide
for themselves. Yet the purpose of such utterances is to guide conduct; it was in terms of this purpose, indeed, that the language of
morals was to be made intelligible. The doctrine is surely somewhat
puzzling. It is clear that if we are to take a test case the particular
decision in question must relate to an ultimate principle; here, where
there is no other more general to appeal to, a moral imperative is
issued—which influences our conduct, though without acting on our
emotions. Again we learn no new matters of fact, for that is a fundamental tenet; no moral utterance can tell us anything of which we
were previously ignorant. Sometimes, perhaps, it serves to hasten a
decision which the agent might otherwise have deferred; but that is
a particular supposition, and a man who asks himself whether he is
to take a given step—the question, according to Hare, that moral
utterance is especially meant to answer—may quite well already
clearly see that he must either do one thing or the other. Inactivity
is also a course of action. Now in this situation we tell him what (as
we say) he ought to do. And that utterance acts on him, it has a
practical function; and yet it acts, not emotionally but rationally.
It does not impugn his own choice but leaves him free to do what he
thinks fit. By hypothesis, however, he would anyway have done
what he thought fit, and moral utterance is left with no function
whatever: unless it is to forgo its claim to rationality, it can do no
more than invite a man to take decisions that he was about to have
taken uninvited.

If the theory of decision is no more adequate to supply a basis for
morals than the traditional theory of intuition, it may be asked what
alternative remains. A reversion to ethical irrationalism may suggest itself as the most promising course. But it is too late for that:

whatever difficulties appear in Hare's work, we shall certainly be much mistaken if we suppose that it merely leaves moral philosophy where it found it. And one important lesson that we may learn from it is that the problem of evaluation is a general one; so that the old simple answer, the doctrine that consigned ethics to one drawer and kept properly rational modes of inquiry—science, mathematics or philosophy—apart in another, will no longer meet our needs. But of this I shall speak more in the following chapter.

# III

## Axiology and the Process of Inquiry

IN any work of moral philosophy we find chapters devoted, as a matter of course, to such topics as the nature of rightness and of goodness—or else, if the writer is up to date, to the use of the words 'right' and 'good'—which in logical or epistemological writings hardly ever get mentioned. One would suppose, then, that these evaluative notions have some plain connexion with human conduct —taking that roughly as the province of morals—which is lacking elsewhere: that they have no such connexion, for instance, with argument or inference, or with answers to questions or beliefs. And that must seem too obvious to need arguing, for this division of topics is usually offered without comment. Yet it cannot be derived from ordinary usage or common thought, for we speak of 'right views' or 'right solutions' quite as often and as naturally as we speak of 'right actions' or the like. The same holds of other evaluative terms; one hears of a good piece of scholarship and takes this expression as a matter of course, no less than when one hears of a good man.

Suppose we were to consider the possibility of some different division of the subject: at least one benefit that the change might bring would be some discussion of morals in works devoted to moral philosophy. For important as these more general problems of evaluation may be, as the status of 'Hume's law', naturalism or the definition of 'right', it is a pity when properly ethical issues are crowded out altogether. Yet the other departments of philosophy, such as logic, epistemology and methodology, would, I suspect, profit still more; a treatise, say, on validity or inference might find room for some clarification of the difference at stake when we call one argument 'good' and another 'bad'—which surely are pertinent questions. The opening chapter, we find indeed, of Mr. Strawson's *Introduction to Logical Theory* has the title 'Logica, Appraisal', and he tells us on the very first page that to call a discourse 'logical' is to commend it; but these topics, it seems, are soon afterwards forgotten.

There is, however, one more hopeful sign; though moral philosophers may concern themselves more with evaluation than with morals, at least they leave us in no doubt of the distinction. They present the former, which is their main interest, wholly generally. We have already given some time to Hare's account of the logic of evaluative words: the rôle that they play and the type of question that they raise remain the same, on his view, whatever sort of object that they are applied to; and further he holds that in principle they are applicable to any class of objects whatever. Much the same position was earlier maintained by Professor Urmson in an article which Hare more than once refers to.[1] When we speak of good people or good books, of good ideas and good arguments and good railways, we can hardly mean something different every time; yet with objects so various as these—and the list might be extended indefinitely— it would be hard to find any one describable feature that they all have in common. What makes it still clearer that the meaning of the word 'good' remains the same here, while the objects which we apply it to vary, is that we naturally ask the same questions in each case and expect the same sort of reply. We can ask of each object what makes it good; it is a question that has to be answered if the claim is to be sustained. Generally speaking, to answer it will be to name or describe certain features—features which serve as criteria for the assessment of object of the relevant sort; and these vary from one sort to another. Different things, for instance, make us call apples good from holidays or railways; a good soldier, say, and a good artist, need not share any of the qualities which they are severally commended for. Yet, variable as they may be, there must be such criteria to point to, if our evaluation is to stand. (We shall find, indeed, that special cases arise where we need to go further, where strictly general criteria no longer suffice; yet even there this is the first step: the appeal to such criteria is always the foundation which we build on.)[2]

---

[1] 'On Grading', *Mind*, lix, 145–69.
[2] On the limits to the applicability of this demand for general criteria, see below, pp. 184 ff.

F

And suppose we commend any one object in virtue of qualities that we find in it: we are bound in logic to commend any other object of the same sort in which the same qualities are to be found. Qualities, for instance, that make one speaking-trumpet commendable must be equally commendable in another—though in objects of other sorts we might not think them commendable at all. Softness may be an excellent thing in a woman's voice, carrying power in a sergeant-major's; but in either case there must be some feature or features that we can point to so as to justify the assessment if we call it good.

This uniform logical pattern surely makes it very unplausible to take the meaning of the word 'good' as differing with all the different sorts of things which it is applied to. And if we were to identify its whole meaning with these criteria that vary from case to case, we should split it up into an infinity of unaccountable meanings—and each one a superfluous synonym for the non-evaluative description of the criteria which, no doubt, we possess already. Hare's and Urmson's account of evaluation has been challenged on various scores, and perhaps rightly; but I do not know that any plausible answer has been made to these telling arguments.[1]

What we say of 'good' may be extended to cover 'right' and other evaluative terms; the logical connexion between 'right' and 'good' is admittedly pretty close. But this will occupy us presently.[2] Here I shall only remark that as between, say, the right way of building a bridge or again of digging a grave; the right adjective to use in a poetical or technical description or the right treatment for juvenile delinquents, it would seem quite as hard to find any common describable feature as between the different good objects that I have listed.

Now we have seen that Hare takes the distinctive function of the

[1] A reversion to the traditional instrumental-intrinsic distinction would perhaps be the most promising course for a critic bent on rejecting this account; but that in turn loses its attraction when we ask whether good reasons or good theories are to be counted as means or as ends. Suppose they are called means 'to truth': the account is then circular. We cannot define 'truth' apart from our means of knowing it.

[2] Cf. below, pp. 178 ff.

word 'good' to be that of commendation, and Urmson in the same context speaks of 'grading'. I shall leave this provisionally an open question and content myself with the neutral word 'evaluation'. What we should stress in the first place is that evaluation is an activity on its own account, that it requires to be studied in itself, apart from any particular subject-matter. That, of course, is not to say that we can evaluate and yet evaluate nothing—neither theories nor people nor radio sets. But, inasmuch as this abstractable function may relate to all sorts of objects indifferently, we must not let our account of evaluation itself be too closely bound up with any one of them. And for this study, since it deserves to have a name of its own, I shall adopt the little-used name axiology—for certainly it is not co-extensive with what we call ethics. And it is as an essay in axiology that what follows is to be taken. First, however, it may be as well to say a few further words in defence of the subject or the notion of such a subject itself.

I do not mean that there are weighty objections to be considered which have been or might be urged against it; if they exist I for my part have not met them. But inquiry has been pressed forward on all sides with such entire disregard of these distinctions—as if axiological questions could have no interest outside morals, where they belong—that some further brief defence of this re-charting of boundaries may seem proper. The literature of the last ten or twenty years teems with uncritical references to this antithesis, variously expressed, between the factual and moral modes of discourse; between description or statement proper, and utterances that are prescriptive or emotive. True, there are dissident voices too, and perhaps they are gathering in volume; certain instrumentalists and pragmatists have always spoken of scientific 'values', along with moral ones, so as to bring out their similarity: it is one of the many merits of that neglected school—neglected in this country at least. We also occasionally find rather puzzled acknowledgements that 'valid' itself, the logician's key term, is a value-word; that the modal verbs 'may' and 'must' have essentially the same part to play in factual and ethical contexts; even that emotive elements are involved in scientific law-statements and the like—though this last is a bewildering claim, that certainly obscures more than it clarifies. Where anything psychologically recognizable as emotion, need enter into the verdict that such and such a theory is sound, such an inference legitimate, is hard to see; and if emotion is not psychological, one may doubt if it is anything at all. But, of course, we know where the usage comes from; its origin appears quite explicitly when, in a still stranger formulation, these same puzzling elements are called 'ethical'. The old picture re-asserts itself, we see, in and in spite of the very attempt to express its inadequacy. There is room, then, for further clarification. At the same time I should say in candour that I have nothing to offer by way of recondite or novel considerations; no dialectical passages which a professional sophist would wish to stake his reputation on. But, supposing I had, so far as the vindication of axiology goes, they scarcely seem called for.

Let us then ask how it can have come about that these questions have been so generally ignored by epistemologists and philosophers of science. One part of the answer may be that the notion of rightness seemed unimportant because attention was fixed on that of truth; once given a sound theory of truth there would be little need of anything more. Now truth, on a view widely held, means simply correspondence with fact; and we have seen that one great problem of ethics—properly of axiology—has been the want of any obvious facts to which its statements, or would-be statements, might correspond. But where there are facts to appeal to, there is no place for the notions of right and wrong: that a given statement corresponds to the facts will itself, if it is true, be a fact. Hence outside ethics, it may have seemed, objectivity could be easily defined—and, further, without resort to Platonism. For that is the great bugbear: intuitable values or standards, as it were, standing at a tangent to the actual world. But the line can be adequately drawn and no axiological questions need arise.

Platonism, we may observe, has the immense merit of posing the problem of objectivity squarely and wholly generally. As to the present account, this papier-mâché wall might stand, I suppose, so long as no one chanced to knock his knuckle against it, but hardly longer. The different status of scientific and moral truths is not in doubt, but our concern at present is not with morals but with axiology: with evaluation in general. Our question here is merely whether the two notions before us, of evaluation and of correspondence to fact, are, so to speak, candidates for the same place; whether, equipping ourselves with the one, we can reasonably hope to dispense with the other. Plainly we cannot: if a statement is thought to correspond to the facts there must be a reason for our thinking so; and that in any instance might intelligibly, even though falsely, be called a bad reason rather than a good one. To say that is to evaluate it, and the evaluation will surely be relevant to the acceptance of the original claim. Suppose even the strongest case one can imagine, that of a man who reports what is before his eyes—which it is sometimes said he cannot even intelligibly doubt. At least another person can always doubt it, believing the speaker to be under an illusion: if we normally reject any such supposition out of hand it is because we have reasons, perhaps overwhelmingly good reasons, for doing so.

We need not ask, for our purpose, whether any class of statements is to be found which are, so to speak, self-supporting, immune from all doubt whatsoever. It suffices that for the vast bulk of our assertions, for our theories, hypotheses or everyday beliefs, we require what we call reasons or evidence. But here it may be objected that what I have been calling 'bad reasons'—or again 'bad evidence'—are not properly reasons or evidence at all; and if not, no question of evaluation arises. But this shift will not alter the argument, at least not substantially; we shall only debate the same points under a different heading. We shall ask what is rightly to be called 'evidence'—whether, let us say, the procedures of some exotic new science or pseudo-science properly come within the terms of the definition—rather than asking whether a given item of evidence is good or bad. 'Evidence' itself is now a value-word, giving a certain status to the material that it serves to introduce. And indeed we find that philosophers of science have spent no little time on determining the criteria for a scientific theory—from which criteria of 'evidence' will naturally follow.

It does not appear that much plausibility attaches to the appeal to the correspondence theory of truth in this exigency. It proves to be of little use to those philosophers who, from militant tough-mindedness, perhaps, or some other commitment or drive, have devoted themselves to this cause, so that they fight the good fight to keep science free of 'values'. But, such as it is, it must surely quite vanish when we turn from simple fact-statements about particular things to theories, general laws and the like. For it is plain that before we accept any theory we must assess the arguments, or evidence put forward to support it; every theory is more or less satisfactorily established or satisfactorily worked out. Here, however, another notion may be brought into play—and one, certainly, of first-rate importance, though not much to the point as regards the present issue. I refer to the notion of a 'decision-procedure'.

The name is borrowed from a discipline where clear-cut distinctions exist between admissible and inadmissible propositions, at least in the generality of cases; where, indeed, there are mechanical procedures for settling the issue should it arise. But the general assimilation of science to mathematics should be expressed by its advocates in the optative mood rather than the indicative. The notion that we have to do with is this: that meaning can be attributed to statements in so far as we know of procedures for determining their truth or falsity. Within certain well-established systems, and pre-eminently those of the sciences, decision-procedures exist —and are indeed what constitute the system. Elsewhere, however, they are lacking, and it is useless to argue over differences where we have no notion of what it would be to settle them; and would-be moral argument, it is often added, is of precisely this kind. In so far as it turns on factual differences, say, on the likely practical consequences of enforcing one rule or another, we have means of deciding the point, at least in principle. Beyond that it will be rationally irresoluble. Here once again, it may seem then, we have a basis on which to define truth and falsity; we can specify conditions that give a use to the terms within any particular system, without raising any question of evaluation. And if so our theory of science will have all that it needs.

I have said that I do not mean to detract from the importance of this concept of a decision-procedure as it may be used either in the theory of science or more generally. My only concern here is with the claims that I have made for the study of axiology, which this new notion may be thought to impugn. As to that a few questions may suffice, questions which naturally arise out of the picture that I have sketched. These are nothing remote or obscure: we may ask, for instance, whether disputes can break out within the sciences as to which among the various procedures are properly applied in a given field, and if so, by what means they are settled; we may ask, again—given that the scientists in the field generally agree on these decision-procedures—whether the agreement must be wholly universal or whether a majority will suffice, and if so, how large a majority; and again whether other considerations, for instance the authority of those specially qualified, may ever tell against the weight of numbers; and if so, by whom the experts are to be recognized and whether one may find better and worse judges; and supposing that the judges and experts differ . . . But it is perhaps superfluous to press these questions further. In all this my intention is not to imply that answers to them could never be forthcoming; quite the reverse. To ask and answer questions of just this sort is the central task of progressive inquiry; but what we are bound to observe is that they all are, or involve, evaluative questions. And scientific thought as it goes lucidly forward, organized in particular departments where ready-made procedures exist, presupposes a basis or larger background where we must work, relatively speaking, in the dark. Indeed we owe it to earlier inquirers, inquirers whose imaginative labours first created these systems without having them to use, that we ourselves are so much better equipped. The procedures that we take for granted all emerged at one point or another in the history of thought, and often were vigorously challenged: the stock example of Galileo and his opponents comes to mind. So it would seem that the logical means of their evaluation could hardly have been dispensed with either by their advocates or their critics.

We may see here clearly enough what this appeal to agreed procedures amounts to in the end. In certain departments of inquiry elaborate techniques having evolved, have gained pretty general acceptance: elsewhere the dispute rages about us. Now science, on the present account, is implicitly defined by the former, the latter being left out of discussion. Let us turn our attention to some of these, to the different schools of analytic or experimental psychology, or look generally at the social sciences or again at those various physiological theories and therapeutic techniques that orthodox medicine refuses to countenance: with this view before us, this notion of a decision-procedure, used as a touchstone by which to test significant inquiry, may lose something of its appeal. Whatever the procedures in question, we must examine them first, before we pass judgement—that at least will be generally agreed on. Their evaluation then, favourable or otherwise, can never be a foregone conclusion. Sometimes revolutionary innovations pass the test after all and survive: here, in the creation of new concepts, of new points of view and ways of thinking, science does its imaginative work. But I fear that the notion which we have been criticizing, rigidly and practically applied, would come near the prohibition of creative thought.

At this point the argument may take a new turn; we may be asked to consider the procedures that science adopts, not now in detail, but generally. Though the particular procedures may vary from one science to another, though, for example, natural and social science may each have methods of their own, it is true at least that all science is empirical; any new science or pseudo-science that stakes its claim must stand or fall by the same empirical tests. With this argument we shift to different ground; a general account of scientific explanation, of what we mean by a scientific theory, is the business of the philosophy of science. I cannot explore the topic in detail here. But let us suppose that we agree at least in broad terms on what we call a good theory: it must serve to bring diverse phenomena under some unifying principle, yielding laws that are independently testable; it must be free from useless complications or *ad hoc* hypotheses to buttress it. If we can imagine that such some broad account were worked out and generally accepted, it would seem that the philosophy of science would have done its work. But for us a further question would remain; we should have to ask what more is involved when theories of this sort are called 'good'. Various answers might be forthcoming: to call them good, it may be suggested, is to ascribe to them some further quality of a special sort, or else it is merely to recommend them, or again to assert that they subserve human ends. But these questions belong to axiology and not specifically to the philosophy of science.

At this point we may meet the same countermove that we anticipated in speaking of evidence: for we have arrived, by hypothesis, at a definition of a scientific theory. Now provided that we know what to call 'theories', it may be said, there will be no need to add this further claim, in pre-scientific language, that such theories are 'good'. Or alternatively let us speak—for it will make the point clearer still—not of theories but rather of explanation; for explanation is the function of anything offered as a scientific theory, and we judge its success or failure accordingly. Now it is plain that a would-be explanation of given phenomena that fails to explain them, simply loses its claim to this title; what we have here is not an explanation at all.

Broadly speaking we may meet this suggestion with the same sort of argument as before. Certainly the tendency exists in ordinary speech: nothing is more natural than to say of a thoroughly bad piece of poetry or of philosophy that it is simply 'not poetry' or 'not philosophy', so that these themselves become evaluative terms. Moreover there are describable differences, broadly describable, between what we call good theories and bad—or again between good and bad poetry, or good and bad pineapples. Now the course we have taken, following Hare—with Moore's work, too, in the background—has been to distinguish these, as criteria, from the value that we ascribe to things on their account; but supposing that another way should prove possible we may not need to use these distinctions after all. We shall simply define the term 'theory' by the presence of the features in question: we do not distinguish theories as good and bad, we distinguish theories—properly so called—from things that are not theories at all. This suggestion might do very well if our concern were merely to classify kinds of object, ascribing names to each to mark the differences; if our true theories and no-theories did not present themselves as rival claimants for the same place. As it is we cannot avoid the task of evaluating their competing claims; the question that science finds itself faced with—not always, as we have seen, an academic one—is what sort of system to adopt and use.

So long as 'theory' remains a strictly neutral non-evaluative term it will be possible, and necessary too, to ask whether theories thus specified—as testable, simple and so forth—are themselves good or bad. Suppose again that 'good' in this context, as applied to scientific theories, is taken as merely referring to the features in question, as representing no more than a shorthand for the descriptive account that we might give in full. If so to call a theory good, when 'theory' itself means whatever exhibits these features, is to express what is no more than tautological, and where there is a choice to be made between one course and another no tautology will serve. But the line of argument will doubtless be familiar and I shall not enlarge on it.

I remarked at the start of this discussion that in ordinary discourse we constantly refer to theories, evidence or arguments as better or worse or sometimes, more positively, as right or wrong. Though philosophers have so often discussed science and logic in complete independence from axiology, we have found no reason for questioning the common practice. If axiological issues underlie ethical ones, as moral philosophers seem to assume—if we are to examine the concept of 'good' before asking what constitutes good conduct—they will underlie similar issues in other departments of philosophy. And here I must let the matter rest. I am more afraid that I shall be accused of labouring the obvious; but I can only point to the current state of discussion. The possibility or the need for any such axiological inquiry, to preface those of epistemology or methodology, has been universally disregarded, and the point, perhaps, for the benefit of tough minds, may bear some repetitive ramming-in. But let us now ask whether some more positive approach to the subject may not be possible.

## II

I have given no account of axiology nor explained what I mean by it, except by reference to the terms 'right' and 'good', or 'well-founded', 'legitimate' and the like. These, we normally say, form a distinct class; we mark them off and call them 'evaluative'. Now the sort of theory that we have examined in the previous chapter will certainly tell us more of the difference; we see better what it consists in—or at least have some mark to satisfy ourselves of its genuineness, or to satisfy other people—when we come to speak of their imperative force: a force that is not to be found in adjectives such as 'sleepy' or 'green'. To point out a value is to point out a reason for doing something, or a *prima facie* reason, at least; it is, in normal circumstances, a sufficient explanation of a choice to say that what one chose was right or good. True, there are things that one might do, one might, for instance, choose to retire to bed, because one was sleepy; or one might choose a crayon because it was green: these, in special contexts, are reasons for actions too—but only in special contexts. We recognize them as such. In the last resort the difference is still intuitive, as it is bound to be: what we can attempt in philosophy is to turn obscure intuitions into plain ones. And we are, I believe, speaking more plainly when we elaborate on our term 'evaluation' with an account of 'imperative force' or of reasons for acting. Another approach to the notion, one that also throws light on it, is by way of an analysis of rule-giving and rules; for where there are rules there is right and wrong. Yet though these conceptual gains are real enough, in the last resort they may not be what we were looking for; anyone looking for a definition or even for what is called an 'account' of evaluation will find that he is no nearer his goal. Though evaluative utterances have the force of imperatives in certain contexts, they are not to be identified with imperatives: we distinguish between obedience and duty—between actions that we do because we are told to, and those that we do because we think them right. So, too, with the concept of rule-giving: however the two notions may be bound up together we still need to make evaluations that distinguish between good and bad rules.

I shall not attempt, in general terms, to say what evaluation is. For all thought progresses self-creatively, bringing forth new concepts as it grows; it creates them because it cannot do without them —or cannot do the same work without them. They are, therefore, irreducibly new. We can hope to teach them, certainly; to make them intelligible and acceptable, at least to people intelligent enough, imaginative and ready to learn. We cannot, however, eliminate them in favour of others: and philosophers are nowadays widely agreed that we cannot define evaluation in wholly non-evaluative terms. In a sense any definition will be circular. That, then, is not my aim: I shall start from our intuitive knowledge of this as a distinct mode of judgement, marking off a certain class of words. What it seems reasonable to hope for is to make this intuition more articulate; to define the concept, in another sense—or to define it more clearly— and at the same time to define the whole process of inquiry more clearly, by picking out the place or function of the one within the other.

Let us turn back to the notion of rules and rule-giving: according to a view widely held we are able to speak of right and wrong so far as we have rules to appeal to. It is in these terms that the notion is analysed, or some sort of analysis at least sketched, for use in epistemology or elsewhere—some such sketch sometimes proving indispensable. And although we have seen reason to doubt its final adequacy, the account makes a useful starting-point. Besides it is only half-inadequate; it serves to point to something like dichotomy in the notion of evaluation itself. A rule is something known and agreed on, for otherwise it could never do its job; we refer to our rules or appeal to them to correct irregularities of conduct, our own or other people's. We teach rules to children and students in all sorts of fields, and punish or reprove them for breaking them. As to the rule itself, suppose we are asked what it is, we shall probably quote some verbal formula; but the crucial point is the rôle in which it serves: as a pointer, like a landmark or a compass; a rod to check the erring, to guide and to reprove.

The rules serve—they function in these ways, so long as their authority is unchallenged. The distinction or dichotomy that I spoke of appears when men's minds first grow critical. It is with rules as with decision-procedures: they are themselves made objects of evaluation, hence they cannot suffice to explain it. We may work within a given system, never looking further than its rules; or again we may feel the need to replace, or reformulate or modify them. We may think it right and requisite to do so. To be sure, the distinction is far from sharp: those rules that philosophers speak so freely of, as the precondition of significant discourse or inquiry, are much more fictitious than real. You hardly ever meet them in practice. A rule in the strict and proper sense will be something clear-cut and well-established, something of known and accepted status; and in the fields that these philosophers chiefly interest themselves in, it would be hard to name anything more strikingly lacking. Otherwise their disputes would be far shorter. Yet they are not merely mistaken in connecting 'right' and 'wrong' with the appeal to rules. It is true in fact that in ordinary discourse, and in the ordinary conduct of our lives, we work with unformulated rules; we find we differ when we first seek to formulate them—yet we may still seek for ways of resolving our differences. We seek for true principles still to be brought to light. Yet these things, though they are so, might have been otherwise: we can imagine a different sort of society living under an immemorial and rigid code, which no one has ever thought of questioning. The code itself could not be called 'right', for there is no right where there is no notion of deviation or difference—nor again, we may notice, where there is mere difference and no notion of resolving or removing it. Yet particular actions would be called right or wrong, simply by appeal to the rules of the code. And here again we meet the dichotomy that I spoke of: we find those who, from weakness or inadvertency, fall short of accepted rules or standards, but we find others who consciously and deliberately reject them. There are dissidents as well as defaulters; and the notion of evaluation, correspondingly, has two separable aspects. We have not exhausted its content in clarifying the notion of a standard, of a mark to which we try to conform, and punish or reprove those who fail; for we may make it our business, too, to determine, to formulate or evaluate the standards themselves.

When we turn from practice to theory we find that the same distinction reappears, with this difference only, that here we can hardly fail through weakness. We do not err knowingly, since once we know it we are no longer in error; our difficulties, then, are difficulties of the intellect rather than the will. Here, too, we may question accepted rules; indeed we may also break them without questioning them—not, however, once our attention has been drawn to it. Those irregularities are called 'slips'—irregularities, that is, that are corrected as soon as they are brought to our notice; and where the rule, or its right application, proves more complex, we speak of 'errors'. The concept is still essentially the same and it is necessary to be clear as to its limits; we are still concerned only with standards and have no notion of evaluation beyond that, even though our failures are intellectual and involuntary. We must presuppose a system of rules which are not themselves called in question; and the rules being clearly understood, and the false step being brought into focus, its falsity must then be apparent. Mathematics, and more especially the sort of mathematics that we learn at school, provides the ideal setting for the notion of an error; and even in the harder parts of the subject substantially the same account will perhaps apply. Here, too, there are rules to appeal to, and an error, once it is properly focused, will be plain to any competent judge: and the rest, that is, the incompetent, are not those who maintain different views but those who have no views at all; we meet incomprehension but not disagreement—or not in the same way or to the same extent as elsewhere.[1] There is, of course, wrong-headedness as well as blindness, both which we meet in philosophy too. A man may first simply slip through want of grasp, and afterwards persist in his error though his attention has been drawn to it; say, in terms that made it difficult to retract. He may defend himself with special pleading—as we call it—or retreat into impenetrable vagueness; we shall still speak quite definitively of his error. Perhaps we are right to; within limits we are bound to trust our own judgement. But this must be borne in mind too, that there exist no clearly formulated rules for identifying wrong-headedness or the like; and to talk as philosophers sometimes talk of their opponents' errors—which these opponents persist in seeing as insights—may carry conviction with their friends, but sounds rather differently to outsiders. We do not inoculate ourselves from dogmatism by banning the term 'intuition'; the logician's term 'error', misused, is quite as dangerous. The concept, we shall find, loses its meaning just in so far as agreed rules are lacking, in so far as simply to point out the would-be error no longer suffices to rectify it. Beyond that we may still call it error: what we mean is that we see the point differently. Our differences concern the rules themselves, and such disagreement is far from rare. Yet even at the most general level, it need not bring inquiry to a halt; rather we make progress by resolving it. We might indeed, for the sake of the formula, prefer to speak of the doubtful interpretation of the rules—much as there was, technically speaking, no new legislation in the Middle Ages but only local re-interpretation of the Natural Law. But fictions are the proper expedient of law rather than of philosophy.

[1] I cannot speak with any specialist knowledge of mathematics, but it seems in several ways to represent a special case, and it is regrettable that it has so often served philosophers and logicians as a paradigm. Even nowadays, despite the work of Professor Wisdom and others, half our apparatus and vocabulary is pseudo-mathematical. Mathematicians may indeed differ and fall into opposing schools as to the general criteria of mathematical proof; but generally speaking in mathematics the solution of a problem, whatever genius or imagination may be needed to find it, will not be disputed over once it is found. Difficulties reflect the complexity of the calculus, not the general acceptability of points of view.

I use this term 'inquiry', for want of a better, wholly generally. Any process directed towards either assertable belief or acceptable procedures may for my purposes be called an inquiry: in some contexts simply 'thought' or 'reflection' would do as well, but it seems that there is no single word that will serve without some forcing here or there. Now we find that such inquiry, so long as it is not at a standstill, involves the progressive resolution of disagreement. Indeed it constantly throws up disagreement too, getting forward rather like someone who successively sets himself obstacles—perhaps to draw out his own energies—which he then must find the means of overcoming. Here we have one point of view from which it is possible to consider this general process; certainly it is not the only one nor perhaps the most natural, for we find that the textbooks hardly notice it. Another concept which we may prefer to use, a concept still more fundamental perhaps, is the old one of 'saving the phenomena'; inquiry begins with the search for ways of reconciling appearances where they strike us as mutually incompatible. What first compels us to reason or speculate is the meeting with phenomena apparently conflicting with one another—or else conflicting with our own expectations and assumptions. But this latter may be only another way of saying the same thing; for we can only say that two appearances conflict against a certain background of assumptions. These apart, the appearance, say, of a white crow or a stone floating on water contains nothing discrepant in itself.

Suppose now at any point in the process of thought our existing assumptions break down. Thus, following procedures that we have previously learnt, or have merely adopted instinctively, we come upon recalcitrant facts and are brought to a halt. So long as the process runs smoothly we shall keep to the habits that we already have as a matter of course; but any jolt leads to some readjustment, which may be either more or less far-reaching. In order to circumvent the obstruction we look for a new point of view; and in changing our point of view we also change the system of our procedures and expectations. Science, to deal with new phenomena, creates new hypotheses and theories—with concepts and languages to go with them

—which serve to present the material in new ways; and even below the level of rationality we may suppose that the pattern is the same. A primitive organism, presumably, proceeds according to its first innate tendencies until it meets with some obstacle that brings it to a halt or disturbs the rhythm; and it, too, will respond to the new phenomenon, either adjusting or failing to adjust—but not merely repeating the same pattern of movement as before. It is, however, the more sophisticated levels of the process that concern us here.

At those higher levels, I have suggested, we can see inquiry in terms of the progressive resolution of disagreement; this is the task it may be said to set itself no less than to save the phenomena. Alternatively, looking at it otherwise, we may say that we find a discrepancy—given the basic attitudes that we have—in this sort of phenomenon too: in the meeting with contrary views, with assumptions and procedures at variance with our own. I say with 'assumptions and procedures': our own practice will not count as a rule until we see others as conflicting with it. The two notions emerge simultaneously: we first take the background for granted, till conflict compels it into consciousness. But this, too, is a phenomenon to be saved. The organism of our thought may in either case be expected to register a certain shock, and some readjustment will be called for. For we cannot rest content with mere differences; here we have a fundamental demand of reason. In the actual divergence of men's views reflection encounters its first obstacle—which also means to say, its first challenge: it is what we are called on to overcome. If we cannot feel its force or respond to it the process will never begin. And one finds, indeed, that certain sluggish minds, minds at the limit of rationality, meet with contradiction and blink, and proceed on their way as before.

The same holds both of communities and individuals. The first great solvent of the primitive rigidity of culture, operating with the development of trade, is found, we are told, in contact with the different customs of other tribes. Even now anthropological discoveries can administer a similar shock, disturbing the faith of modern Europeans or Americans in the validity of their own ethical codes. Again many children or adolescents may have something of a similar experience on first meeting the moral world outside; for here are people, it may be, who merely disregard attitudes and views which, in their own milieu, were so far from being questioned that no one had even thought of defending them. This discovery is a disturbing one at any level, and much turns on our way of responding to it: it may be worth dwelling a little on three general patterns that appear.

The most natural, I suppose, and in a sense the most basic, is mere withdrawal, the response that, as it were, denying that the thing has really happened, makes believe that the world is still intact. We ignore the strange cults of outsiders—who, being outsiders, do not count. This way of disposing of experience that one cannot assimilate is commoner and even, within limits, much more workable than might be thought: it proves useful, at all sorts of levels, to minds of a certain peasant-like cast, who combine narrowness and toughness with practicality, who can learn how to dig their own plot—and never ask whether rich men believe in God. Indeed where we cannot make terms with views that conflict with our own, then we have no course but to ignore them: unless we are to face the other alternative, which is simply scepticism or despair. We may be led to abandon the whole notion, at least within the relevant field of discourse, of a view for which we shall claim universal validity: and that is to say any view at all, for what is taken as only 'valid for me' may be a preference or a choice—perhaps part of a system of preferences deliberately adopted—but cannot be properly a view or a belief.

This consequence follows necessarily once we accept the principle that truth holds universally. For these possibilities exhaust the field; where it proves that differences remain, differences which we can neither account for nor remove, then either we merely ignore them or else relinquish the whole search for truth—for any attainable view to be held up as universally valid. In practice, of course, the situation does not present itself in black and white; we have many sorts of half-way accommodation: scholars find ways of accounting for the success and popularity of rival views that (as they agree quietly among themselves or affirm in their own minds) in truth are self-evidently absurd. The ideal of universal agreement which I have called a demand of reason is not an attainable reality; we must nonetheless proceed as it prescribes. Hence disagreement wherever we encounter it calls for some response; and the two simplest are those that I have named, either mere withdrawal, shutting our eyes, or else the abandonment of any positive view. But a third though a harder course remains, which is the one that I am most concerned with here. We may recognize the existence of divergent views and yet keep hold of the notions of right and wrong so long as we undertake to remove or at least explain them—to search for ways in which these differences may be resolved. Here rationality gets a foothold; we get our first contact with other minds and the process of inquiry is set in motion.

The first mark of rationality is found in puzzlement; it is in doubts, not in knowledge or belief, that we must look for its beginning. The same holds whether new natural phenomena or other people's divergent beliefs are what confront us, first disturbing our primitive complacency. To be puzzled is not merely to be sceptical; indeed at bottom it is antithetical to that sophisticated virtue of the twenties. For what we find in puzzlement is evidently a kind of protest—an inarticulate protest, let us say. What it tells us is that something is wrong—an intimation which, followed up, points beyond our present perplexity to the idea of its possible resolution. It demands that what is wrong be put right.

The pattern that we are to picture, then, is the same throughout. Certain views that we have naturally adopted or certain procedures that we have followed—at the lowest level mere organic adjustments—are brought into collision either with different views or with new and unexpected phenomena. Out of this, reflection is set to work. Moreover the whole process is progressive. In the course of a co-operative inquiry—and the mere attempt to understand opposing views is the beginning of such co-operation—our minds are developed and changed; their first tendencies are redirected or redefined. For nobody can learn by himself, whatever his initial endowment, to experiment or calculate or argue. Thus his 'mind', which is to say, the processes of his thinking, his intellectual capacities and performances, will be part of the mind of a larger group. What we call a tradition or a culture, a common body of theory and practice, emerges where individual minds work together, being formed and reformed in the process. In some measure, then, they are mutually assimilated; proclivities that originally differ are educated by working contact, and brought into line. To share in a culture, in an intellectual tradition is to share ways of thinking and working, to use the same concepts and procedures. It is only on the basis of such agreement that further fruitful differences can appear—differences that serve to set further problems, problems, perhaps, at a deeper level, that call for resolution in turn.

The Greeks were, it would seem, the first people to develop a tradition of this sort that concerns us, namely a dialectical tradition; a custom of talking, of discourse, where the talk was a form of inquiry and, further, the inquiry was free. A purely dialectical tradition may have its dangers, and the name 'sophistry' was turned by Plato and Aristotle into a term of contempt; yet where such a tradition is wholly lacking fruitful thinking, we may say quite as definitely, is not to be hoped for. I suppose that it will hardly be denied that Greek inquisitiveness was the starting-point of all European thought; and along with inquisitiveness there went a readiness to try different views. To be sure not all traditions are progressive, and it may be that in every tradition we find also an opposite tendency—a tendency to ossify and resist change. The existence of a culture and a tradition makes progress possible, yet sometimes it restricts and retards that very forward movement that depends on it. We might well ask, then, what keeps an intellectual tradition alive and moving; but thanks to its several champions we can give the answer with tolerable confidence—we find it in the freedom of critical inquiry that welcomes rather than silences divergent views.[1] The first essential is that different voices should be

---

[1] To refer to Mill in this connexion is no doubt superfluous. Professor Popper, in more recent years, has pressed the case further, and his name is especially connected with

audible; so much will probably be granted. And yet mere disagreement marks no more than the breakdown of inquiry. What carries us forward in argument is not simply the fact that we now differ but that we think of our differences as removable—though the search for agreement finds no place in common works on methodology and logic. The notion does indeed play a large part in the thought of one modern philosopher whose ideas have been profoundly influential —in that, namely, of Wittgenstein. Wittgenstein spoke of agreement in what he called a 'form of life' as the precondition of all discourse whatever. For two persons or two living creatures not agreeing in certain basic tendencies could have no common language at all.[1]

This view, plainly, is one to pause and ponder over. Taken in one way, or at one level, what Wittgenstein says is indisputable; for if we are to communicate in words, here at least our practices must agree. To use language in similar ways is already to share in 'forms of life', to have certain tendencies in common. But these in turn presuppose others—though it seems that the fundamental proclivities that serve to make our minds what they are, are all too easily taken for granted. Let us consider the use of any general word such as 'red': it seems that we normally take it for granted that anyone who has been shown a few samples of red things and has, as we say, been taught the word—the sound being correlated with the samples —will continue to use it as we do; that being asked, for instance, to choose red apples at the grocer's or to bring the red book from the shelf, and meaning to comply, he will select the same object as we would. One might imagine a creature who acted differently, or who went with us to a certain point and then changed. But thenceforth there would be no way of talking to him. The mere possibility of language depends on our sharing certain tendencies; and these

these lines of thought: he has seen in the scientific tradition the development of systems of procedures designed specifically to ensure the difficulties should be felt and not baulked, that divergent views should not remain unheard. I am conscious, further, that my general account of our reasoning on the basis of existing views owes something to what I have learnt from Professor Popper, though I fear that he will not greatly approve of the use that I have made of his teaching.

[1] Cf. *Philosophical Investigations*, e.g., i, 238–41.

tendencies, taken together, define our attitudes or constitute our form of life. Thus in our world certain concepts apply; they apply, that is to say, in the world as we see and think of it, as opposed to some conceivable alternative—for we can at least form the idea of an alternative without claiming its detail as conceivable. Our discourse and our thinking are cast in terms of certain basic notions that we share: of material things and of people, of causes and growth and the like. Our ordinary use of these terms always presupposes common procedures, common ways of responding to what we meet. Now to imagine that such agreement might after all break down, that we might find ourselves proceeding differently even in basic things, is to imagine the disruption of all language.

The speculation may seem a remote one; outside philosophical discussion we do not often contemplate such possibilities. And Wittgenstein himself hardly uses it except, as one might say, to mark a limit; his concern is with the point beyond which inquiry cannot sensibly be pushed. It is no doubt true that in many cases the idea of a breakdown of this sort seems strange enough—but we must observe, not in all. In some fields it is nothing unheard of. One may be surprised, certainly, taken aback even, to find another person reacting differently, say, to a new acquaintance or a new kind of art— or again to discoveries made about the behaviour of rats or dogs in special conditions, or of human beings. Yet what we have here, surely, is not something outside normal experience. Still less do we think it abnormal when we differ decidedly in our reactions to apricots or Camembert cheese. But those, you say, are matters of taste; and no doubt there is no harm in saying so. For it is true certainly that we no longer try to argue—if we ever tried to argue in these things—with any different feelings that appear. In any of these cases, in fact, we may merely accept our differences, or at least bring ourselves to accept them; but I suspect that our first tendency everywhere, even in matters of 'taste', is, as it were, to resist the fact, to push to get past it. We keep up the attempt for a period, shorter or longer, but where we make no progress we at last give up; where neither existing techniques, nor any that we can formulate or find, even point towards any resolution, then, naturally, we write off our losses. We discover then that taste is not to be disputed over, and whatever in this sense we call 'taste' is excluded from rational inquiry. The saying 'De gustibus . . .' is in effect a tautology; or rather —more significant than a tautology—it is a schema that serves to define for us a certain area of our experience.[1]

Happily, however, the other outcome is also not unknown; not all

[1] Wittgenstein himself, I believe, never inquires as to the relations between different forms of life; he never asks what can happen where they impinge on each other or come into collision. The examples that he gives are of practices—the systems of reasoning on which our ordinary or our scientific beliefs are based—whose rejection we can hardly contemplate seriously. Perhaps outside philosophical discussion we do not contemplate it at all. Yet collisions are, after all, possible; even science has not always been what it is today. And science and the form of life it brings with it have often been thought to conflict with that of religion; with certain religious practices it undoubtedly conflicts.

'What has to be accepted, the given, is—so one could say—*forms of life*'. (*Philosophical Investigations*, p. 226.) Wittgenstein also tells us (op. cit., i, 217), that we reach bed-rock of argument here, and no further justification can be sought. If so, the differences at issue between the adherents and the critics of some religious creed are things merely to be accepted; they are unarguable. I do not mean to deny that that is a tenable and plausible view; I would only remark this, that it is a view that will hardly serve the purposes of religious proselytizers. But now suppose that proselytizing is an integral part—as it very well may be—of some particular religious way of life. If what must be accepted is a way of life, it seems that we must accept contradictories. Or, alternatively, if therapeutic philosophy is committed to condemning—perhaps even as 'irrational'—whatever way of life claims to change others by rational means, a host of further questions arise: but in general it would be welcome to find so sharp a descent from the Olympian withdrawal to which this descriptive philosophy, advancing no theses, leaving everything as it is (op. cit., i, 124 and 8), seemed to confine us.

The fact is that men do argue about religion, and many believe, rightly or wrongly, that their views have been changed by rational argument. Universal agreement, to be sure, is hardly to be hoped for; that might be a reason for dismissing all such argument as idle or empty—but it would be a dangerous reason for a philosopher to give. Universal agreement is hardly less remote in philosophy itself, and this, therefore, as a philosophical view, would be self-defeating. There is however, a deeper, more intrinsic difficulty. It appears in what I may call the monadism of what seems to be Wittgenstein's notion of 'forms of life'; each one is what it is, and we hear nothing of their changing or overlapping. Yet we lack any principle of individuation. Perhaps the mediaeval world had one form of life and we another. But if we say so, what account can we give of the infinite complexity of changes, involving many rational processes as well as irrational ones, whereby different forms have evolved from it? The truth is, I fear, that though the notion is pivotal in Wittgenstein's thinking, it is merely invoked with little elucidation or working-out.

disagreement proves so hopeless—nor can we know in advance whether it will prove hopeless or not. This last is a point of some importance; we embark on the process of inquiry in any field with no prior guarantee of success, but we can never pre-judge the issue against it either.

We find, then, that the notion of agreement appears in two different places or different rôles. We may see it, as Wittgenstein does, as precondition of discourse, and hence, in some sense, its supporting framework: it constitutes the basis of our thought. But it functions dynamically, too, as an end, as the ideal that we work under. And disagreement, conversely, can be seen either as marking the limit, the conceivable break-down of thought, or again as its starting-point—the first challenge that it meets, that calls it into active being. The ideal can never wholly be realized: even where agreement seems most solid, say, in parts of natural science and mathematics, there will still be odd cases to discount of prejudice or even mere crankiness—these descriptions themselves bearing witness to our faith in the orthodox positions. But at least we may say this, that agreement, emerging as inquiry advances—as new problems are tackled and new methods establish themselves, progressive agreement—is involved in the process itself; it is part of the notion of such a process. But here there is another point to notice. Socrates told his disciples to follow the argument—not him but the argument—without professing to know where it would lead. Once we are collectively launched on the current of rational inquiry, the process in some measure takes over; the workings of individual minds are involved in the course of a larger movement whose direction is never wholly predictable. We call reason 'objective' in this sense: without talking nonsense we cannot describe ourselves as choosing what views shall emerge from a genuine inquiry—views which we shall adopt and advocate as 'rational'. We should not let etymology constrict our thinking: objectivity, as philosophers have sought to frame the notion, is not bound up with the presence of an object. Even given some appropriate object we shall need more; for our belief in the object in question will itself need to claim objectivity. If that in turn requires the presence of an object to make it objective, it is plain that the sequence will be infinite. Some philosophers have spoken, more clearly if also more clumsily, of universal bindingness; and this notion is given significance in contrast to mere preference or choice. Those systems that base all our thinking on a personal decision—a decision to adopt certain principles or definitions—can have, properly speaking, no place for the opposition of objective and subjective; both terms are left empty of meaning.[1]

It is plain that a man who can encounter views contrary to his own without the least sense of disturbance—the system of his old intellectual habits registering not the least repercussion from the jolt— is likely to finish his days with much the same outlook as he began with. But once we treat mere disagreement as something that is rationally unacceptable, once we commit ourselves to the attempt to overcome it, the event is beyond our control. To resolve differences we must first understand them; we must, that is to say, understand how views that we might ourselves have dismissed out of hand, can seem natural or even self-evident to someone else. Thus we encounter and engage with the workings of other people's minds; we adopt— hypothetically at least—and seek to enter into their points of view: and out of that initial experiment we cannot tell what else may ensue. But suppose that no movement towards agreement appeared; that in the general process of inquiry and all the more special processes that it may generate, our initial divergent assumption showed no tendency to come into line: here thought itself would have broken down and the whole work of the mind could go no further.

Now discourse—argument or reasoning—forms an essential part of the general process. We say, indeed, that seeing is believing, and positivism seems to erect the proverb into a philosophy. Science appeals to the evidence of the senses, and here stable systems are

---

[1] Hare, arguing against objectivism, (op. cit., p. 195), deals indeed with the Moorean or Platonist, but, I would suggest, he altogether misses the deeper issue, the antithesis between the freely chosen and the rationally binding. On his premisses, evidently, he would have to deny sense to the latter, except perhaps in a secondary way; but in fact this sense of 'objective' is not discussed. Nowell-Smith seeks to mediate between objectivist and subjectivist on a similar basis. (Cf. *Ethics*, Penguin, pp. 178-80.)

built up. Here, it may be said, we must look for solid agreement, but mere argument may go on for ever. Indeed mathematics remains as a fair-sized exception to the principle—there is, however, no need to quarrel over it. For in general, we may grant, it is true enough that where we can appeal to our senses to check the theories, the conceptual views that we frame, agreement appears at its most substantial. The ideal we might wish for, no doubt, would be perfect testability in every sphere; but lacking that, I suppose, it is sensible to make the best of what we have. A historical theory, for instance, can never be tested as one might test the predictions of the Gallup Poll, by waiting to observe the event: that does not seem a good reason for abandoning historical scholarship. But let us confine ourselves to science itself: whatever the value we set on observations it is plain that without concepts and theories that serve to knit them up into a whole—without some attainable agreement in rational as well as sensible material—our knowledge of things would never advance an inch. In some fields our best theories may remain speculative; and mere dialectic may have its limits. Nonetheless it is no exaggerated importance which we have given to this possibility of agreement.

For the rest some objection might perhaps be raised against the verisimilitude of the picture I have sketched of rational inquiry; of this co-operative activity of men, seeking agreement, striving to enter into one another's minds. That, I may be told, is a pleasing image but not strikingly like. Supposing we turn back to the original and follow the stream of controversy in its actual course, we may find it flowing less sweetly. For irrational processes swamp rational ones, or carry them along on the tide. Self-assertion or contra-suggestibility, or the antipathy to all orthodox views, or conversely the solidarity of the establishment united in putting down outsiders —these currents may sometimes seem stronger, or sound more audibly, than the voice which we came to hear of discursive reason. So they may; and so, often enough, they do. Each picture shows a part of the normal truth; yet after all, this is true too, that even the shadowiest image of rationality must also be more than a shadow.

For whatever the other forces at work, they must, if they are to get a hearing at all, at least disguise themselves in rational forms: the disguise is never merely an epiphenomenon, it is the pattern of reason and counter-reason that decides what is actually said. We can only win by the rules of the contest, whatever interest we first engaged to fight in.

In the process of inquiry, I have suggested, we must always progress towards agreement; an inquiry that was permanently at a standstill would lose its right to the description. But the idea of agreement serves, further, as the end under which we work; this latter point requires more attention. What we have here, let us observe, is not a straightforward prediction; rather it is in the nature of a postulate—but even so a postulate of a special sort. No doubt it is often possible to make predictions about the views or beliefs that other people will adopt, even where they adopt them on rational grounds. Nonetheless what we commit ourselves to as participants in the process is not a prediction; and though we may make predictions about other people and their views, in doing so we ourselves are, at a different logical level, engaging in inquiry too.

Whatever account we are to give of the relation between a prediction and what it predicts, here we shall need a different one. The notion of attainable agreement is involved in the process of inquiry with a closer or another sort of intimacy. What we seek here is agreement of a special kind, for it is defined by its origins—by the procedures out of which it emerges. The ways in which a man's mind may be worked on are very various; we may influence the procedures that he adopts and even the view-points that he finds natural. And presumably, if we can influence individuals, we could in suitable circumstances produce agreement among a given collection of individuals. One way of influencing their opinions is to train them in the processes of rational inquiry and, that being done, to show them the relevant evidence—which, let us suppose, all points in one direction. Another might be to bombard them gently but continually with slogans from hoardings, television screens and elsewhere. Or, invoking the resources of romance, we can imagine a new sort of drug, working after the manner of a philtre, inducing or wiping away a whole set of convictions overnight. We hear accounts, too, of uglier methods, and whether or not the reality fully answers to the description, the thing is presumably conceivable; and we can imagine a technician who should predict, inasmuch as he himself intends to ensure, that the divergent views of some half-dozen people will within a given period be brought into perfect harmony. Now to clarify the notion of inquiry and of the sort of agreement at which it aims, I have said, we must ask how it comes into being; in general we give meaning to this notion by distinguishing what we call rational procedures from others, from hypnosis, suggestion or the like.

Let us say that we distinguish mere agreement from right agreement. Right agreement is what we seek in inquiry; we postulate a solution to be found. But a solution, again, is a point of view on which, generally speaking, rational people will agree: inquiry is the search for a solution, and a solution is the outcome of an inquiry in so far as the process is successful. Lastly we call those people 'rational' who accept and adopt such procedures as emerge in the process itself. Our concepts, then, define one another; they form a system that is logically interlinked. Of such systems we normally say that they may or may not have application; for that depends on the facts, not on logic. But unless the present system were applicable there would be no such thing as thinking at all. We are able to distinguish, in fact, between a successful and unsuccessful outcome to any particular attempted inquiry; but what all our discourse presupposes is a fair measure of success in a fair proportion of the inquiries that we attempt.

Now taking inquiry as a whole we cannot predict its success; for any such prediction presupposes established criteria which we appeal to. We may, as I have said, predict the outcome of any given inquiry, arguing from the analogy of others; but to do that is itself to engage in the process. The possibility of agreement remains a postulate—but a postulate, we must add, necessarily involved in any conception of rational discourse.

We may notice in passing another consequence that follows from this account. Inquirers are engaged in asking questions, they are looking for a solution, for a right view, that is to say, or a view commanding rational agreement. These, plainly, are evaluative terms, and we cannot describe the process without using them. Hence, in the use of the term 'description' that is currently popular—'descriptive utterances' being contra-distinguished from evaluative ones—there can be no neat description of inquiry. Indeed this theory leaves it doubtful whether what we do in inquiry can be meaningfully expressed even in language that is avowedly evaluative; for we have seen that where the use of evaluative terms is identified with the use of imperatives—imperatives of a special sort, to be sure, but that makes no difference here—no interrogative forms, no strictly ethical or axiological questions, are possible. We could not, strictly speaking, ask 'What is right?' Yet to engage in inquiry is to ask precisely that; what we seek for are views to adopt. And still more clearly when we press forward beyond the guidance of procedures formulated at any given time, this will be the question that we ask. But here, I imagine, adherents of the imperativist account will not allow that we can ever go beyond it on any other basis than our own decisions.

I say that our account of these things involves evaluation: that, of course, is not to deny that it involves description too; these phrases—'reason', 'rational procedure' and the like—all have their own descriptive content. But in some ways that, too, is of a special kind. At any point in the history of inquiry we can specify established procedures, ways of reasoning and calculating and experimenting; a given body of practice exists, and that primarily is what we refer to when we speak of particular rational or irrational judgements. So far we have a straightforward description, as one might, say, describe a worshipper's actions by saying that he follows such and such a ritual. But this body of practice is also changing: the descriptive content of all these terms, therefore, will vary from one age to another or even one decade to another. That is quite natural and proper; it lies in the nature of the case: further, whenever we use them, they must be partly vague, for there is never universal agreement on right procedures. Any one man's view of what constitutes reason may differ more or less from another's. What is noteworthy is that we can still use the word intelligibly without committing ourselves on the points at issue between them; we may speak in much the same way of the 'future champion' without being able to name the person whom we are referring to. We use the word 'reason' quite generally, to refer not only to those procedures we know but also to those that have yet to emerge. The usage is not merely empty; we know, at least, what general conditions they must satisfy, however much remains indeterminate.

This indeterminateness that I speak of will always be a matter of degree. At all levels we must work with some sort of specification, some conception already formed, of what sort of object we are in search of. And yet there is also a searching for something—we hardly know what. If puzzlement is, as I have suggested, a kind of pre-rational inquiry, as it were, an indeterminate questioning, it also must obscurely contain the postulate of an attainable answer—at least of some possible appearance or different view of things that would set our present mental uneasiness to rest. The two notions we have to deal with are correlative: the questions that we frame are determinate in proportion to the answers that we envisage. Few things, however, could be better adapted to distort our conception of inquiry than a definition of 'meaning' or of 'problem' that only takes account of the two extremes, leaving nothing on the one side but strictly meaningful questions to which, as we so often hear, 'we know what counts as an answer': and, on the other, meaningless ones where we do not know at all. Even within developed systems, systems of established procedures, we ask many questions of different sorts; in an adequate account of them we shall need to indicate their place on this scale, the scale of determinateness, along with their other logical characteristics.

And this first point leads on to another. It is not necessarily the wisest course to take one's notion of inquiry from an exclusive study of well-developed systems. That is what is sometimes recommended; we are told that philosophy should concentrate its attention on the methods of science—that is, of the well-developed natural sciences—

for this obvious reason, that here we have the work of inquiry in its best and most advanced form. Now leaving aside the study of human beings, of history and of social relations or even morals, which are, perhaps, important too—and may not be wholly amenable to just the same methods that triumph in the study of nature—there is in any field, we must observe, a theoretical danger in gathering only specimens that are already full-blown. These are systems that may plausibly be claimed as the finest expression of human thought. Yet those features which show in the final flowering cannot characterize the process as a whole; and fascinated by what we find here, a pattern of intricate order, we may forget the more general stock from which they have grown. But inquiry, we see, is a process which passes through many stages, it admits of all degrees of actuality. What we reach in the end may be a system of procedures, agreed on and established, and wonderfully fine and sure in their working. But what we agree on at first may be little more than to persist in the search, the attempt to understand some other point of view different from our own—the point of view (it may prove to be) of a rational being who on his side is trying to understand ours. I say we agree on 'little more', but how much or little this may be I shall leave the conscientious reader to decide.

## III

I have now, I hope, made tolerably clear my general conception of inquiry, and I shall seek to develop it further in the following chapter. But with the main outline sketched in, it may be useful to pause before proceeding, to anticipate certain possible objections. One I will touch on but not spend long over. The notion of agreement has played a large part in this account. A critic may object that its right to that place cannot be taken for granted; it must be justified. And since I myself have envisaged some process parallel to inquiry at a pre-rational level in a single organism, it seems that this agreement of different minds cannot be indispensable. I shall not here raise the issue of the possibility of what has been called a private language; certainly it seems that the adjustments of an organism to its environment prior to the development of language are the forerunners of what we call reasoning. But it suffices for my purposes that inquiry develops as it does; at anything but its lowest levels it appears as a social process, and that lies in the nature of its development. I suppose that any study of physical science, for example, will concern itself, among much else, with the use of mathematical calculi in the explanation of natural events; yet there was certainly a time before the need or the possibility of such techniques was thought of at all. But if we take the matter as we find it we shall see the publicity of testable results—the point is one on which almost all theorists agree—as essential to the method of science. Indeed the fundamental distinction between reality and illusion leans heavily on it in more ordinary spheres; a man who finds that no one else can see what he seems to see, no matter how vivid it is to him, may reasonably judge himself to be the victim of an illusion. And again we cannot seriously conceive even of significant observation and experiment except against a background of discussion—a critical, dialectical process in which ideas are tried out and explored.

But now suppose that our critic should press his objection and urge that though these things are so, they might yet be otherwise; that some other test of acceptability might play the part that agreement and publicity play now: that supposition need not disturb us. It is indeed pretty hard to conceive, but there is no need to urge the difficulty. For if not agreement, then some other test must fill the same rôle; that is what we are asked to imagine. And as long as there is something to fill it, our general account of inquiry can stand. If alternatively what we are asked to imagine is that inquiry might go forward working neither with this concept, guided by this goal, nor any other that fills the same place, then, it seems to me, we may ignore the supposition until it is somehow made intelligible.

We may, therefore, stand by our use of the notion of agreement. But if so, it will seem perhaps, we shall only have to face a more serious difficulty from the other side; for now it may be objected that the weight which we propose to put on it is more than in fact it will bear. If agreement is to be our test, it must surely follow that the greater body of agreement must outweigh the less, mere numbers will carry the day. And hence, it seems, superstition and prejudice, provided only that they are sufficiently widespread, will be firmly and legitimately installed.

Ignorance may often be voluble, so much is true: but that does not mean that it is wholly unteachable. For people generally are able to follow where they would not have been able to lead. Aristotle's implicit advice to ordinary people in the conduct of life is worth bearing in mind: they are, it seems, to seek the guidance and follow the example of some person of practical wisdom—one whose better judgement they can trust. The proposal is open to a well-known sophistical objection. It would seem that to follow a suitable example we must first be able to recognize it: but we shall not be able to recognize it unless we already know right conduct from wrong— and if we do, we shall not need an exemplar. This difficulty need not detain us; we need only reassert the fact that people are found capable of recognizing, when they are shown it, what they could not have discovered for themselves. And whether or not we say in these circumstances that they know or have knowledge of it is im- material: but the fact is important. You may remember a man's name, or the right form of a quotation, once you are told it, though you could never have found it for yourself; and with the example of a man of practical wisdom before us we may recognize the right way to act though we should have done differently left to ourselves.

It follows that mere general acceptance need not be a conclusive test of excellence; and finding a whole suburbia of sameness we may still remain reasonably unconvinced. Whether or not we share Plato's or Socrates' intellectual contempt for the views and ideas of 'the many', we may still distinguish levels both above and below the mean. We not only recognize experts but also those whom we may perhaps call sub-experts—whose mental reach, no less exceeding their grasp, enables them to recognize the higher expertise of their superiors; and who in turn may be recognized by those below them. Beneath these there will be another level again, and so downwards. This scale is not without its importance even socially, for it binds up

H

the various levels which would otherwise merely fall apart. The lowest could never make direct contact with the highest; the gap is too wide. Yet every man capable of learning, where learning means more than acquiring information, must be capable, too, of recognizing those competent to teach, his immediate moral or intellectual superiors. Shaw says that we hate the highest when we see it—that we crucify it or stone it to death—but the greater probability is that we shall not understand it at all. What we are able to recognize is a not-too-much greater than ourselves; and mature people at all levels alike know how to defer to moral and mental superiority that they recognize.

We have our criteria, then, for distinguishing competent judges; and even following the views of the incompetent, we find that they may indirectly authorize judgements that would run counter to those that they themselves explicitly profess. But the problem has still another side to it: we have to deal not only with ignorance but also with the perversion of judgement. And here, too—though it may be harder to discount the sheer weight of numbers than in the former case—the test cannot be merely numerical. Suppose we reject as perverted the common judgement of the solid majority, that we set it aside in favour of our own; in theory the position is a wholly possible one, but in practice we might find it embarrassing to defend. Perverted judgement, we normally feel, must appear only among relatively few people and, what is more important, in special circumstances: or, if we may sometimes be prompted to call the judgement of a whole nation perverted, at least it must stand by itself in the history and among the community of nations. Nonetheless we take notice of the 'special circumstances' as well as the 'few people'. There are two independent factors here, and the greater strength of the one may partly compensate in any instance for the relative weakness of the other; majority agreement does not settle the issue by itself. But here, when we go against it, our primary appeal is not to the authority of experts; the judgement of any given expert might on a particular matter be perverted too.

I have spoken of the ideal under which we work as the universal agreement of those who engage in inquiry; this, though we can never wholly realize it in practice, provides our great measure of success or failure. But now we may add another clause. Where disagreement appears we shall first, as a matter of course, seek to remove it by rational means; but failing that, we shall seek to explain it, and an explanation, if we find one, will serve instead. What we cannot rest content with is mere unexplained disagreement. If another man sees something, physically or mentally, differently from me, then in some measure my own views are cast in doubt. But once I can show how the discrepancy comes about—I may, for instance, point out some special medium distorting his vision—I need no longer take account of it; it ceases to tell against my original view. Hence a more adequate statement of the ideal that we use will be that all differences of view must either be explained or removed. On the title-page of his *The Psychology of Perception* Mr. Hamlyn quotes Malebranche as saying 'Cette science en effect n'apprend que la manière de tromper les yeux.' This is what calls for psychological explanation: our special aberrations and errors, not our normal conduct and judgement—there can be no general explanation of the latter. But when we describe a point of view as 'perverted' we clearly hint that some explanation is to be found. I do not say that we could always produce it on demand; but then we are not always ideally careful in pronouncing judgement. But if in favourable circumstance the search for the explanation makes no progress, a rational person will feel its failure as casting doubt on his original charge.

We may still, then, with these qualifications, insist on the importance of agreement as a test of the acceptability of possible views. But what I have said raises one other issue which, I fear, it is impossible to ignore. We have found that the theme which we have been concerned with—right answers, rational agreement—cannot be adequately expressed without the use of evaluative language. Actual agreement may be a matter of fact, and so may actual progress towards agreement; yet from that, it would seem, nothing follows. For, as anyone with a nodding acquaintance with our contemporary moral philosophy must know, from statements of fact such as this is, no evaluative conclusions may be inferred: we cannot get norms out of facts. This truth is, it seems, universally recognized; logic vouches for it—though how it arrives at it is less clear. One would expect logicians to make it their job to formalize and systematize ordinary, accepted modes of reasoning; but certainly it is not by any mere formalization of the procedures that we actually adopt, outside our text-books or schools, that the present sort of argument can be condemned. For in actual argument we draw such inferences every day. But if they derive it from some source other than common practice, it is puzzling to know what it can be—unless perhaps *a priori* intuition. Even that unlikely expedient would not serve, for we with our different intuition may always testify against theirs. Intuition, as we saw in Chapter I, is not an infallible guide, but other things being equal the common sense or intuition of the majority must carry the day. And here the majority we have to take account of, who join in rejecting the dogma that forbids us to infer values from facts, is no less than the whole body of people who reason—even, in non-professional moments, the logicians themselves. For my part I am content to state existing principles as I find them, until I meet positive reason to alter them; and, in the present case, so far from such positive reason, I find that this proposed alteration would disrupt the whole business of inquiry.

First, then, let us lay it down that the fact that men agree—and still more that they are brought to agree—creates a presumption, even though a weak one to start with, that the view they agree on is sound or right. That they disagree has, of course, no such tendency; but further, that within some particular field they continue despite all efforts to disagree, creates a presumption that nothing that we could call a solution is to be found: that the terms 'right' and 'wrong' have no place here. And lastly where within a certain sphere they come to agree up to a point, and more so as inquiry is pressed forward, it creates a presumption that outstanding problems are problems indeed: that is, that they will prove to be soluble in the end. These, roughly stated, are the principles as far as I can discover them, on which we all ordinarily proceed, which underlie the whole body of our accepted views. But any philosopher may, if he prefers, treat them rather as unproven postulates or again as first principles on which we are to 'decide'. But if so, as we previously saw, he deprives himself of any logical means of enforcing his own doctrine on those who reject it; and for the rest, if he himself should decide against them, we shall have to leave 'him to find another way of carrying on the business of inquiry.

This may seem too summary a dismissal of a dogma so widely subscribed to, one quoted again and again as if its mere statement sufficed, and no further defence of it could be called for. It is incumbent on one who rejects it, a critic may urge, at least to give some account of its charm, to explain how it has come to have such a hold. Perhaps it is so; though to explain the success of every false view that has ever gained widespread acceptance among philosophers would be no small undertaking. But for the time being I must leave the matter as it stands; the relation of thought and practice will concern me in a later chapter. I shall only say this by way of anticipation: that a certain model of argument or inference, one which consistently applied would forbid all substantial inferences whatever, has (for various natural causes) come to dominate the thinking of philosophers. And the sort of inference of which we have been speaking is certainly a substantial one. This model first owed its ascendancy, perhaps, to the peculiar beauty and clarity of mathematical reasoning; and, further, to its resounding success as the instrument of science in explaining nature. It kept it because philosophers failed to see what they had committed themselves to, and when they saw their habits were too firmly fixed to change; they failed to distinguish between operations within a symbolic system, which keep all their virtue intact but in themselves are of no concern to logic or ordinary reasoning, and the possible application of such systems, their use in drawing substantial conclusions. For the rest it appears that there were, in Hume's phrase, certain 'vulgar systems of morality'—for instance, the evolutionary system, or the appeal to the necessity of conforming to our own true psychological nature—which this prohibition, once accepted, served to refute; perhaps it seemed the simplest and surest way of refuting them. And there has been more than one distinguished general who, having made his name on a single great victory, where the real feebleness of the enemy was unknown, has lived the rest of his life on prestige. The continued authority of Hume's principle may, in part at least, be explained along similar lines.

# IV

## The Development of Judgement

IT is a pity that the word 'scientist' etymologically at least, means not one who asks but one who knows; and a pity, too, that we have no serviceable general term less academic than 'discipline' and less narrow than 'science' has become: for the latter, nowadays, is bound to bring the developed natural sciences, with their special features, foremost to the mind. Imagine these qualifications away and I may say that what I shall be concerned with in the present chapter is the growth of science and of the judgement of people who engage in it. For the process has two sides which are correlative. The body of science is extended and grows in bulk, while the judgement of the scientists who study it is deepened, and thus changes in character. The difference between the judgement, say, of an experienced historian or lawyer and a novice confronting the same material is admittedly vast; nor does it consist only in erudition, in a stock of like cases to draw on, invaluable as that may well be. It also lies in something more organic, an acquired bent or bias of the mind; a trained mind is chiefly distinguished by its different and more significant grasp of the data presented to it. And that is something very different from any prize-winning mental capacity, stretched to the utmost; from a mind stuffed with facts like a card-index and bulging in uncreative bigness. Rather the picture we are to form is of an organ modified by every impression that it receives and hence responding differently to the next: or else, more simply, we may speak, as we normally speak, of the growth of a man's judgement.

This process is familiar to everybody—except perhaps to logicians and epistemologists, who either have never encountered it or else consider it foreign to their work. But we have learnt in recent years that it is unsafe to leave out of account the normal context in which a notion operates; and the notion of judgement, presupposing or bringing with it this sort of background, plays so large a part in our ordinary thinking that it may repay further study. The expert, we say, sees the same material differently; his attention is differently directed so that he notices what a novice overlooks. So far so good; certainly he sees it differently, for that is the fact that we wish to understand, but it is less clear how far talk of attention or of noticing will serve to illuminate the difference. For there is no need to suppose our novice inattentive; let him stare no matter how long and conscientiously, he will still fail to find what the expert finds—and not only finds, but very likely sees at a glance. The notion of 'noticing' may be a more promising one, though it, too, is in need of some stretching; we must seek to deepen it or extend its capacity if it is to carry the burden of the present distinction. It will, however, bear stretching, I think; for the process is common and often fruitful. Formalists are too little aware that the stuff of our concepts is elastic —whence we find that the enlargement of understanding is, generally speaking, not impossible; it is only impossible to certain minute philosophers.

Yet there may after all be something surreptitious in the process; for the very attraction of this term 'notice' will be, for many philosophers, that it appears not to break with certain implanted ways of thought—which, in stretching it, we must break with after all. I have in mind philosophers committed to the empiricist tradition, who nonetheless recognize the need for some account of these familiar differences of which I have been speaking: here the term 'notice' may seem to provide a bridge. Let us suppose that two people see the same object differently: the facts are all there, we shall say, but one notices what the other overlooks. Thus, availing ourselves of this useful term, it may seem that we can still confidently speak of those strictly describable 'facts', the findings of undoubted observation, on which different percipients will agree; and no question of interpretation need arise. These facts, and what belongs to them, can hardly need more than pointing out, even though unobservant people may fail to notice them. Now it is true that we use the word 'notice' in just these contexts: a picture has been replaced upside down, a letter has been left out of a word in typescript—we see it as soon as our attention is drawn to it even though we missed it at first.

It is for just that reason, however, that the concept needs stretching. Its attraction may be that it seems to keep intact a clean notion of the 'facts', but here we have its limitation too; and this was our starting-point. For to see these same facts as an expert sees them, to find what a layman fails to find, requires or may well require much more than merely that our attention should be drawn to them; it may require a lifetime of training and study, so say nothing of initial endowment. Adherence to the doctrine of 'clean facts' is incompatible with any real theory of judgement; for judgement appears in the interpretation of facts. But then again, once we accept the interpretation, we shall describe different things as facts, speaking as we could not have spoken before. The notion that must be rejected—to state it more accurately—is of any one level of facts such that these and these alone are ideally hard and ideally public: facts over which there can be no dispute, and which serve to supply the real content or to test the legitimacy of anything that we can say at any level. Certainly it may often be useful to oppose the two notions, to speak in terms of facts which are relatively undisputed as against the judgement or interpretation we make of them; but this is only a local and provisional distinction, not one that we can generalize, building it into a metaphysic or a theory of knowledge.

These differences are familiar in more ordinary fields. It is a commonplace that the features of other races, those of negroid faces, say, to a European who has never met them before—and doubtless the reverse also holds—seem hardly distinguishable; and yet there is no difference plainer than the difference between one man's face and another or even the different moods of the same face. Imagine, for example, a nervous false smile with twitching lips, and then in contrast a permanent grin, the image of content, of assured complacency: they are almost as obviously different as any two objects can be; we could no more ignore or not notice them than we could miss the grossest natural phenomena. Yet what we see here are muscular movements, a momentary quivering, that physically measured may be minute, and which anywhere else than in a human face—in grasses, clouds or the like—would hardly have caught our eye at all. Again consider the tiny differences in the pronunciation of certain vowel sounds in English which leap to the ear: whence, indeed, the extreme pains often spent on eliminating them—or those of them, at least, by which gentility sets store. Social differences interest men in general more than most matters; but that apart, so much turns for us on the tones of a speaking voice, its slight shifts of emphasis and the like, that it is no wonder that we have long since learned to scan these things. They strike us now with no effort of attention on our part.

Here we have a kind of perceptual judgement: even within sense-experience, which I suppose is where these differences fall, it is a factor that we cannot discount. But let me develop, rather more fully, another example. Imagine a piece of paper or a canvas variously patched and covered with coloured paint. One observer may pick out the profile of a face or some regular sequence or pattern where another can see only confusion. Now what one sees will depend on what one looks for; one may see a beetle or a bear or alternatively the features of a Turk: hence the psychologists have hit on this way of getting at men's preoccupying thoughts. But let us go a little further and it will prove that what we look for or, rather, are prepared for, depends not only on our character with its conscious or unconscious structure but, more specifically, on our training: and here we have differences of the type we noticed before. If we are trained to look for faces among the confused shapes before us, or if we are trained to look for ellipses, we shall soon succeed in finding them where other people fail. But again the pattern that we find in those shapes, now standing out clearly, will itself direct our further attention; it will, so to speak, emphasize or underline certain features —features that might otherwise have passed unnoticed. A tiny dot on a piece of white paper will certainly fix our gaze, at least momentarily, supposing that for some reason a set of concentric arrows point towards it; and the North Star, that would otherwise be lost among the infinite pin-pointing of the night sky, makes the focus of a pattern revolving round it.

But the process may go further. Once these new features are brought into prominence the first pattern that served to high-light them cannot itself remain unchanged: for they become the new focal points of our attention, and between them, in turn, new relations appear. So further differences and likenesses emerge and a new pattern is superimposed on the old one; and, this being so, the interaction of the two may transform the whole painted surface yet again. But we need not pursue the process any further; though indeed the development of judgement in any science, which this extended analogy is meant to illustrate—which works not on colours and shapes but on the abstract material of language and everything that such language relates to—may perhaps be extended indefinitely. At least with this picture before us it may no longer seem strange that a trained mind will seize on connexions that a novice, perhaps, can hardly see; which he may still fail to see even after they are deliberately pointed out to him. For, in terms of our analogy, we may say that it is only when the deeper pattern has once crystallized, and in virtue of that well-established ground—and that itself may not be easy to grasp or hold—that these further features and connexions, the points that the expert picks out, can ever be visible at all.[1]

---

[1] It may be worth noticing in what terms modern commentators discuss what seems to them the obvious confusion of Socrates' argument in the *Phaedo* (96–7 and 101), his objection that the same thing cannot serve to account for two different sorts of difference: eight cannot both be more than six 'by two' and less than ten 'by two'. Plato, it is evident, sets no little store by the argument; but a different logical training has made it appear differently. I have noticed within my own experience that the so-called refutation of the naturalistic fallacy makes a similar first impression on the non-philosophical; they take it as a piece of ingenious but quite unconvincing verbal trickery. Yet philosophers have been so deeply impressed by it, rightly or wrongly, that ethical discussion has revolved around this same point for fifty years. We are apt to imagine, apparently, that whatever seems obvious to us, must have seemed equally obvious to any rational person no matter how remote in time and place. On this matter I cannot do better than refer to Mr. Robinson's *Plato's Early Dialectic*, which is, anything else apart, a fascinating document of the development of logical judgement—its earlier development no doubt, but still in a mind of high genius. 'Evidently,' Robinson writes, 'there must have been a time when the human race, or its immediate ancestor, possessed no logical propositions

## II

What we need is a notion of judgement which shows it to us as a developing faculty, that takes account of the process of its evolution. And then on the other side we must see the body of any science or branch of study—the concepts and the language in which it works —as developing too. Ways of thinking and ways of speaking—the two must reflect one another—reveal a pattern of progress or growth, and to understand them we must study them accordingly. Further, unless reflection and inquiry led, in general, to better and truer views rather than otherwise there could be no such thing as rationality at all.

But since all that I have offered so far are only images and analogies of the way in which growing judgement finds new points of view, it may be useful to add a few more concrete illustrations. I may give one, perhaps, from a field with which I myself have little direct acquaintance: for in Chapter II of Professor Toulmin's illuminating little book *The Philosophy of Science*, I find the section-heading 'New points of view come with new inferring techniques'.[1] Toulmin's account of a scientific theory is broadly speaking this, that it provides us with certain conceptual apparatus, with terminologies, calculi or diagrams in terms of which we may present or re-present familiar things; and what we gain by the new presentation is the possibility of inferring from given data factual conclusions which we could not have drawn otherwise. Thus the phenomena of light and shade are pretty familiar, we all know more or less how shadows fall in sunlight or candle-light. But Toulmin asks what sort of difference was at issue or what could be gained by the first introduction of the principle of the rectilinear propagation of light; light is said to travel in straight lines. The notion, we must notice

at all, true or false. Nor is there any necessity that logical propositions when they did arise, should at once be those that seem obvious to us. . . . The history of thought cannot succeed if we assume from the beginning that some idea or other is innate and necessary to the human mind' (op. cit., pp. 28–9).

[1] Op. cit., p. 23.

to start with, is a genuinely new one; we are familiar enough with the travelling of horses or of rolling stones but that light should be said to travel is another conception. Not that the change would matter to us much, it would be no more than an oddity, or a possible metaphor like the falling of dusk, if this verbal innovation stood by itself; but in fact much more goes with it. The new concept gets its meaning because now, once we speak of light as travelling, we may draw diagrams of different situations with a straight line to represent its path. Then, given certain other data—as the position of the source of light, the height of obstacles and the level of the ground—we shall be able to infer with some precision which area will be in light and which in shadow. The new point of view, as Toulmin says, brings with it a new type of inference.

Subsequently he complicates the example, for so far it may seem elementary—though the simple case is a model for many harder ones. But later difficulties raise further questions; we ask 'What is it that travels?' a question that has no place in the earlier picture. There we simply drew a straight line for the travelling light and let that suffice. But now, to explain such further phenomena as refraction, we construct a further concept; we speak, for instance, of waves or particles of light.[1] We naturally picture such a particle on the analogy, say, of a grain of sand, and to some extent, I presume, the analogy must hold: for otherwise the notion would not serve as the vehicle to introduce our new point of view. But that view itself, what it is and involves, can only appear in the use that we make of the term, in those operations and techniques and new sorts of inference from phenomena, that it serves to make possible. What will be analogous, then, though only pretty broadly so, will be the two systems of thought as a whole (for no doubt our talk of grains of sand, though we may ordinarily take it for granted, has its own system too). But what concerns us here is the emergence of new ways of thinking, of seeing particular material, which, formed on the analogy of old ones, arise in the course of inquiry: and, on the other side, the development of judgement that will accompany them. For judgement is

[1] Cf. op. cit., pp. 65 ff.

nothing else than a capacity for seeing things, with the eye of the mind, in appropriate ways: an acquired bent that has become second nature. We must note lastly—a point that will concern us more later—that our new or emerging points of view are in no sense a deductive consequence of the old ones. They never, perhaps, represent a sheer break, but they are intellectual creations in a real sense, with new models and systems of thought, and linguistic and other operations. But deduction, as it is normally thought of, moves within a system already established.

I must leave the development of further technical illustrations to those qualified to handle them; though I shall have occasion to glance at others drawn from the study of history in the course of the present chapter. But there are problems nearer home, or nearer the main themes that concern us here, not least within philosophy itself. It is here, indeed, that we seem to find the widest range or greatest variety of cases, which may make it instructive: we find analogies closely argued for, models systematically applied; and again pictures, illustration and the like, which may serve merely as imaginative aids. Even so the distinction is not sharp. We get a new view of human language when, say, we first learn to think of it on the analogy of games, such as cricket or hide-and-seek; or we first treat the terms 'logic' and 'grammar' as interchangeable. 'Logical grammar' is a new notion; yet new notions are only evolved by adapting or building on old ones. Now we need conceptual apparatus to think at all; but to grasp or assimilate complex and strange material we shall need more —some central focus or point of view. The notion of the travelling of light brings a vast diversity of phenomena within our grasp; and philosophers trying to think, for instance, of the mind, picture it as a miniature republic, as a closed room or a theatre or again as an ever-flowing stream. The pictures, of course, may compete, and each and all in the end may prove inadequate: we may prefer to frame our thought in wholly abstract terms. Yet in their very inadequacy they have their value; for here we have something to fasten on, something to work with and correct.

Now suppose that we adopt one view or another: all our ordinary reasoning will reflect the change; the inferences that we make and allow—though we reckon them rigorously deductive, as perhaps they are—will be subtly but systematically modified. It follows that to other philosophers who assume different concepts or models, and hence different rules, they will simply be errors; yet that, perhaps, is a discovery of limited value until they have seriously explored or entered into these alternative modes of thought. In saying so I do not mean to advocate vagueness or mere mental laxity; though I confess that I should wish to see—what is really a harder task not an easier one—a trained use of judgement in reasoning that might be rather sensitive than formalist. At least we should distinguish and recognize the diversity of cases to be met with: in general a scientific model brings with it conceptual apparatus whose distinct mode of functioning is pretty plain; in philosophy the line may be less sharp. We sometimes coin technical terms whose logical grammar is unique—not replaceable, even at the cost of clumsiness, by anything that we already possess. At others the effect of the change may rather be to give a new slant or emphasis to linguistic systems already in use: we take this step now with increased confidence, and qualify that one. We use the same words as before but no longer with quite the same force. (I am conscious that throughout the present argument I have slipped in 'conceptual apparatus' as an amplification of 'concept'; preparing the reader, I hope, for a use to be made of the latter, which might otherwise have brought some slight jolt.) And again we may work from within, never crystallizing our viewpoint in a single image, but gradually establishing new patterns, enforcing new habits of thought; reflection thus moulding imperceptibly the way in which argument goes forward.

Here ethics provides examples. Moral judgement, no less than scientific judgement, is a faculty that develops gradually, growing with experience and training; and moral concepts have developed concurrently. For it is here, in his grasp and his handling of those concepts, that an individual's judgement appears. We find a familiar example in what has been called, in a monstrously over-sized word, the universalizability of moral judgements; in the requirement, namely, that any moral judgement passed on a given object must be applied equally to any other objects of the same sort except in so far as relevant differences can be shown. And many moral philosophers have made that part of the definition of a moral judgement.

Now any philosophical study of a given concept—'morality', 'judgement' or what you will—seems to meet with this difficulty, that its subject-matter is not static but changing. Morality is not a single concept clearly defined: rather we find a growing tangle of fibres that overlap, branch, and join again; and to pick out any single strand seems merely arbitrary. We might instead try to set out a complete and impartial description, to reproduce with photographical neutrality the whole complex as it actually presents itself —though what we should gain by such a replica is less clear, even supposing that we could get it. The truth is that every description partly systematizes; it always seeks for a pattern in its material, and, quite rightly, represents it accordingly. The business of intellectual inquiry everywhere is to find a significant order in data or phenomena that seemed senseless at first—given and arbitrary, a mere manifold. Hence we need neither cut off at random a given slice to study, nor yet to attempt to retrace all the multiform whole —omitting no detail however trifling for want of criteria to judge of trifles. For what we find in a body of concepts where thought or reflection are at work is a pattern of development or growth; we can indicate the main lines of evolution and make the distinction between forms that are more and less developed.

Some moral philosophers, as I remarked, make it a defining property of moral judgement that it admits of universalization; so that any judgement lacking this feature cannot be classed as moral at all. This, plainly, is an arbitrary course; ostensibly it represents nothing more than a decision to use the phrase 'moral judgement' in a certain way. I suspect that it really expresses something more —an attempt to formulate or study the concept in what is, after all, felt to be its most developed or most adequate form. And to do that is at least to go beyond any would-be neutral description. It must at the same time be plain that this black-and-white distinction cannot in fact adequately express the material that it claims to apply to; the practical application of this test of universalization in ordinary argument can only be a matter of degree. If what we require, to be allowed to speak of moral utterances at all, is its rigorous and consistent application then the consequences may be strange; for my part I should hesitate to commit myself to any very wide generalization even about the practice of English-speaking people. All that I would confidently say is that they vary greatly both in clarity of mind and in moral development; the safest supposition is, perhaps, that in their application of this or any other logical procedure they will vary no less. Apply this test strictly, then, and we may find that many of them never express moral attitudes or pass moral judgements at all.

But let us imagine a community in which certain terms are in use similar to our terms 'right' and 'wrong'; they serve to prohibit or promote sorts of action whose performance is punished or rewarded —or brings self-congratulation or remorse. We may say, then, in a sense, that moral judgements are passed here; but these judgements, we may further suppose, are never consistently universalized. The thing is surely conceivable and not even particularly remote; if so, ethics is bound to give some sort of account of it. Different accounts may be possible, but at least we must not put ourselves in a position that logically obliges us, *qua* moral philosophers, to ignore it altogether. One culprit, perhaps, is punished for an action—is made to suffer by reason of what he has done—while another man who did the same thing goes scot-free. That may seem absurd to imagine; it would be unjust, certainly, though I believe that I have seen certain homes where the justice meted out to different children follows much this pattern. Besides the system might have its own justification after a fashion. The tribesmen who follow these practices might tell us that it is enough that one man should suffer: some penalty has to be paid for what has been done, they say, but which individual is made to pay it is immaterial. That might, indeed, be a tolerably rational view if, say, they had not yet struck on the notion of varying the severity of punishments with different offences: suppose

I

there is one and only one fixed penalty in every case, and that the measure of suffering that it represents if two men separately suffer seems out of proportion to the present wrongdoing. To expiate the crime, perhaps, one man's-worth of penalty is required, but who pays it is an arbitrary matter. Religion and mythology, indeed, often tell us of penalties incurred—yet penalties that may be paid either by the innocent or the guilty.

No doubt there are various possibilities of such pre-moral or semi-moral systems, and again of more or less developed morality; there are systems in which much remains that seems to us arbitrary or crude where we yet see a kind of groping reason. But now let us return to our example and suppose a particular system in which the demand for universality is simply not recognized; two people who have done just the same action are yet quite differently judged. We might expect to be told that one, say, is senior in rank or is older or belongs to some different group; and that, whether or not we should think it good morality, would serve to save the logic of the argument. Any normal person, you would think, could not but feel the discrepancy, and therefore feel, too, the need to give some sort of account of it. We certainly should feel it; and like so many steps in every learning-process—steps that afterwards get built into our judgement —it may, once we have assimilated it, seem inescapable. One may marvel how one ever failed to see the force of an argument which now stands out like black on white, though at first, perhaps, one groped, at a loss. This process is the formation of concepts, of ways of thinking that serve to guide the work and movement of our minds along new channels. Thus, to take quite a different example, children up to the age of five or six suppose that a quantity of liquid in a given vessel changes on being poured into another vessel of a different shape; or, more properly, the concept of quantity, which is defined by its constancy through such changes, is one that they have not yet formed adequately.[1] Yet before long they may puzzle or

[1] Cf. Evelyn Lawrence, *Children's Idea of Number* in *Some Aspects of Piaget's Work*, (National Froebel Foundation), p. 2. Many other fascinating examples will be found in this pamphlet. The concept of quantity whose first formation we see here, answers at a

laugh at the very absurdity of the question that would have defeated them six months or a year before.

I am far from denying, then, that we should rightly expect a normal person, brought to reflect on the point, to feel the need to account for the discrepancy in the case that we have imagined, that of identical actions judged and handled totally differently. What we must bear in mind is only this, that not all people are equally reflective or equally penetrating; nor does every moral system in which their natural powers—great or small—have been trained, belong to the same level of development. To insist on the test of universality to define moral judgement, wholly excluding whatever falls short of it, would, as I have said, be grossly arbitrary; and it would be worse than arbitrary to take no account of it at all. What we need is no more than to recognize a progressive direction in our thinking—to acknowledge and yet place its more primitive forms: for judgement, here as elsewhere, has its laws of growth. We are carried forward by the force of the process, and new principles emerge and establish themselves. Or, making a single clearer step forward, we may introduce pictures or models to formulate a new point of view: our intellectual attitude is modified, and the operations that we make or allow, either with objects or with words, will be modified as well. It is in these, then, progressive modifications, more or less gradual or abrupt, that the development of judgement consists.

## III

I have spoken so far of the development of judgement on the one side and of systems of concepts on the other; but it is time to go further and speak of language. For language, it is plain, reflects our concepts, those concepts are embodied in language. And here I find myself in conflict with a view of language—a whole orthodoxy, I

more basic level to those new concepts, or points of view, which Toulmin finds in the development of science. The world as we see it reflects through and through our previous learning and thinking—the conceptual apparatus that, in striving to cope with things about us, we have slowly built up. Again, on the grasp of what we come to call logical relations, cf. the note to p. 107, above.

fear that I must say—that has dominated contemporary philosophy: broadly one may call it linguistic conventionalism.

I have said that reflective thinking, inquiry in any form, has its necessary tendency or growth; and it follows that we must say the same of language. The precise point is not altogether easy to put into words; the word 'logic' has been so straightened in recent years that to speak of a 'logical' necessity or 'logical' superiority of one form of language over another would be to invite misunderstanding. It may be better to use old-fashioned language and speak of what is binding on rational beings. If we can recognize certain ways of thinking, and hence of speaking too, as better or more adequate in themselves, then, in so far as we are rational, it naturally follows that we shall accept them. The distinction that we shall require to draw is between what falls under mere choice or preference and what, whether we choose it or not, remains nonetheless objectively valid; and though this 'valid' is another term that has been narrowed in technical usage it retains more, perhaps, of its older meaning as well. Non-philosophers, at least, speak happily enough of a 'valid point of view'.

Now the view which we come in conflict with here may perhaps be summed up in the slogan that all necessity is conventional; and this is perhaps a sort of shadowy counterpart to the Humean denial that necessity can ever be found in nature. Facts are contingent through and through; an appeal to the authority of logic is always an appeal to linguistic rules. It may be that some obscure feeling or conviction of the metaphysical force or (after all) necessity of Hume's view, of the impossibility of real connexions in nature, is what leads the adherents of conventionalism to cling to it as they do through thick and thin. For apart from Hume's own powerful argument—an argument which the present account does not conflict with—that all particular matters of fact might imaginably be otherwise than they are, we find little ground offered for conventionalism. But what we continually meet is the absolute dichotomy of facts and language; languages are systems that we construct, and we are free to construct them as we please—though doubtless we do not normally proceed arbitrarily. We have purposes in view; some systems are more workable than others, some modes of expression are 'misleading'. But these strictly are not logical predicates. When we speak of statements as true or false we must look beyond language to the facts, to those facts which are what they are, and verify or falsify what we say, regardless of any such constructions.[1]

This view is so general and so familiar that coming to challenge it one may well hesitate, as one hesitates near the edge of a gross paradox. And yet this is no paradox after all, rather one would have thought it a commonplace that our thought can be no subtler than our language; that a deficient or unsuitable linguistic instrument, like flawed glass in the pane of a window, will distort what it was meant to reveal. The very terms we use may block our thinking; a true presentation is impossible in too inappropriate an idiom. And yet they need not block it altogether—nor are we bound to wait in silence for the Promethean gift of a perfect language.

Let us imagine, for instance, a chronicler or early historian writing at some time during the Middle Ages and meaning to tell the story

[1] It is not easy to document a view which is part almost of our philosophical atmosphere: and doubtless the conventionalist position is held in many various forms. But my concern is less to refute any particular alternative view than to clarify my own; so a somewhat loose general statement may perhaps be forgiven. For the rest one may refer to A. J. Ayer, *Language, Truth and Logic*, ch. iv, esp. pp. 78–82 for a classical statement of the doctrine. And we found, too, in Chapter II (cf. above, pp. 42–4) that Hare's moral theory presupposed a similar theory of inference; and the two are built into each other. Again Wittgenstein has insisted that mathematical and logical systems are things that we construct and do not discover, and has denied any sort of compulsiveness—beyond what follows from our acceptance of a given system—as attaching to a logical 'must'. (Cf. *Philosophical Investigations*, i, 492, and *Remarks on the Foundations of Mathematics*, i, 121 and ii, 167.) But he, no doubt, would not have acceded to the notion of the facts that I indicated; of facts which we merely find, wholly independently of our conceptual or linguistic structures. That may set some limits to his conventionalism; but perhaps the different strands in his thought were not in the end wholly consistent. A better view sees logical rules or principles as involved in the nature of inquiry so far as it sets itself certain general goals, such as comprehensiveness, precision and the like—which goals themselves will presumably remain a matter for sheer decision in the sense criticized in Chapter II. But the truth is surely that both 'goals' and principles emerge in the same process, and each is involved in the notion or application of the other. We cannot make precision our goal without logical principles to give the idea content: both at least may count as criteria, and science discovers its criteria in working.

of Ancient Rome. Shakespeare's *Cymbeline* or Chaucer's Troy will give some idea of what I have in mind. This historian will naturally write, in the English of his time, of the Senate as 'the Parliament' or ('parlement'), meaning, of course, such Parliaments as the Plantagenets summoned to Westminster; he also refers to the Roman plebs as 'serfs' or 'villeins', to proconsuls as 'viscounts' or 'earls', and to centurions, possibly, as 'knights'. Now in such a history we might be tempted to say that Brutus and Cicero would appear in fancy dress. The story that it told would be systematically distorted, or partly coherent but blurred in patches—like the discourse of an inmate of a mental asylum, which may often begin rationally enough; or like a programme picked up on a wireless-set from a station not quite within its range. For what the chronicler is to retrace is a chain of connected events, the story of men who in their own eyes acted on sufficient grounds and aligned themselves with causes that had meaning. The parts that they play in the plot are unintelligible except in their setting—in a nexus of social relations and ideas as to social relations, which, by hypothesis, our historian cannot penetrate. He cannot, that is to say, penetrate them wholly; and with the progress of historical science it would be easy to point to his shortcomings. Yet the question to ask of his work, a more significant question as well as a more candid one, will be how far and where it succeeds. For if science is ever to make itself better tools or arrive at more adequate statements we owe it to such beginnings as these; to understand whatever is unfamiliar we plainly have no other way than first to present it in terms of what we know. Here we have concepts to work with—and imperfect concepts are corrigible, we correct them in the process of using them: but out of nothing nothing can come.

But now, granting all this, the reader may ask what the illustration serves to establish. Broadly we may say that conventionalism might constitute an account of a science whose forms were wholly final and fixed; where our concepts never grew on our hands, nor were criticized or modified in use, but rose perfect like Venus from the sea; and again of a world of inquiry where every possible subject of study was amenable to the methods of mathematics—where precise rules were applicable throughout. What the present illustration represents, along with the others that we have glanced at—the notion of the travelling of light (and hence of its travelling in straight lines) and of moral judgements as implicitly universal—is the emergence of new forms of thought, of conceptual and linguistic innovations. These, further, are assessed as good or bad. Our general concern in the present chapter has been with the development of judgement —and hence, too, with these conceptual developments that form, so to speak, its objective correlate. We must now ask in what terms these latter are assessed when one among them is preferred to another. Here the conventionalist has no better account to give than to speak of the laying-down of new usages, making it a matter of decision and legislation; whatever terms of valuation we may use, then, the issue is not strictly a logical one. Logical evaluation is confined to what falls within a system already laid down; there, when procedures come in question, we test them by recognized rules. I have said that I do not mean to quarrel over the term 'logical': judgements of the sort that concern us here are certainly different from those that may be thought of as logical *par excellence*, from judgements of validity or invalidity in deductive reasoning; no purpose would be served by confusing them. But the real danger of confusion may lie elsewhere: these cases are no less different from the evaluation of an instrument or an artifact designed to subserve human ends, as a knife or a dynamo for instance. And they are different, once again, from any judgement of practical convenience; say, the preference of one notation or another on the ground that it is easier to work with. And that also falls outside logic. As to the former, our assessment of instruments or tools: the end that we pursue, where these 'tools' that we speak of are theoretical structures or concepts, may be nothing but understanding of the world; all that we seek, it may be, is to satisfy intellectual curiosity. It is at least an intelligible purpose if not a common one; and any system that serves to advance it, and on that account is evaluated favourably, must be one that gets us nearer the truth. And this truth, once again, is not something detachable, something given in itself or explicable apart from those modes of inquiry, from the tests and procedures that we use in the relevant field. We may frame some general account of truth: it still has to be made concrete in terms of these special concepts.

Hence to say that we assess these concepts as tools, is no more than to say that we assess them. Again the evaluation in question is not one of practical convenience; for in working with a poor linguistic instrument, suppose it is all that we have, the statements that we are led to assert can never be strictly the same as those that we might have made with a better one—the same, their truth-value unaffected, despite their obscure or awkward form. Rather, any statement that we make is bound to use a particular conceptual framework, and hence to presuppose a point of view. And the less adequate the point of view the less adequate will be the statement that reflects it; it may be true, perhaps, but partly distorted, and the truth and the distortion are inseparable. But this must be shown in more detail.

Let us ask what account conventionalism can give of the matter. A true statement agrees with the facts: what we have are these facts on one side, untouched by linguistic constructions, which our statements either mirror or fail to mirror, and the rules of those constructions on the other. Strict truth or falsity, and again formal validity within a system, are all the kinds of logical value that a conventionalist can allow. Where statements that are not merely false fail in some other third way—where we require not an absolute black-and-white but rather a continuous scale—it would seem there is nothing that he can say of them but that, though true, they are 'misleadingly expressed'. They are cast, it may be, in terms of some imperfect linguistic medium, like those of our mediaeval chronicler. Yet that is a matter of lucidity, of ease or speed of working or the like; that is to say, of convenience, not strictly of logic. It would count as psychologism, I suppose, to confuse the intelligibility or the ease of a particular notation—to this individual or that—with anything like validity or truth. If, then, we have a third notion of adequacy as forming a value *sui generis*, it has no place in any system such as this.

Conventionalism, we see, relies heavily on a distinction between these 'true statements misleadingly expressed' and those that are simply called false. It further requires exact rules, rules which must be rigidly applicable, for determining to which class any given statement belongs. But where our concepts are partly indeterminate it would seem that no such rules are to hand; here we can no longer draw a line to mark off the area of their application. Take a predicate expressing such a concept: we make a statement, in the conventionalist's idiom, that is either merely true or merely false, or again is 'true though misleadingly expressed'. Now this last will be a matter of more or less; we can, therefore, imagine the same statement expressed in forms that are progressively misleading—until a point is reached in the series at which we no longer call it misleading but simply false. The one will pass over into the other, for our concept, by hypothesis, is indeterminate: and yet, for the conventionalist, it cannot. For the former predicate belongs to psychology and the latter to a would-be pure logic; the two cannot fall on the same scale. To mislead is to mislead given people: they, certainly, may report that they cannot tell whether a given statement is indeed false or merely difficult or puzzling—that is, puzzling to them. What is hard to conceive is how anyone could sensibly say, 'This statement is so difficult to me as to be not merely puzzling but false.' In some spheres, no doubt, we can solve our problems by legislation, the conventionalist's favourite recourse; we can draw a merely arbitrary line. But here, by hypothesis, our subject-matter is inexact, and though we might lay down what is to count as truth or falsity in any one instance, we shall no sooner come to apply these same terms to new cases than the old difficulties will meet us again. We shall be unable to say with precision whether the stipulated conditions are fulfilled or not.

There are, we find, certain regions of discourse, or possible regions where the conventionalist account is unworkable, those, namely, where we lack precise tests of truth or falsity. But this possibility is also actual. Ordinary language, it is plain, equips us with nothing of the kind: and even though the progress of science should substitute exact methods for rule-of-thumb, large areas remain in which we seem unlikely ever to possess them. The demand for precision is out of place—it is no more than a truism to say—in proportion as what we are to deal with are intangible or immeasurable things. I suspect that there may be philosophers—in some writings, at least, the impression is hard to escape—who feel in their hearts that the only material, ideally speaking, fit for philosophy to recognize is what is amenable to the methods of mathematics. But let us look at the study of society, and ask how far the strength of social forces admits of expression in decimals. We read, perhaps, in some work of history that the greatest single influence on the acceleration of industrial development in Great Britain in the later eighteenth century was—not such factors, say, as labour or invention—but the accumulation of capital from the India trade: we speak here of the relative strength of forces which do not admit of precise measurement. Nor indeed—since inventiveness responds to demand, and industrial development reflects both—do they admit of strict mutual separation. Yet we can still sensibly, although within limits, weigh the importance of one against another. But let us take the example a little further; we may find the same assertion made—what we shall roughly call the same assertion—in the different idiom that we probably heard at school: we read this time, perhaps in a textbook, that this same amassing of capital was 'the chief cause of the Industrial Revolution'. Now a historian might question this choice of terms: but suppose, first, that he accepts the former statement as true (it is immaterial here whether it is so); then he must presumably say of this latter, if he is to speak in the conventionalist's idiom, that it is 'true but misleadingly expressed'. But we can imagine the sequence carried still further; for this, surely, is not the worst mode of expression, the most misleading that we could imagine or devise. Suppose, then, that the same historical processes are still more ineptly described: a point will surely come at which what is predicated of them can no longer be called misleading, it is merely false.

And again doubtful cases will arise where no test or criteria that we can possess will suffice to provide a clear answer; we cannot say to which class they belong. Now this situation, we have seen, is one that conventionalism cannot contemplate: these two notions, the false and the misleading, are essentially disparate, so that the one cannot pass over into the other: nor yet can we recognize any borderline or no-man's-land where possible indeterminate statements might fall—statements which could properly be described as somehow partaking of both.

All that we need on the other side, to avoid the difficulty, is to accept the situation as we find it, redescribing it in more realistic terms. For when historians abandon the notion of some single episode, of a well-differentiated unity, standing out, to be called 'The Industrial Revolution' and ascribed to other such unit-factors as its 'causes'—indeed wherever we replace less with more adequate conceptual forms—no uncommitted commentator, I suggest, could see the process as no more than a change of the notation in which 'the same facts' are expressed: facts that are neutral or merely given. Some such common ground must exist indeed, the hard data on which different parties agree—on which, therefore, further building can go forward. Even here what we have are not facts that stand beyond even possible dispute, but rather, all we need for the purpose, agreement or substantial agreement on the right way of presenting or interpreting them; that suffices to let us speak of 'the same facts' which different further accounts present differently. But these later interpretations—interpretations of greater depth, as we may say—are not merely ways of arranging, or different notations for describing, basic facts that never come in question. The historians whose interpretations differ may indeed revert, if need be, to the lower-level description as presenting material that they share; they may go back to common ground to restate an argument. But once the higher-level language is readopted the very material in question appears differently; the 'same fact' is differently described according to the interpretation that we adopt. Historians may agree, say, that such and such specified persons were elected to Parliament, but disagree heartily in interpreting what occurred: say, as to whether 'The Whig Party' was consolidated at the election; or whether it really was no more than that the machinery of eighteenth-century political patronage shifted the group interests around—operating in its ordinary way. We may come in the end, if you wish, to a man's own reports of his sense-perceptions, which still stand open to question and interpretation. A historical issue may turn on a partisan's description or report of something that he claims to have witnessed; we do not, to take an extreme case, accept the evidence on oath of Titus Oates. Oates himself was no doubt a plain rogue; yet the time was a time of doubt and fear, and probably many honest witnesses too, their thinking coloured by false or distorted concepts —their concept of 'Popery', for instance—gave equally dubious reports of what they saw.

This, in different philosophical contexts, has often enough been pointed out. What is less often noticed, perhaps, is in default of such ground-level or clean facts no conventionalist account can suffice. For all assessment of statements as true or false will now involve, not only comparison with the facts, but a further assessment as well of the conceptual scheme in which they are formulated.

Take any statement of dubious status—dubious from the conventionalist point of view. The theory requires an analysis into two distinct and ultimate factors: on the one side its truth-value determined by merely observable facts, and on the other its conformity or nonconformity with the rules of the language to which it belongs. And the latter, it is said, are conventional. But these are requirements, we find, that cannot be met; at a certain point the distinction breaks down. Our judgement as to the truth of any statement, its agreement with the facts that serve to verify it, is bound to be partly a judgement of the conceptual terms in which it is cast. Hence if this assessment of concepts is called conventional discourse must be conventional through and through; for we cannot separate or unfuse the two elements so as to isolate anything solely testable by reference to given matters of fact. Since the would-be pure facts, clean of all interpretation, fall outside discourse as a sort of unknowable noumenon, they cannot help us in judging actual statements: real facts, of course, do nothing of the sort, facts as perceived and interpreted, well or badly, in right terms or wrong. Here indeed we shall find truth and falsity, but we shall find conceptual adequacy or inadequacy as well.

In all this I do not, of course, deny that there is a broad distinction to be drawn, nonetheless important for being vague, between an appeal to reason and an appeal to fact. Pure reason would mean a bare conceptual scheme, an uninterpreted calculus, perhaps; not yet what we normally call a language. Interpret it, giving it substance, and at once you get a view of the world; which, rightly or wrongly, a critic may call a false or distorted one. Again pure fact, though sometimes we approach it—we recognize different degrees of 'givenness' —is not something we can ever attain. 'Reason' means the structures we have; for what other first appeal can we make? To work within them is so far to think rationally. Yet they in turn may develop or may break down; be changed or enlarged. What we are bound to suppose is that in general with progressive reflection, working with and within existing moulds, we get nearer to adequate views.

## IV

In the previous chapter I spoke of the general process of inquiry as a communal thing; procedures and views emerge and establish themselves among people who share a culture and a tradition, so that differences are brought into line. And on this basis, moreover, we shall find that further differences arise, pointing to new possibilities and requiring to be resolved in turn. I have sought here to fill in the picture: I have spoken of the development of judgement—which is essentially the same process, we may notice, whether we look at the history of thought as a whole or at the training of an individual within an existing tradition. For there the individual assimilates and makes his own, what earlier generations have acquired more slowly, the conceptual apparatus, the terms and forms, in which growing judgement finds expression—which make it objective and substantial.

For it is this that the new student must learn, structures that inquiry has built up, and in learning them he forms his own judgement. I shall return in the following chapter to my main theme, namely evaluation; but there remains one possible objection which it will be as well to examine before proceeding.

The process I have described is a temporal one. I have spoken of an individual's judgement as gradually developed through training and experience, and again of inquiry in general as looking forward towards what we see as attainable agreement. So far so good: but it seems an intelligible supposition, even if a strange one, that a person might appear on the scene equipped with a fully formed legal or scientific judgement, without having had to acquire it in the normal ways. We can imagine that this prodigy walks in, picks up the relevant documents and seizes on the key-points at once, and yet cannot say how he learnt. One morning, perhaps, the gift came to him. Now how, if so, will this possibility affect our account? So long as what we are to imagine is no more than an individual with special powers its philosophical significance is slight. For if we say of his judgement, as perhaps we may, that it is equal to the judgement of experts who have spent a lifetime at their job, we shall still have to appeal to established tests. Let us suppose that given some new problem he produces the right solution at a glance: to say so we must refer to criteria—criteria already established, presumably, in the ordinary way. To bear on the philosophical issue the supposition must be taken much further: we must leave behind us the world that we know and imagine a whole community of beings born, like this, with their faculties complete. In this new world, we are to suppose, we find sciences and systems of thought—with procedures for resolving problems that arise—but systems that never change or develop. They exist as they always have existed, in their present perfection, as far as memory goes back; or perhaps they emerged one morning sympathetically in all the race—as if they should suddenly find themselves all talking together in French.

I shall not merely dismiss this supposition or content myself with calling it inconceivable; conceivability is a matter of degree. But the interest of this sort of fancy is precisely in its dissimilarity to the ordinary world that we know. Reasoning and science in such a world would lack many features that are essential to them in ours; there is much that we are bound to do, that they would have no occasion for. Differences of this sort, which throw light on the connexion of elements in our own system, may be what this sort of supposition serves best to bring out. It would seem, however, that philosophers of certain schools are more inclined to go to work the other way, to think and speak rather as if this hypothetical world were the actual one; and hence, in effect, they ignore all philosophical problems which arise out of those features of thought that belong only to a developing system.

In this hypothetical world there could be no question of pressing inquiry beyond its present limits, of new sciences with procedures of their own—that might establish or fail to establish their disputed claims. And such problems as those that we have been discussing would be a great deal easier than they are. Take the universality of moral judgement for instance; we should lay it down without further ado that this test either was or was not a defining feature of morality —or again, supposing existing practice were mixed and variable, we could only say so and leave the matter there. For it would be useless to seek to bring to light the best or most rational sort of practice. In general we may say that in this imaginable world philosophy would be much simpler than it is. But now suppose that philosophizing, as we must, in the actual world, we always talk as if it were that hypothetical one: it follows that the account we shall give of things will also be proportionately simplified. It is somewhat as if we should project the image of a curved surface on a plane, so that many of its features are distorted or even disappear altogether.

Other consequences of this sort of approach, ignoring the temporal background of our actual thinking, are too far-reaching to pursue here; and the following chapter will be concerned with the emergence and adoption of new principles in the process of thought. But that apart, we might pause over the confused and patchwork picture that we should be left with if, on these principles, we were to survey all the beliefs that men have ever held, in any civilization or age. Philosophy sets out to make sense of whatever presents itself as a mere manifold, but it can hardly expect to succeed if it ignores the part that progressive reflection plays in our thinking itself. Hence, whatever illumination may be got from such fancies, or from this notion in particular of a static and unchangeable world of thought, in our ordinary theorizing we do better to keep our eyes on the real one.

# V

## Knowledge of Principles

PHILOSOPHERS have made it their special business to inquire into the status of so-called first principles; for it seems that there are fundamental laws or practices on which any body of thinking depends—the principle of induction, for instance, or whatever is to be put in its place, or the principle of rational benevolence. And these may well seem the natural starting-point; we shall begin with what is basic and thence derive the rest. Here, however, I mean to take the opposite course, and my justification for doing so must be left to the development of the argument; it will appear in whatever light this procedure may throw on the subject—though in fact I have, in Chapter I, already indicated a general approach.

There are also particular rules or principles which we use and appeal to in inquiry, short of those that may be thought fundamental, and it is time to say something of these. I have spoken so far of evaluation within the general context that serves to make it intelligible; of judgement as it is exercised in one special field or another within a developed school of thought or branch of science. But this account as it stands may seem defective, if not radically perverse: for judgement must have principles to appeal to, otherwise it could claim no authority. And if that is the crux of this issue all that has been said so far is beside the point. For what has still to be shown is how we come to be equipped with these principles—and that was precisely the question to which the rival doctrines which we examined at the start, intuitionism and the theory of decisions, set out to provide answers.

Now principles have a curious dual status; they belong both to theory and practice. A practitioner, it is plain, can follow principles without knowing it, and in this sense practice precedes theory. Our first tendency, perhaps, in the notion that we form of these things, is to picture them the other way round; principles, we feel, come

K

first, they stand at the top. We were taught them in the first place by superiors, by authorities who, we say, stand over us; and again in the linear setting-out of argument convention has given them pride of place. The truth is, however, a familiar one that the order of discovery may differ from that of demonstration; and even our teachers had to learn. Where there are no teachers to learn from it seems that certain skills may develop nonetheless; here patterns of activity emerge and the principles that govern them are followed unreflectively long before they are explicitly formulated. Thus, to take a common illustration, it is much eaiser for a native to speak tolerably correct English than to state the rules governing, say, the use of the past subjective (as, 'If I came . . .'): and it is easier to conduct a fair argument than to formulate the principles of logic. Here, then, we find a simple answer to our question, the first source of our ordinary principles is not far to seek: we learn them by reflection on practice, by observing what we previously did unreflectively.

In any ordinary activity, working or playing or talking, the course that we follow unreflectively will prove to have been regular, not random—in some measure at least. Pausing in the midst of the process and looking back over the ground that we have covered, we find regularities or patterns; and these we shall henceforth call principles. We followed them long before we recognized them, and it seems that once they are recognized they enjoy an immediate authority. *De facto* is changed to *de jure*; their mere past acceptance suffices— and to know what we have done in the past requires neither intuition nor decision. But if we are asked on what grounds we adopt these principles rather than others, by what right we proceed after this fashion, we may perhaps turn the question round on our questioners: for surely not to follow them—in default of apparent ground for any change—would call more for explanation. I shall assume that our critics, like ourselves, are concerned with the business of inquiry, are ready to give reasons for their views, appealing to procedures that command acceptance. For no one can argue with silence. But now, if inquiry is to go forward, it is hard to see on what basis that can be contemplated, supposing we are to start by rejecting wholesale whatever practices or principles have been followed or observed hitherto. What line of progress can remain? We can only speak of 'reasoning' or 'inquiry', only give content and meaning to the words, inasmuch as we can refer to some body of procedures that are generally accepted and agreed on. Certainly they may always be alterable; but if our concern is with particular principles which we propose to reject, and, dealing not wholesale but singly, can show reason for rejecting, that can only be by appeal to some other principle—a principle which, therefore, we continue to recognize.

There is, then, no great difficulty about the general source from which our principles are derived; but the solution of this first problem, it may seem, only raises another more serious one. For what we shall have to account for is not only the fact of our having such principles but also of our needing them; they must have some function to fulfil and the present account may seem to leave them with none. The rôle in which principles normally serve is tolerably plain; we appeal to them either for justification or guidance in face, say, of challenge or of doubt. Now so long as our appeal is to authority, or to principles laid down by authority, then the part that they play is not, perhaps, hard to explain. But the present view leaves the point more obscure. Our only appeal is to past practice, for it is from practice that our principles derive. Now provided our progress runs smoothly no special guidance can be required; nor can justification. Not until some hitch or impediment halts or disturbs us—or other people's views, which we come up against, prove to conflict with our own—will we feel the need to appeal to principles at all. It seems that principles represent nothing but a statement of past practice; yet no need for such principles can arise until the practice in question has broken down. Or again, if other people's views collide with ours, the most we can do, on this account, will be to formulate on either side the very practices which we have previously followed—those, namely, which have led to the collision.

This inference appears pretty plain, yet it is not quite plain that common sense would endorse it; our first instinct in face of a difficulty is to review our own previous practice, and I believe that most people would say that we may sometimes get new light merely in stating it explicitly. We were brought to a halt by some obstacle; we resurvey the course that we have followed, and thence adjust our bearings and proceed. But that in turn, I may be told, is simply explicable, we need no special theory to account for it. The statement of our own habitual practice will help us only if we treat it as a rule, which is the very thing we set out to account for; but again, we are able to treat it as a rule only in virtue of this, that where our progress is blocked we normally expect to find some discrepancy that may explain it. We expect to be able to show a difference between our procedure hitherto and our procedure on the present occasion. Where the two diverge we can correct one by the other, but failing that there would be nothing to gain.

So far, it would seem then, we are left with our dilemma on our hands: rules that do no more than reflect our past practice will be useless, while those that go beyond it remain arbitrary; we cannot tell either their source or their justification. Yet our briefly sketched account of our normal response to present difficulties may, for all that, have its significance: there is, it would seem, some sort of natural response, a procedure that we immediately adopt, that sets the processes of our thinking going again. First we review our previous practice—yet we review it, it would seem, in a special light. What we look for and speak of now is not only a practice but a rule, though one followed unreflectively in the past, and never yet formulated. Indeed it cannot have been followed universally, or else the problem could never have arisen; we could not correct present practice by reference to the past if the one never differed from the other. Rather, it is the general or prevalent practice which we now see in this light and call the 'rule'; and other practices now appear as 'deviations'. The use of this conceptual machinery is involved or is implicit, at least, in our normal response to a difficulty; it is, no doubt, simple machinery, reflecting no very sophisticated point of view, but not less important on that account. But more is involved too; we eliminate those discrepancies—those that we see as discrepancies—we set out to bring them into line. Thus the effect of reflection is twofold: first to set the picture in a certain light, to reduce it to some sort of order, for instead of an arbitrary manifold we now see a sequence of conduct in which a regularity is imperfectly observed. Secondly its tendency is to reinforce any regularity that it finds. Our natural feeling is, I have suggested, that the mere statement or review of past practice is often of use in face of difficulties; that feeling, after all, may be justified. What we seek in such a restatement is not any ideally neutral or merely photographic description—omitting and emphasizing nothing, and presumably illuminating nothing either—but a description, a new account of the material, which will help us to understand what it presents. We look for a pattern in past practice, and that pattern is to serve as our guide.

Any description, let us remember, must bring its own categories to what it describes. To say that is not to say that it need falsify it, far less render the real object unknowable. How much or how little it falsifies will depend on the categories in question; in the last chapter we took notice of certain descriptions cast in more or less unsuitable terms. But here we shall do better to confine ourselves to the illustration that we began with, that of the rules of linguistic practice: for on being asked any point of usage in one's own language, I remarked, it is natural to try out a few sentences experimentally in hope of eliciting a rule from them. For simplicity's sake let us ignore written English, so that what we have to do with will be nothing but a broken or varied flow of sound. One might think of the language in this way, as one sometimes hears the hubbub of a crowded room, losing the sense of particular differences: and then again we may focus our attention; we discriminate, and soon separate voices and separate threads of discourse emerge. Similarly in a grammatical account: we first distinguish certain recurrent units called words, and grammarians classify these further as substantives, verbs with their inflexions, prepositions, pronouns and the like; they give names, and that is to give prominence, to certain relations and to certain terms. Reflection, having set itself to work in what seemed a merely arbitrary manifold, a heterogeneous mass—

and significantly ignoring an infinity of interesting differences, as of key, loudness or rapidity of speech—finds a pattern of intricate order; it contrives to reduce this material (barring a few intractable 'idioms') to an elaborately systematic syntactical scheme. Yet this scheme, in turn, is nothing final; English grammar as traditionally taught is borrowed from Latin and only fits the language with some little forcing here and there. Other systems and perhaps better ones may be devised, or others at least equally good; the same material admits of presentation in very various ways. We also find cases where our current usage (as of the past subjective mentioned above) will hardly be reduced to order on any terms; and to make sense out of these we need to seek further afield, to examine our language, not only as it is, but as it has been. Then, taking up a new point of view, we unearth another and different sort of pattern, a deeper and more comprehensive one, which has a place for what seemed arbitrary at first sight.

But grammar in its traditional rôle does not aim at any radical treatment; there are doubtless criteria by which to judge of better or worse grammatical systems, yet none of them sets out to make sense of the basic operations of language. That task, oddly enough, has been assumed in recent years not only by philologists but by philosophers; and we ourselves have spent some space on one notable product of the method. For sentences, we have seen, may be classified at a more-than-grammatical level as falling into the indicative mood or the imperative; and moral utterances are ascribed to the latter. The material is familiar enough but the point of view from which we are now asked to regard it is new; we have seen that it is not for nothing that the innovation is introduced. We need to look for a new point of view wherever we fail to make sense of what we seem to see from the old one. And perhaps no coherent account of moral concepts is to be had on the standpoint that we examined at the start, which this revision is intended to correct—roughly the assimilation, implied in the term 'intuition', of moral judgement to physical seeing. Such is the claim, at least. But adopting a different angle of vision we may find that the whole scene is altered, though perhaps each single object remains the same: features that stood out as discrepancies may all fall coherently into place. What we have reached might still be called a description—for instance, of the language of morals—but the view of ethics that it leaves us with is new.[1]

But our present concern is not with the legitimacy of the imperativist's contention, of which I have spoken at some length already; what I wish to speak of here is the character of such innovations in general. Other examples might serve as well. So much has been said in recent years of the unlikeness of philosophy to science that it may be useful to remind ourselves of certain resemblances that may prove important too. When, for instance, we first say that light travels— and travels in straight lines—or think of what travels as waves or particles, we are not handling phenomena that are new and strange: we are not primarily concerned with those 'new facts' which science is supposed to discover as against the familiar material of philosophy. For we have all, no doubt, seen sunshine and shadow. What is new is the system of concepts in terms of which we are now taught to think of them. And the charge is introduced for good reasons; new points of view, Toulmin says, bring with them new techniques of inference. Perhaps we were previously held up by certain intractable phenomena—phenomena which, in the light of our new view-point, may appear as a special case of a given law, while

---

[1] I am conscious of a great debt to the work of Professor Wisdom; yet I cannot refrain from remarking that for an example of a method that is purely descriptive or neutral one could hardly do worse than psycho-analysis. Psycho-analysis sets itself the task of interpretation, and the material which it undertakes to interpret might serve as a very exemplar of anarchic heterogeneity. For where shall we look for the negation of rhyme and reason if not in dreams and undirected mental ramblings? It is here that psychoanalysis seeks for a significant pattern, and succeeds only so far as it finds it. On the other hand I am far from denying that here, and in philosophy itself, a closer encounter with known facts, or a description that serves to bring them home to the imagination, may also have its particular efficacy. It, too, represents in its own way a new point of view, at least a new emphasis; and that may serve, for instance, to make us abandon some ill-fitting, perhaps too abstract conceptual scheme, which we had sought to force on the material. I should add that, in so far as I have criticized Wisdom, I have done so largely with weapons stolen from his own armoury (cf. e.g. *Philosophy and Psycho-Analysis*, pp. 248–54).

before they were merely discrepant or fell outside the system altogether.

I may seem to have digressed in this discussion; but the original issue is not far off. We imagined a critic who complained that the account so far given of evaluation said nothing of the status of principles; yet these principles are the crux of the matter, and if so it is a question of some importance to ask how we acquire or establish them. Now the answer that immediately suggested itself was that we get them from past practice; we first merely proceed in certain ways and afterwards make rules of our own procedures. But here the objection was renewed: so long as our practice runs smoothly we shall never feel any need of such principles, no occasion to appeal to them will arise. To make the use of principles intelligible we must suppose ourselves in some sort of *impasse*; but if so, it was our own practice that got us there—certainly it was nobody else's. A principle, then, that represents no more than a summary of practice, and is only invoked when the practice in question has broken down, would seem the most useless thing imaginable.

The objection has evident force; but we shall answer, first, that to arrive even at a bare formulation of our previous practice—to know as an idea, held up to view, what before we knew only as a process—is already one step towards clarity. We may admit, indeed, that the sort of redescription which we may conceive as ideally descriptive would be a thing of very limited utility: one that attempts no distinction between the significant and the trivial, the relevant and the merely accidental; and which, presumably, would go on for ever for want of any notion of what to leave out—for there may well be an infinity of things that can truly be said of any given subject-matter. But the real situation is different. Any description that we give will be cast in terms of certain concepts or categories, and might always have been cast in terms of others. We at least distinguish 'regularities' and 'deviations', and we see material accordingly. And, further, where such patterns emerge the course that we instinctively adopt is to sharpen them or observe them more consistently; we eliminate whatever, from our new point of view, we see as

irregular. (And here, too, we may notice in passing, we have a principle which we follow and may appeal to: one that itself is, as all
principles must be, elicited from a survey of normal practice—and
is therefore, in this sense, homological.) But we not only use a given
system or see a certain pattern in our material; the particular pattern
that we find there will depend on the view-point that we adopt.

I have said that the standard grammatical account of current
English or again Hare's distinction made at a different level, are
only two amongst endless possibilities, and some will be better and
others worse; for to emphasize the diversity of conceptual schemes is
not to put them all on equal footing. On the contrary, our concern
is to evaluate them. Some obstacle or apparent discrepancy, we supposed, had blocked our progress. The difficulty may be more or less
obstinate; a mere statement of past practice may suffice, or again a
deeper search may be called for, or a wider survey. In general the
further we stand back from the immediate blockage—the more comprehensive the view-point that we thus take up—the more various
will be the patterns that reveal themselves. Here we find our hope of
further progress; from one standpoint we may see no way through
the problem, but with another, perhaps, the perspective shifts and
new possibilities come into view.

Our first general rule, it appears, is to seek for existing regularities
—which, where we find them, we reinforce. We conform to them
with closer consistency. But that is not all: with the particular position that we take up and hence the pattern that we find, say, on
changing our view-point, the practices that we see as regular or as
divergent will alter too. Grammar again provides examples. Suppose
that the monosyllable 'than' is classed (as by most speakers nowadays it seems to be), not with 'and' and 'although', but with 'from',
'by' or 'with'—as a preposition and not a conjunction: then to say
'less than me' will not be to diverge from the rule but to conform
to it. A new point of view, it will be observed, also gives us new
rules to follow; we shall alter our conduct—correct it—on quite
different lines and different principles according to the pattern that
we select. To speak, in this sense, of a 'point of view' is, primarily at

least, to speak of what things we treat as analogous, of what cases we put into the same class. Any concept, say of 'ferrous metal' or 'neurosis' or 'the baroque', is made by our recognizing resemblances, by grouping given cases together; so much will probably be agreed. Again we find concepts in use whose right application we deny, perhaps to a particular subject-matter or again quite generally; we deny it wherever the differences between the qualities or things in question are, to us, more salient than their likenesses. What things we see as like or different define the point of view that we adopt. Suppose now that there are alternatives to choose from: if so, the rational preference will be for the view that makes best sense of the material; that yields, let us say, the widest harmonious accommodation of relevant data, inasmuch as it finds room for what otherwise would remain discrepant. But again we can only speak of discrepancies, can only see them as such, in virtue of a system in use, of pre-existing practices and views.

In saying this we have gone a little beyond the position and the problem that we began with. A point of view, we say, shows us different things as like and unlike; and inquiry broadly may be thought of as the search for a generally acceptable point of view. Given this account it is now plain enough how, from a review of past practice, we may find regularities or rules—henceforth we shall treat them as rules—by which we may correct our present course. Our instinct, it seems, is to search for them; we take it for granted that they may be found, though they need not be obvious at a glance: to grasp principles embodied in practice we may need a more or less comprehensive survey, a more superficial or deeper inquiry. But at this point another question arises: we must ask whether after all this instinct may not sometimes prove false. The basis on which all inquiry must proceed is to be found in such instinct—or 'intuition'. (The two terms hardly differ, except in that intuition is called 'instinct' where it is practical; a difference which does not affect the present issue.) For all that their guidance is not infallible: in the end cases may be met with for which previous practice provides no precedent, where we find ourselves on wholly new ground. Now, if so, it would be easy to reply, there can be no question of an appeal to accepted rules or principles; and hence, however important these issues may be in themselves, we are not called on to deal with them so far as the present argument goes. But such an answer is hardly satisfactory. For, if it is true that we turn for guidance to past practice, we are bound to ask where our practice itself comes from: human thought in the course of its history may have met with wholly unprecedented problems from time to time, but it has not in all cases failed to solve them. Where it succeeds new practices will accordingly be introduced, and these in turn will be appealed to as yielding principles.

No doubt a resourceful man in the face of a difficulty ransacks all his experience of like cases; he seeks, not necessarily for a rule directly applicable in the immediate instance, but for anything that may give him a lead. But suppose that every precedent fails: then progress must come, if it comes at all, from sheer intellectual creativeness, from new thought. Sometimes we frame bare hypotheses as well as unearthing further principles from systems already in use; and though observation, the systematic re-examination of available data, has contributed much to the progress of science, imagination has perhaps done still more. At the same time this distinction is not absolute: all reflection must in some measure be 'speculative', it implies some wider survey, some standing-back from the material —which consequently is grasped in new ways. That already is an imaginative thing. At one extreme we find the sort of search that I have spoken of, where a man tries out his stock of material for any promising analogy or the like; and at the other the much simpler procedure of referring to accepted practice for a rule: the difference is still one of degree. Nonetheless the break may be so sharp that it becomes absurd to persist in the same description; to speak, as we have spoken hitherto, of a pattern educed from existing practice. And these further cases remain to be dealt with.

One other point arises first. My approach here has been primarily methodological; and, though we might find it natural to speak, say, of the trying-out of a new treatment or technique, it would seem a solecism to call it a 'hypothesis'. But this difference is more verbal than real (though doubtless some reason underlies the different vocabulary normally appropriated to theory and practice). If the new procedure in question is not itself to be called a 'hypothesis', at least we proceed on the hypothesis that its use will yield acceptable results. Any theory brings with it procedures which we follow, though in following them we may always meet difficulties; if the difficulties prove thoroughly intractable we shall say that the theory has broken down. But in either case our problem remains. Any procedure or any theory that we adopt provides us with principles to be appealed to; we have still to settle the status of these principles which we set up without precedent or practice to authorize them.

We shall find, however, that the problem requires us to seek for no standpoint widely different from that which we have adopted so far. Let us suppose that some well-established theory runs into difficulties. A new experiment, perhaps, produces a counter-example; so that, in the situation that we are left with, theory and observation are in conflict. There is one rule that we cannot abandon—that of testing our views by observation: for that rule is built into all our science, so that to reject it would be to reject everything that has arisen from and rests on its use. But the theory that has come under challenge is one, perhaps, that covers a whole range of well-attested phenomena which we know no other way of accounting for. Our thinking is consequently paralysed throughout this whole area—or would be, if we took the refutation wholly seriously; though mere necessity may suffice for its practical use until some better theory appears. Suppose now, however, that such a theory is framed: some new concept or new view-point takes shape which enables us to accommodate without conflict both the laws that the old theory entailed and the newly found discrepancy too. In such a case we shall surely not puzzle ourselves long with asking by what right or reason we adopt it. Before we were left with a deadlock: now we are shown a way through—the new hypothesis serves to save the phenomena, which is the fundamental task of all our thought. What would call for justification, if anything, would be *not* to accept it in such a case.

Speculation can only build on the basis of a pre-existing system; we take our stand on common ground, on established foundations, even in laying down what is new. Problems can only arise and only be dealt with within a given body of thought. What we have in effect, is an unfinished picture, a mosaic with some area not yet filled in, and what we seek is a piece to fit the gap. Or, altering the illustration a little, let us imagine an artist at work, say, a portrait painter, held up by some difficulty. He has realized what it is his picture needs: he must strengthen the line of the brow, yet without spoiling, and hence without altering—here is his peculiar problem—the effect of the feature of the face. And let us now imagine a solution too: he may set to work on some quite different part of the canvas, developing the curve of the left hand, say; and thus, in turn, strengthening the diagonal which the line of the brow prolongs. So that, thrown back, there now falls on the brow itself that heightened emphasis that he seeks. Such a proposed solution, it is plain, would be unintelligible unless the face and the rest of the picture were already largely painted in; (or if for theory's sake, we are to suppose the whole problem posed intellectually before a single brush-stroke has been applied, at least we are bound to suppose, too, the image or idea of these features is already clear).

So likewise with the process of inquiry: we can only envisage new procedures, if the innovation is to have any point to it, against some determinate background. We cannot either conceive or state problems except in terms of pre-existing systems; and the same therefore holds of solutions. A new point of view, I have suggested, needs no further justification than this, that it enables us to accommodate material that could not be accommodated within the previous one. But it is plain that in saying so we take our stand on the existing system as substantially valid. We can only evaluate the new because in general we stand by the old; for out of mere indeterminateness neither questions nor answers can ever come. Hence supposing that we are to seek to think at all we must give some general acceptance to those procedures which we already possess; further, in so far as they fail us, where the system within which we operate has broken down, we must accept whatever changes will make it work again. And lastly, where we are led to adopt such new procedures—where, therefore, we assess them as more or less workable—we can only appeal to criteria or tests which are part of the main system that we still accept. But as to what criteria we ought to use in detail, in face of particular problems—these, plainly, are questions for specialists; philosophy cannot deal with them in general terms.

In all this I have said nothing of deductive reasoning, which has, of course, its own rules or principles; but so far, at least, as we reason not in special symbols but in words—and I must leave mathematics with its peculiar problems on one side—these raise no new issues or difficulties. We deduce $p$ from $q$, it is often said, when the proposition '$p$ implies $q$' is analytic; and analytic propositions are those that reflect the rules of the language that we are speaking. We need not embark on a search for some impossible non-circular definition of sameness of meaning; we must know broadly, if we know how to speak at all, what sorts of utterance are permissible. Yet these rules are only implicit until the propositions in question are formulated; when we speak of the rules of the language it is our own normal practice that we appeal to. Our previous account therefore will suffice to cover the present case. It may, however, be useful to add a few words concerning one special field, that of philosophical reasoning; for that, too, is often thought of as deductive.

Philosophical difficulties hardly arise until we find language itself pulling us in different ways; common practice, differently interpreted, can be fairly invoked to justify diverse forms of speech. To ask in these circumstances whether or not such a proposition is analytic, is to put a question that admits of no answer—though one that has been a favourite with logical positivists. Indeed they hardly recognize any other; philosophy for them is 'analysis'. And on these terms, it seems, unless we are to make it all legislation—so far as we still recognize questions, answerable questions, for philosophy— they can only take the form 'Is $p$ analytic?' And this in fact is the question that we find arising again and again, for instance, in the work of Professor Ayer; in his more recent no less than his earlier work. If, then, the question proves in strict terms to be a meaningless one, that perhaps is fitting in a way. We may wish, indeed, to weigh the respective merits of possible systems of usage, or commit ourselves in favour of one or the other. We shall then call our proposition analytic—as it is within the system that we have now adopted. Perhaps when a philosopher speaks of a given proposition as analytic, without further explanation, it is best taken as a way of announcing his commitment.[1] It is analytic if he says so—it is so, that is to say, in his language and for him.

Principles in general, we found, are derived from implicit rules of practice; but sometimes, too, new notions are advanced which go beyond anything in previous use. Now deductive argument, again, may be thought of as representing operation within existing systems —and therefore within systems established by some other means than deductive argument itself. We inherit our systems of thought; large bodies of unreflecting practice have progressively been raised to intellectual form, or extended by dint of reflection working from within, in accordance with its own laws or tendencies. But in philosophy our typical concern is with the creation of concepts: deduction in fact has a chiefly negative use, and it is anyway plain that it can never provide us with premisses. As to constructive argument in philosophy, we may perhaps distinguish two typical phases. First, in advancing any doctrine, a philosopher must establish an original view-point, or formulate and gain acceptance for some new way of thinking and speaking; say, of a 'monad' or a 'language-game'—or of the difference between 'analytic' and 'synthetic statements' conceived in terms of a new theory of meaning. Here he uses analogies and examples, re-surveys familiar material, emphasizing this aspect or that, to clarify or fix his new terms. He must proceed next to justify and apply them; and to justify them is to exhibit them as applicable. He must tackle apparent exceptions and show that the

---

[1] Cf. for a broadly similar view and a statement much more thoroughly worked out, D. W. Hamlyn, 'Analytic Truths', *Mind*, lxv, 1956, pp. 359-67.

material in question in fact admits of accommodation within the new scheme: that all propositions, for instance, are classifiable as either analytic or synthetic. And then again he must be able to claim that discrepancies that remain unresolved on the old way of thinking disappear once the new view is adopted: but that, most often, will have been plain from the start, for otherwise he would hardly have embarked on the undertaking at all.

As to deduction itself, its use, I have said, is chiefly negative; it serves us to eliminate rival views. For deduction, moving within existing systems, may well serve to expose hidden inconsistencies. The distinction is not a sharp one, however, for ordinary language is not a formal calculus. Rather, it is partly elastic, and is stretched and remoulded in use, like a stiff garment or a shoe that gets shaped with wearing. Or suppose again that we start our philosophical inquiry from whatever seems obvious or natural to us, 'hypothe-sizing' the best hypothesis, as Plato says: we shall often find it difficult to say whether a statement of this sort clearly has or lacks the warrant of usage. The statement that we cannot ever perceive moral truths is, we found, analytically false; but what of the state-ment that there are no standards in nature? Yet we know, perhaps, how to argue for or against such views: how to marshal the relevant material, presenting the picture in one light or another—the ordinary method of philosophical polemic, even though you only call it 'assembling reminders'. But even what we call deduction, we have seen, will have, as it were, a bias or emphasis. Philosophers argue for the most part, where language itself gives no unambiguous answer; and the line between the application and the development of a concept, between linguistic conformity and innovation, cannot be rigidly drawn.[1]

To this account there is only a brief postscript to add. I have been speaking of the origin and the justification of our principles, and the account that I have given is wholly general; but it may be objected that many, if not the greater part, of the principles that we use derive

---

[1] I have developed this view more fully in a paper called 'Logical Rigidity and Licence' *Proceedings of the Aristotelian Society*, lv, 1955, pp. 133–56.

from a much more obvious source, we simply accept them from authority. It still remains to give an account of these. Indeed it may seem that if only we had taken this as our starting-point we might have made much shorter work of the whole subject, for authority provides a sufficient source for the great part of the principles that we acknowledge. In morals, for instance, the attitude due originally to the person who was the source of the principles is transferred to the principles themselves: indeed it has often been held that the status that we attribute to them ultimately derives solely from the authority of the parental voice that first laid them down. That view loses some of its persuasiveness when we extend our study of such words as 'right' and 'wrong'—words which prove to play essentially the same rôle in morals as in any other department of thought. But at least, it may be said, the use of principles is plainly an instructor's device. If practical knowledge is to be passed on it must be reduced to some manageable form, and principles are both manageable and memorable; they serve to epitomize past learning and make it available for the future. Even an individual working alone may seek to formulate and teach himself principles, and that may serve to accelerate the process; but instructional situations remain more striking. For the rest it is natural enough that we should appeal to those principles that we have been taught, whether for guidance or for justification.

All this is true enough; and yet an account in these terms must plainly be logically secondary, for, as I previously remarked, these teachers and authorities had to learn. It is impossible, as Ross has pointed out, that authority should be the general source of principles. Yet more needs to be said of the rôle that it plays. Generally speaking our acceptance of an authority as a source of principles of any sort is itself a judgment, which might, of course, be challenged or justified. We treat this as a competent authority, as a power that has also a right to speak—though indeed the recognition of the right may remain largely obscure or indeterminate.[1] On particular matters

[1] Cf. on the whole question R. S. Peters, 'Authority', *Proceedings of the Aristotelian Society, Supplementary Volume*, xxxii, pp. 207-24.

L

the decisions that we defer to may sometimes be more or less arbitrary; perhaps all that we require is that some definite ruling should be given. Yet we are proceeding even here on some general principle; and indeed we may even obey authorities that we think incompetent. But so long as it is authority that we defer to—so long as we are not submitting to mere force—there must be some sort of principle that we appeal to; we may make it a principle, for instance, that, competent or not, duly constituted authorities should be obeyed.

For the rest it will be found that the appeal to authority turns out to be a special case falling within the general account already given. Where our authorities lay down principles, they, presumably, have learnt or acquired them, not through an arbitrary choice, but out of their own wider experience. We adopt new principles, on our previous account, in so far as new patterns become apparent on a wider view of the relevant material. Now let us suppose that we have some one principle whose prestige stands so high that it carries the day against its rivals; its authority alone is sufficient. Thus to gain our point in any argument where some particular case is in dispute, all that we need is to establish that it falls under the principle in question. That claim may be questioned, perhaps, but hardly the principle itself. Even here it is plain that we do not defer to mere authority; principles, after all, do not acquire their authority for nothing. One principle will carry more weight than another when a greater sacrifice would be involved in surrendering it; a principle may be integral to a given theory, it may serve to organize and unify a whole range of phenomena which we could otherwise make no sense of at all. If so we shall not give it up lightly. But the outcome is the same as before, that in appealing to the authority of principles we are adopting implicitly what we take to be a more comprehensive or adequate general point of view.

## II

So far I have spoken chiefly of 'principles', though sometimes of 'rules', availing myself of various senses which the term allows, but, I fear, leaving them vague. Broadly there are three notions to distinguish: that of a mere uniform practice actually or generally followed; that of a uniform practice taken as authoritative; and that, lastly, of an ideal practice, which may hardly be followed at all. In current discussion the two terms 'principle' and 'rule' seem to be treated as interchangeable, and doubtless our usage is far from rigid; nonetheless there is ground enough for insisting on the distinction.

Our rules in some sense, we may feel, are less elevated or at least less solemn things than our principles; a different atmosphere attaches to the two notions. Rules, normally, are laid down by authority, or else (where authority is lacking) by the agreement of different contracting parties: thus we can suppose, for instance, that two children make up a game, and that afterwards one accuses the other of infringing the rules. Further, being made in this way, they can also be unmade by their originators; the children may alter the game or the authorities may revoke their former edicts. But there are also customary rules, codes of etiquette, grammar and the like, which are not always so easily alterable. In certain eastern countries, I believe, grammar is changed by decree; and given some arbiter of fashion—such that what The Prince does is correct by definition— much the same would hold of etiquette. But if we extend the notion of a rule to include these cases it is rather because there are arbiters and models whose authority, as a body, is not in dispute; among whom there is general agreement. We speak here of 'breaches of rule' in so far as there are known ways of identifying them. A breach of a rule is a kind of error, and the same account will be found to hold of both: let differences break out among those authorities, who are the setters of tone, or let their title be challenged, and the notion soon ceases to be applicable.

Legislators proceed freely, on good or bad grounds. Even minor customary rules, such as rules of etiquette, may contain some hidden wisdom. But here there are two things to be distinguished: a rule might be instituted because it was, or seemed to its makers, right or good; but that fact, supposing it a fact, is not what would make it a rule. Rules, in this sense, are conventional, which principles are not; and indeed the whole feeling of the word 'rule' is less weighty.

A still lighter notion of the same sort is that of a 'ruling'. Rulings rest on merely occasional decisions, where authorities are called on to settle some point that the established rules have left unclear or undecided. But this concept of a ruling raises no special philosophical questions; rules on the other hand have played a great part in recent discussion, especially of logic and of language. We find that two fields, almost exclusively, have provided the illustrations or analogies in terms of which language has been thought of: it has been compared, or its parts have been compared, first to games and secondly to the deductive systems of symbolic logic and mathematics. These are fields in which rules in the strongest sense—rules that are clearly formulated and easily known—are most in evidence. Indeed they are indispensable. Given these analogies, then, it is not to be wondered at that we have heard so much of the 'rules of language'; an idiom that may often be misleading—on other lips, that is to say, than those of *bona fide* grammarians. So far as our concern is with the fundamental working of the system we ought to speak not of rules but of principles; though these principles, once they are recognized, will certainly supply or serve as rules.

Principles are things to be discovered not to be made; and they are discovered in the first place, as we have seen, in previous practice and usage. Some authorized body such as the Historical Association might, if need arose, lay down rules for the use of document material and the like, but it would be absurd for it or any other authority to undertake to promulgate the principles of historical scholarship—or of farming or banking or golf. These are not fields in which there is room to legislate. The appropriate powers may, no doubt, alter the rules of championship golf, but the principles of sound play are only to be learnt by long practice or by studying the play of an expert who has got practice behind him.

We may regard it as a matter of some importance to determine the principles—the true principles—of any science or art that we engage in. It is notable that we never speak of 'true rules'; that sort of depth, that dimension, does not belong to the notion of a rule. There cannot be anything here that is hidden or needs to be brought to light.

Rules, not already publicly known, would lose their whole purpose; or supposing that no one obeyed or acknowledged them, then we should cease to call them rules. But with principles the case is very different; the practitioner of any technique or discipline may well be ignorant of its principles, even though he himself has been pretty well following them all the while. To discover them he will need, first, to survey his own practice and pick out the pattern that it reveals. But suppose that he is successful so far: it does not follow that these principles, which are formulated now, are the 'true principles' of the art or science in question. We may have an accurate statement of the practice of given practitioners, but their practice, plainly, may be imperfect. That is what marks the word 'principle'; it retains an ambiguous middle status somewhere between ideal and actuality. We have seen that in the course of inquiry new principles may always emerge or the old ones be modified; that we correct and develop them in use. We refer, certainly, to the body of practice to establish the principles of any science; those that are currently followed are what we first seek to elicit. But we may, in the working out of these, be led on to others—others which we shall recognize as the true principles when they emerge. 'Principle', unlike 'rule', is itself a term of commendation; in speaking of the principles of this or that form of activity we have already committed ourselves in their favour. It is partly for this reason, perhaps, that we need the further phrase 'true principles'—for after all we may not wish to commit ourselves. To speak thus explicitly of 'the true principles' —principles of scientific sociolatry or whatever it may be[1]—is to let one's hearers know, in effect, that there are practitioners in the field from whose practice one means to dissociate oneself. But in merely reporting the rules, that is, whatever rules are publicly recognized, we shall be stating a matter of fact which commits us neither one way nor the other. At the same time, to speak of a principle is not merely to speak of a rule with the added implication that the speaker himself endorses it; for if it were there could be no

---

[1] 'Sociolatry' is defined, for the reader's guidance, as the idolatrous worship of so-called scientific method in the social sciences.

question of a search for true principles, imperfectly known but yet discoverable.

The two notions, then, are radically different, yet in many contexts either, we find, will serve. A formulated principle is *eo ipso* a rule: for unless we endorse a given practice we never should speak of it as a 'principle', and again where we have once endorsed it we shall use it to regulate conduct. At the same time we must certainly reject the view that the very possibility of evaluation presupposes the acceptance of rules; what we require are not known rules but discoverable principles. We suppose, further, that with their discovery present conflicts and differences may be resolved. Judgements on particular matters are made and challenged in every sort of field long before the formulation of rules; and this observation, commonplace as it is, suffices to refute the notion that all evaluation requires existing or recognized rules—far less the decisions of rule-givers.

The real process of the excogitation of principles was described long ago by Aristotle—the process, that is, whereby a universal is extracted from particulars—and we may content ourselves with recalling his account.[1] Suppose that we recognize some object as belonging to a particular class: to do so is to discriminate special features. For the most part we take our classification of objects for granted; but supposing that we are challenged, we may, on reflection, be able, with or without difficulty, to make the principles that we have been using explicit. 'That creature', you say, 'is a cat'; and being challenged, 'Well, obviously . . . Look at its ears, and whiskers.' Or again, 'That is a late Titian . . . less obviously, perhaps, but consider the brushwork and the chiaroscuro.' And the principle, once explicitly stated, gives us a rule for identifying cats or late Titians.

Aristotle says that we disengage the form, the universal, from a series of particulars. A universal, from our present point of view, may be seen as a principle of classification—one unreflectively adopted and used in many practical judgements, as principles

[1] An. Post. 100 a–b.

generally are, long before it is made explicit or formulated. Further it yields rules of inference, for there are numerous things we can infer of a creature once identified as a cat; and in this way we first discover principles and thenceforth apply them as rules. Otherwise these experiences, our groping for principles, and the sudden crystallization of features that makes a given pattern stand out as obvious, are to be renamed 'decisions'—a more-than-linguistic oddity with little to recommend it.

In the context of progressive inquiry evaluation is intelligible, but not otherwise. The old faith of rationalism is that truth is to be found. And it is singular that so many of our modern irrationalists— who rest everything on voluntary decisions, who have, in effect, abrogated the whole essence and tradition of rational inquiry— seem to regard themselves in some special sense as the guardians of the scientific outlook. The new slogan would be different from the old; it would rather be that 'truth is to be promulgated'. Yet that, perhaps, is not altogether new; for it seems that Hobbes long ago had much the same notion, though his critics and commentators during three centuries have hardly brought themselves to treat it with great seriousness.[1]

So far I have, I hope, made my own approach tolerably clear; but it remains to speak fully and explicitly of those main arguments which have proved the chief teasers in the theory of evaluation. We have still to tackle the problem of first principles—as distinct from those particular principles which emerge in the process of inquiry—and also of the metaphor of vision that has proved such a hard hurdle to empiricists. Suppose it said, in ordinary idiom, that a given course of action is right or wrong: we say that we can see that it is wrong—that is the verb that we use. Now it would appear that

---

[1] Hobbes writes in the *Leviathan* (Everyman Edition, p. 15) that 'truth consisteth in the right ordering of names in our affirmations', and draws the conclusion (in a phrase no doubt echoing *Hamlet*) that we may find ourselves—unless we keep clear in our minds what every name stands for—'entangled in words, as a bird in lime twigs, the more he struggles the more belimed'. In *De Cive* he wrote that truth 'depends on the compacts and consents of men'. *English Works of Thomas Hobbes*, ed. Molesworth, p. 295, quoted by Richard Peters, *Hobbes*, p. 58.

seeing requires an object; and philosophers faced with such statements ask, naturally and properly enough, what it can be that we
see. We found here the great objection to intuition, one that has,
perhaps, weighed more heavily than all the rest: there are, they tell
us, no standards in nature. Suppose, for instance, that the cat is on
the mat. This statement is verified or falsified by facts that we take
to be independent of it; our problem is what can serve to verify or
falsify any evaluative utterance, where there is nothing of this sort
that we can point to.

To all this a pedantic reply, and no doubt an accurate one, would
be that such verbs as 'to see' normally take a noun clause as predicate; what one sees, for instance, is simply 'that a given action is
right'. We have before us the known facts of linguistic usage; we may
be asked what more we can want. But the critic will, I fear, ask for
more: the noting of small points of idiom may not wholly quiet his
doubts. Let us say that there are certain demands of reason that we
can still recognize, though the name may have gone out of fashion:
even at a bare linguistic level we shall hardly be satisfied with a
system so little systematic that the same verb takes two quite different
sorts of predicate. Going a degree deeper, it is surely proper to ask
why we should use the notion of seeing where the most obvious
conditions of ordinary perception are unfulfilled. There are, however, two things to be distinguished here: in using the verb 'to see'
we not only commit ourselves to a given claim, we commit ourselves
with a certain assurance. To report that one has seen something is,
in normal circumstances, to put an end to argument; we treat the
evidence of our senses as final. But let us distinguish the claim itself
from the confidence with which we choose to make it; it would at
least seem to be conceivable that every judgement ever made should
be tentative, and we might still use the terms 'right' or 'valid'.
Here, however, verificationism itself shows us the way: what
we need to make sense of the verb 'to see' in such expressions as
'I saw that it was right' is some rational way of distinguishing, with
or without special certainty, those views from others, from wrong
ones. Now here I can only refer to the previous course of our general

argument: a right view is a view taken as testable by procedures established, or to be established, within the whole matrix of thought. Where the process as we have sketched it goes forward, where the conditions of rational inquiry are sufficiently fulfilled, we can use the word and know what we mean by it.

## III

All our discussion so far has revolved around particular views or principles emerging in the course of inquiry; but these are not principles of the sort which philosophers have chiefly concerned themselves with. There are, it seems, principles on which whole departments of thought depend, and these as yet we have hardly touched on. Examples of such principles, or supposed principles—their validity or right formulation does not concern us at present—would be the *dictum de omne*, the principle of induction or the principle of rational benevolence. These have often been thought to serve as first premisses for all sorts of particular arguments; and, as we saw, the provision of such premisses was just what the exponents of the rival theories of intuition and decision were concerned with.

The issue is evidently a large one, virtually coextensive, on some views, with philosophy itself—which, it used to be said in the past, is nothing but the science of first principles. Yet it seems that we have no choice but to intervene, at least to indicate a possible approach —not that I have anything very recondite to contribute. But where, among the theories that hold the field, we find that one appeals to nothing better than intuition, it tells us that we merely see and know these truths, that beyond that there is no room for dispute; while the other, its main rival, merely invites us to choose or decide —where doctrines such as these represent the best light profound research has to throw, there may be room for a few further rather obvious words.

Now as to particular principles, I have said that we persist in existing practices so long as no better course presents itself; and that if we come to call any new course 'better', the assessment can only make sense with reference to the body of existing practice,

whose further development it must promote. We cannot speak of
better or worse in the void. And again where existing practice breaks
down so that wider speculation is set to work, and new views or
techniques are created, we still have no other ground than this for
accepting them. We are driven to speculate where the process of
inquiry is halted by some impediment in its path; we naturally
accept any new approach that removes the obstacle and allows us
to proceed. Further, what holds generally will be found to hold of
philosophy too. Here what we are faced with are conflicts or apparent
conflicts in the structure of those concepts that we use: with such
a conflict, for example, as seems to be involved in our ordinary talk
of seeing that given practices are wrong—joined with the want of
any obvious entity that might serve as an object for this vision. And
what we seek is a new point of view that enables us to see round the
obstacle. Practice, made consistent with itself, stands in no need of
further justification.[1]

Now returning to our first or fundamental principles: we shall
find that we need not give any very different account. Philosophy, as
I conceive it, is not a science of first principles; I do not believe such
a science possible—and besides we find work enough elsewhere.
Every inquiry begins, and is indeed bound to begin, with a body
of existing thought and practice; and suppose that we push the
question back to imagine the earliest beginnings, we shall still not
find any *tabula rasa*—though certainly we may arrive at a point at
which form has yet hardly been imposed on the primitive matter of
the mind. We may find barely conscious adjustments or organic
processes or the like, out of which by progressive correction, progressive articulation, all our sophisticated procedures emerge. But
though we find our starting-point in views actually held, we need

---

[1] I speak here of 'apparent conflicts' in the concepts that we have hitherto worked
with; for the term 'concept' has the same sort of dual status that we have already discovered in 'principle'. In retrospect we shall never admit that what could show this
internal incoherence was indeed the concept itself. We say, perhaps, that the concept
'wrongly formulated' appeared incoherent; the fault, then, was with the formulation, not
the concept itself. What we express in this usage is a faith, partly sustained by fiction,
that all conceptual conflicts must prove resoluble in the end.

make no claim to indubitable intuitions. These fundamental principles that we adopt are so far from being the clearest and most evident of things that we are often hardly conscious of using them; generally speaking we first bring them forward into clear consciousness on finding ourselves challenged to justify them—and then it will prove for the most part that their right formulation is far from easy. Nonetheless we work with those principles that we have, and for this good reason, that otherwise we shall have no way of working at all. We shall not take it as a methodological rule to start by razing every existing structure to the ground—hoping like Descartes, perhaps, that the desert will blossom forth a deity. (Indeed supposing that we have reserved one grain all the while, and have planted an innate idea in the apparent waste, we may manage to make a flowery showing after all.)

We work with the principles that we have until some better alternative appears. Or again we can imagine—what may be thought theoretically possible—that we find an alternative principle which proves neither better nor worse. That would not alter the situation, for to say that is still to evaluate the two principles: we should, of course, treat them accordingly and take it as a matter of indifference which one we adopted. In theory, too, even these fundamental principles are always held subject to correction—certainly to clarification and redefinition. We do not treat them as unalterable or final; for our test of the acceptability of all our views is that they stand this ordeal, that they survive the process of criticism: of whatever more particular tests the general process brings forth. Here, however, we must seek to distinguish between different sorts of difficulty that may be raised; between the bull-dozing scepticism that flattens everything and the probing of discriminating doubt. Merely as a psychological experiment it may be possible to believe or doubt anything; certainly it is possible to say 'I doubt it', and perhaps with conviction in one's voice. That is of no philosophical interest. Where doubt is to be given serious attention we shall require, not the mere possibility of doubting, but some positive grounds for it.

When I speak of positive ground, I mean any sort of philosophical argument that raises substantial or real difficulties. The difficulties which we have been concerned with in the present chapter—the apparent conflict between our ordinary talk of seeing that given actions are right or wrong, and the want of any ordinary entities that could serve for the objects of this vision—are of a different sort from the mere fact that we can imagine people who doubt what we normally believe. And to meet these difficulties we must either accept the conclusion that such talk of seeing is illegitimate or else account for it in some other way. Another source of ethical scepticism has been the apparent relativity of moral beliefs; and here, too, we have a serious argument. For all disagreement certainly casts doubt on whatever views are in question, and persistent disagreement still more so. Or we may recall another view that philosophers have found grounds for doubting, the normal assumption of human freedom: for this assumption, it has often been maintained, conflicts with certain postulates or principles on which the whole progress of science depends. Supposing that could be shown, we should certainly have good reason for questioning it; but the mere fact that, here as elsewhere, doubt is actually possible or conceivable is of no significance.

What we say of doubt we must also say of beliefs: just as we can, in a certain sense, imagine a man who makes the experiment of doubting anything so we can imagine someone who believes anything. That may seem to alter the philosophical issue, but in reality it is no different. It seems that we may meet two different sorts of critic: in the first place we shall hear of the doubters who find it possible merely to suspend their belief in some given principle; and then again of those who find it possible to adopt some positive alternative, and one, perhaps, incompatible with ours. Now here we may seem to have a more serious difficulty; for certainly all disagreement casts some measure of doubt on our beliefs, and further, we are authoritatively told that philosophy deals with the possible not the actual. Yet really the case is the same: anyone can announce that he believes any new notion he likes and challenge us to prove that he is wrong. Suppose that we should find some sort of proof —and this concept, which belongs to mathematics and courts of law, is hardly in place here—it will still be to no purpose unless our supposed critic at least accepts the procedures or criteria that we use for proving it; and if he can doubt the one he can doubt the other. Nor is that a merely fanciful speculation; the situation actually arises. Nor yet does it mean, as might be thought, that he has rendered his whole thesis empty, merely withdrawing himself from rational discourse; he may still stop short of that extreme, as I shall seek to show directly.

But let us look first at the immediate issue and see what it involves. We are to suppose that an alternative procedure is proposed which is to replace one of the commonly accepted principles of moral or scientific reasoning; what we shall require for it to be taken seriously is that it can plausibly promise to fill the same rôle in inquiry that the old principle adequately filled. And that requirement is not easily to be met; for the principles that we are concerned with are those on which a whole department of inquiry has been built up. We find principles embodied in existing practice; when some philosopher, for the sake of argument, suggests a new principle out of nothing, we shall ask him to show us in detail that this proposed innovation will in fact prove workable as the old one has. For our previous principle, by hypothesis, has served to sustain a whole growing and ramifying process of human thought; further systems of particular procedures, founded in its application and use, have progressively developed and established themselves. It is useless to ask in the abstract whether this or that possible principle might imaginably be found acceptable; we must see how far it admits of integration within a given body of thought—and that is always a matter of degree. There can be no general philosophical justification of those principles that we at present adopt; it is after all in some sense conceivable that alternatives should be proposed and accepted, and such proposals would have to be examined on their merits.

This comprehensive talk of systems and procedures may seem unsatisfactory, but plainly so long as the problem is posed in merely general terms it is all that the case allows; in a later chapter, however, I shall seek to fill it out or reinforce it with some more concrete consideration of the actual procedures that we adopt in morals.[1] For the rest we may say this much generally, that any principle that we are to reckon with seriously must at least stand some chance of gaining the acceptance of reflective people. In moral discourse it would seem that we actually adopt some sort of fundamental and broad principle that enjoins the consideration of other people's feelings or interests; and in ethical discussion one hears sometimes of possible Satanists who propose a principle directly contrary to that—whose rule would be, perhaps, never to take the interests of others into account, or even to damage them wherever possible. Now anything else apart, we may remark here that it is only in open discussion where divergent views may be brought into line, that any principle can prove itself at all. And the principle before us seems unlikely to survive that central and fundamental test; men in general will hardly agree with me if I tell them that I do right when I act on this principle, to do everything possible to thwart their wishes.[2]

The principles we adopt, I have said, are to be integrated into a system of thought; more particular principles have emerged through their use, and proved acceptable. But now we can imagine a critic who rejects these criteria or tests—the test of fertility in effect, for that is what we are really appealing to: one which we commonly use, too, in evaluating scientific hypotheses. But we must notice that he may reject it on various sorts of grounds. At best, we have seen— what is in some sense theoretically possible—what he offers is a positive alternative, a different system with procedures and criteria of its own; and in that case we shall have to consider the proposal on its merits. But the alternative may be less thorough-going; it may amount to no more than a modification of the practices that we already adopt, a sort of partial dismantling of the existing system. Or we may find something different again, that that system is

---

[1] See Chapter VII, below.
[2] This point, in a rather different form, has been made to me by Mr. A. P. Griffiths; I do not know how far he would wish to go along with the use I have made of it.

avowedly maintained and applied, but applied, as we wish to say, with persistent distortions or eccentricities. And after all it will still be a sort of system; the question is never one of black and white. We cannot make it an issue, as many philosophers have (and I myself at certain points for simplicity's sake), between either this way of working or none at all. The alternative need not be a total abandonment of rational thought and meaningful discourse; the difference may be one of degree.

It is sometimes said that some principle of induction is involved in any use of past experience as evidence for further beliefs. Now I do not mean to discuss that problem in any detail here, but it may nonetheless be worth noting that it is possible to use experience in our thinking and yet use it erratically or wrong-headedly. We may, for example, imagine an astrologer whose predictions are consistently falsified, or falsified in a high proportion of instances, who yet never loses faith in his own methods. Such cases, indeed, are not unknown. This astrologer, no doubt, will explain his disappointments *ad hoc* or he will redescribe or reinterpret events to show that what we took for failures were really successes after all—and thus, one way or another, will keep in business. It might be useful, perhaps, if—instead of that imaginary sceptic or the believer in improbable new principles so often introduced into philosophical discussion—we sometimes met the views of this pretty real astrologer. We might well hear the same difficulties urged: 'Here is a possible position, a possible dissident: how would you convince him that he is wrong?' Now the answer, of course, is that we never shall. Certainly we can argue with him—we shall very likely find him eminently argumentative—yet it remains improbable that we shall convince him that he is wrong. Nor, perhaps, rightly or wrongly, would let ourselves be much troubled by our failure.

But let us ask how the argument might proceed. First perhaps we shall seek to elicit in the usual way the principles our opponent adopts elsewhere, in all the ordinary business of life, on the assumption that these at least will broadly agree with our own—for no doubt it is only in the practice of astrology that his methods are eccentric. We ask him, then, to reflect on his own practice and to consider what principle he follows: in general, as we have seen, principles are got at by reflection on existing practice. Supposing that so far we are successful, we shall go on to point out the evident discrepancy between the different principles that, as we find, he follows in different fields. That would no doubt be a fair argument: it is just because people in the main feel the force of considerations such as this that inquiry in general goes forward. But if you fancy that the matter is now settled you may find that you have been over-optimistic. 'To be sure,' our astrologer may reply, 'we employ special methods in astrology; but why should you make such a pother over that? Are the methods that historians employ the same as those of physicists or mathematicians? Don't psycho-analysts use methods that are different again? Astrologers are like other scientists; they have their own methods too.'

I shall not pursue the course of the argument further; perhaps it would be unprofitable. What we need to notice is this, that a person such as the astrologer we are imagining—and the same goes for all muddle-headed reasoners, as well as for many accomplished pseudo-scientists—still follows his own pattern or system; an unsystematic system, you may say, but still the choice is not between all and nothing. Here are certain interknitting procedures—around which we also find that new language-games develop. For pseudo-science is prolific of language. Moreover these new concepts that emerge, belonging to astrology or any other similar system (whether or not it is taught in universities), only function and only have meaning within this special system that gave them birth: for there is some sense in which one could be said to know or not to know what they mean. But now let us return to our previous question and ask again by what means we are to adjudicate between the rival claims of different systems of thought—allowing, however, for all levels of rationality, of obtuseness or muddle; of sterile formalism or imaginative depth. It is surely plain that there can be no general answer. We must learn the particular language in any instance; we must enter into and follow the argument and assess it to the best of our powers. It is only within actual argument, and for minds trained to recognize such niceties, that the difference between clear and confused thinking emerges; or between subtler discrimination on the one hand and more ingenious special pleading on the other. Supposing that we could lay down general laws beforehand we should have less need for working intelligence than we actually find. But this again is not to deny that we are able to formulate and use general tests for the assessment of arguments, for distinguishing good reasoning from bad. The very reverse is the case: the argument we have been envisaging consists primarily in the application of just such tests.

It is certainly neither arbitrarily nor irrationally that we would condemn the procedures employed by our imaginary astrologer—and no doubt by many real ones as well. But only because we commit ourselves to the general process of argument—only in so far as criteria in fact establish themselves, emerging and taking form within the process—can such judgements be possible at all. We appeal to a consensus of opinion, certainly: the chief test of an acceptable view is that any fair judge will accept it. Yet perhaps it is hardly less important that we find means for distinguishing experts too; for it is plain that clear-headedness in face of confusion and sophistry is not the commonest of all human gifts.

But these considerations lead us on to another way of dealing with first principles; or of dealing, at least, with the sceptic who calls them in question. Such scepticism is sometimes said to be self-defeating; and we find accordingly that Mr. Strawson writes, 'His doubts are unreal,' (that is, the sceptic's) 'not simply because they are logically irresoluble doubts, but because they amount to the rejection of the whole conceptual scheme within which alone such doubts make sense.'[1] Thus, for example, the sceptic who professes to doubt the reality of other people's minds—he has, so he tells us, no assurance as to their inward experience, which he can never

---

[1] P. F. Strawson, *Individuals*, p. 35. The illustration that follows, which I have chosen for the sake of its relative simplicity, is not taken from the issues that Strawson is concerned with in the passage quoted.

M

directly observe—cannot even express what he doubts without employing the language that he seeks to challenge; without distinguishing himself from other people. And in making the distinction, it may be argued, he already implicitly commits himself to the very thing that he intends to deny.

I have said that I do not detract from the importance of general criteria; much the same view will hold in the present case. The position of such a sceptic as Strawson describes would no doubt be a self-defeating one; and, for the purposes he has in view, to demonstrate so much may suffice. Further he explicitly sets on one side the other possible development of such questions—the case, not of the mere sceptic, but of a metaphysician bent on revising the general pattern of the language that we possess. But this alternative is one which our present inquiry demands that we examine further. Our problem concerns the status of first principles, and the possible objection that we were faced with was that some set of alternative principles might always be put forward in place of ours. If so, and if anyone preferred them, it appears we have no way of proving him wrong. Now arguments such as Strawson uses have only a limited use here; the adherents of such alternative principles need not be driven to any self-defeating modes of speech—though they may be obliged to accept other unwelcome consequences of the position that they take up. Suppose that in any instance we should succeed in showing them, after the present line of argument, that the new principles that they profess to prefer amount in effect to 'the rejection of the whole conceptual scheme within which alone such doubts' (or such arguments in general) 'make sense'. After all they may choose the second alternative and reject the whole system—which may not prove so huge a step after all. Perhaps nothing more will be required than a small adjustment in the criteria to be used for 'making sense', and this once made, the argument or doubts in question will pass muster after all. It now no longer matters whether we say that what this involves is in fact the rejection of the whole system or merely its slight modification; either way the logical innovator need not be reduced to silence. And if this suggestion sounds a far-fetched or unlikely one, let us recall the example of the astrologer and the pattern of argument that we found there: the two cases are not really very different. In each we shall tinker with an existing system— leaving, no doubt, what is a worse system, or less of a system (for we have other criteria whereby to judge of that) but after all in some sense a possible one: possible in that it is actually used. And the motive for such tinkering is normally the same; our object is to save some single element which we are loath to part with—though it can only be kept and accommodated at the cost of radical adjustments elsewhere. The reasons for this unwillingness, in both these two examples, are doubtless bad ones; in saying so we reaffirm our faith in those broadly based tests and procedures which the process of thought has established. The astrologer's reluctance to abandon his theories, whatever its source, does not reflect or belong to what we call scientific judgement; his feelings and attitudes have not been formed in any such school, by any similar discipline. For the rest we should notice that, though in general, no doubt, we are rightly reluctant to admit radical readjustments in a system that has established itself in long use, yet sometimes the recalcitrant element may be something too substantial to be dismissed; here, as always, we must judge the case on its merits, and draw a line between sensible conservatism and rigidity or mere blindness.

Let us return to our initial problem; we were called on to justify our present principles in preference to some conceivable innovation. But it is useless to think of justifying principles apart from the system in which they operate; what we should justify, if anything, would be the system as a whole. But that is superfluous. What may be possible, indeed, is to exhibit a particular principle as one deeply built into the whole system; we may even maintain that its rejection would dislocate or demolish the whole structure. And that would be a truth of some importance. Yet in saying so we presuppose our present views; we have a notion of what constitutes a system, or again the dislocation of a system, which our innovator, as we see, may not accept. If so he will no doubt be wrong, but we cannot prove him wrong by further appeal to general principles; and there is no clutch that cannot be eluded by a free enough use of the *ad hoc*, with 'unique qualities' and the like. Meanwhile, whatever principle we give him, he may apply them eccentrically.

Let us look at the question in another way. Suppose that we succeed in unearthing some connexion, some fundamental principle, involved in a whole field of discourse: without it, we may rightly claim, the whole system or structure would collapse. Now our concern is with a system of concepts—each, therefore, representing a sort of smaller system of its own. For a concept is expressed in a word, with patterns of inference belonging to it. The operations that we make or allow are, in existing language, thus and thus, and might always be more or less modified; a given concept is formed in a certain way, and conceivably—sometimes barely conceivably, sometimes easily enough—might have been formed rather differently. Our general or basic principles, certainly, are not useless or empty; but in default of the judgement to apply them they would be both. The law of contradiction, it may be argued, is involved in the very possibility of discourse; without it the structure would collapse. We cannot talk at all where a statement and its contradictory can both be asserted at once. All this may be granted; but in detail what we call a contradiction will depend on the concepts that we work with—or perhaps on the way in which we work with them. The whole system of these workings is our language, the objective embodiment of judgement. Both these together are built up and handed on within our culture, in the common medium of our thought.

Patterns of practice develop, are altered or extended imperceptibly. Later, being led to reflect, we may seek to dig out the principles underlying them—the deeper and fundamental principles, as well as those nearer the surface. But let us return now to the sceptic—the sort of sceptic who wants to have his cake and eat it: if he does, these principles that we can perhaps exhibit will themselves be sufficient to silence him; but where the choice lies between rival systems, then, in default of common judgement, general principles no longer suffice. A principle can always be applied so as to yield a sort of conceptual system that is, to our way of thinking, very far from systematic. So we can only ask men to go on reasoning as best they can and trust in what emerges in the process. Where we meet with irrationalism in examples such as those that I have given our real view is that on these terms inquiry could no longer go forward; the whole collective undertaking would come to a standstill.[1]

All that remains, as I have said, is to justify the system as a whole, which may be thought an impossible demand or an unnecessary one. But at least we can justify it in this sense, that we can go through it process by process making it progressively acceptable, and teach it to anyone who is prepared to learn. Now so far as this teaching succeeds we shall be equipped with the means of assessing proposed new departures or innovations: with the rules or criteria to be applied and also the trained judgement to apply them. Our real assumption throughout is that this system, as against hypothetical alternatives, will in fact prove learnable and workable; that where men engage in inquiry their attitudes and views, progressively taking form, will evolve or, as it were, tend to grow into some common structure.

---

[1] In speaking of scepticism it may be proper to refer to that one favoured class of statements—so-called necessary statements—which have been thought to escape even the possibility of doubt. For statements of this sort do no more than express the rules of given systems of usage; hence merely to understand them will be to accept them, for what we understand is the usage in question. As to this it will suffice to say here—leaving aside the many large questions that we might explore—that a mere system of unapplied symbols is not yet a language; it is a thing of limited philosophical interest. But once language is employed in inquiry a different sort of system arises; for here the contexts in which it has its use form an integral part of the working whole: they, together with the merely symbolic procedures, constitute the more significant, larger system that concerns us. So-called analytic propositions are thought not to be falsifiable even in principle; and that is of course true in a sense. In any given system that we use there is much whose possible alteration we hardly even contemplate. In principle, however, the possibility remains open that whatever we apply at present in one way, we might later reapply in another; and to say that the old usage—or the 'analytic statement' that expressed it—remains nonetheless unrefuted, is only to say that it remains as a procedure within a possible system which we no longer apply. But that is not a 'statement' at all. Philosophy is surely concerned in the use of language in the guidance of conduct and the understanding of the world; beyond that we cannot speak of language.

# VI

## Theory and Conduct

THE title of the present chapter, let me warn the reader at once, gives a rather partial indication of its contents. There remain in fact a number of miscellaneous issues which would have held up the argument too much if they had been dealt with as they arose; but most of these fall under the general heading of the relation of theory and practice. We have already met this problem at one point; for there is one principle that is fundamental to all inquiry, namely that we infer the acceptability of a given view, or at least its strong *prima facie* claim, from the fact of its general acceptance. And this principle plainly contravenes another—a negative principle that is certainly less generally followed, but much more widely acclaimed —forbidding us to infer evaluative conclusions from matters of fact. It will be necessary to attempt some more positive account, too, of the relations between those two aspects of inquiry, views and procedures, of which I have been speaking all along; but first let us look at this famous, or should we say notorious, prohibition.

Inferences of the sort that we are concerned with are made by ordinary people every day and seem to stand in need of no special apology; rather, the denial of their legitimacy should be thought paradoxical. Yet what in fact we meet is little more than assertion. Or if the rule forbidding this mode of inference is something self-evident to those who lay it down, then, for my own part, I can only answer that to me it is a great deal less evident than many others, among them the principle stated above, with which it conflicts. Besides self-evidence has no place in the systems of the philosophers whom we are chiefly concerned with here. Nor again can it derive from general practice; all practice, as we see, contravenes it. Hume himself demands that a reason be given for what, he says, seems inconceivable 'how this new relation can be a deduction from others which are entirely different from it'.[1] This is a proposition to make one pause: can Hume mean to call it inconceivable that argument or inference can ever lead to ideas that are different from those that we started with? If so he makes it impossible to conceive of any advance of thought whatever. But no doubt the sort of advance represented by a geometrical deduction would not have troubled him; there he would not have felt the need for some 'new relation' deduced from different ones. Hence it would seem that the real objection is to this as representing a substantial step in argument; he objects to the non-deductive or non-mathematical character of the inference. But even this distinction is far from clear. We shall find, perhaps, that mathematical inference, once we treat it as more than a merely formal matter, as more than a matter of operating within some particular symbolic system—once we apply it, that is to say, either in theory or practice—becomes a substantial thing, too. And hence, if this requirement that 'a reason be given' is legitimate anywhere, it will be equally legitimate here.

The truth of the matter seems to be this, that logicians, taking pure mathematics as their pattern, have devised a sort of paradigm or a formal scheme in accordance with which they require all argument to be set out; this is what I previously called the Euclidean or linear model. And here, as so often in human thought, a process that proves useful or illuminating in certain particular applications is then applied generally—it is forced on everything. Now the consequence, roughly stated, is this, that any substantial step in argument must, so to speak, be abstracted from the mass and installed in the new system as a premiss; for that is what the model requires. The step we are at present concerned with is certainly a substantial one, and must appear, therefore, either as a premiss or not at all. And as a premiss it seems to stand stark and lonely, in need of some justification that can never come. It is notable that for some reason the present principle—that forbidding us to infer statements of value from facts—is not itself justified further. Perhaps we are to take it as a postulate laid down within a given formal system—which

[1] *A Treatise of Human Nature*, Book III, ed. Selby-Bigge, p. 469.

we are then invited to apply, say, in the discussion of moral theory. But of course we can construct what systems we will, and perhaps we can apply them as we will. Premisses authorizing the present step will present no more difficulty than others, and indeed all *a priori* moral systems insert them as a matter of course: and these formally are no worse than their rivals. Asked if any statement is 'analytic'—say, the rule authorizing or the rule forbidding us to infer evaluative statements from factual ones—we should answer with a further question, 'In what system?' If the answer is 'In ordinary English', we know what to say; if some system other than the ordinary one we may ask again why or whether it should be used.

To say this is not to blur or throw overboard the distinction, one that we have used from the start, between evaluative and non-evaluative forms of language. In some contexts its sharpness may be lost, and again critics may point out that the term 'description' in ordinary speech covers many abusive or laudatory phrases—'scoundrel', 'lickspittle' and the like—which, of course, are evaluative too. Yet the very possibility of the criticism presupposes the distinction in question; the objection could never be urged unless the critic himself could tell the one sort of language from the other. And for the rest, it may well happen that philosophy, adopting a wider viewpoint, seeking out the deeper patterns of things, should find the need of distinctions which do not occur to common sense; we ordinarily have no occasion for them, and therefore no language. We shall, then, follow Hare's analysis of words such as these, or as 'honest' or 'sweet-tempered'; we shall distinguish their descriptive from their evaluative element. On the one hand there are certain roughly determinate patterns of behaviour which might in principle be described in evaluatively neutral terms, and on the other the implicit commendation that the mere use of these epithets involves. We may claim so much but not necessarily more: that in all cases this analysis can be pressed through to the limit has not been shown, and does not need to be: it can certainly be carried a long way, and there seems little prospect of an adequate account of thought or language that merely disregards it. Value words, bound up as they are with practice and preference, form a family that we cannot ignore.

On the other hand we must recognize that as far as linguistic usage goes 'honest' is a thoroughly legitimate word too; and hence, given a mere description of a certain conduct, namely honest conduct, we can infer—'analytically' if you wish—that other things being equal it is also right. The point may be thought a rather trivial one, as indeed the possibility of analytic inference usually is. Yet it seems that the rule forbidding us to infer values from facts has no better basis than its status or supposed status as analytic.

The question, here as elsewhere, concerns the application of such a system; for it is plain that no formal system can prescribe terms for its own application—or, to put the same point in different terms, it cannot serve to justify its own premises. I call this the same point, as it is essentially, because until the system in question is to be applied no issue of this sort can arise. Prior to that there can be no question of justifying our premises; within the system itself they may stand merely as postulates or axioms laid down. They are sensibly treated as justified or unjustified, as true or false, only in some interpretation when the system is applied to a given subject-matter.

But here, with any such application, we go beyond the bare system; we undertake to talk and think in new terms. I said that in the nature of the case no system can justify its own application in any field; nor again—what comes to the same thing—can it justify the assertion of its own premises. But that is a loose way of speaking, for so long as we confine ourselves to the language of the system itself no such question can arise; we cannot even intelligibly ask whether the system is applicable or not. We do, of course, ask it, but not as formalists. This is no very startling discovery—that some systems are legitimately applicable; that statements exist which are true, that we can assert them. Yet it is a discovery we shall never make so long as we confine ourselves to the terms of a formal 'language', that is, a system of symbolism, and recognize no other way of speaking. Having once adopted the Euclidean plan we are bound to require that any substantial truth should be withdrawn from the process of argument and installed as a premiss; next we shall naturally ask how this bare premiss is to be justified. Our very use of the model entails that the system itself cannot justify them, and so long as we allow no other language no justification can be forthcoming. The outcome is one, to be sure, that some logically-minded philosophers, who get near to acknowledging it, seem surprisingly little disturbed by; for my part I cannot imagine any *reductio ad absurdum* more complete than the conclusion that no application of any system, no proposition or verbal form that claims to be more than the substitution of symbols in an unapplied calculus, can ever be justified at all.

And we may apply the argument to the very principle that we have been concerned with, the negative principle that forbids us to infer evaluative statements from factual ones. For this principle, like any other, is no use unless it is applied; as a formal rule belonging to some possible system it is, no doubt, unexceptionable, but not part of moral philosophy. What we must ask is how its application is to be justified; for in applying it the step that we shall have to take is no longer a merely formal but a substantial one. And when we search for the sources of this principle itself, when we ask on what grounds it can be maintained, what we find is nothing but this: that no inference can be logically legitimate that represents more than a move within a system or requires more than a formal guarantee. Now the right to apply any system, or any formula belonging to any system, can never be formally guaranteed; and the conclusion to which we are driven is that this principle, consistently followed, must forbid its own application as well. It not only runs counter to universal practice, not only is no positive ground adduced to justify it, but consistently applied and followed out it itself proves to be condemning too.

I remarked that the Euclidean model, strictly observed, would raise all substantial steps to the status of premisses. The decisionist system which adopts the model will of course have the same consequence: and then on these substantial principles as premisses we shall, as always, be asked to decide. The conclusion is wholly general: all the principles of natural science or of historical scholarship, of any sort of activity whatever, are extracted from the mass, so to speak; and then shown—in accordance with the paradigm—as entailing (together with appropriate fact-statements) whatever conclusions or views we can ever claim to have any right to assert. The principle that forbids the inference of evaluations from matters of fact would stand as a premiss along with the rest; there too, we should have to decide, and even apart from the previous argument, we shall always be free to decide against it.[1]

## II

Something has been done, I hope, to clear the field of dogma, and it is time to turn to a more positive view of the subject. We hear much of the impossibility of this step from description to evaluation, or from theory to conduct: we might ask how far the two things are distinguishable before we madden ourselves over the difficulty of getting from one to the other. For the point is much less clear than might be thought. The topic is generally raised in ethical contexts,

---

[1] In the text I have spoken for simplicity's sake of this or that as a 'substantial' step or a 'substantial' statement—as if there were such things as non-substantial statements to which these might be contrasted. But really neither expression is legitimate; the phrase a 'substantial statement' is strictly a pleonasm. A formula in an unapplied system, is—one might say—what such a statement would be if *per impossibile* we could find a specimen. But an unapplied formula is not yet a statement at all. And, on the other hand, even to say that an uncle is a mother's or father's brother, or that a whole is greater than any part of that whole, is at least to adopt and to commit oneself to certain concepts or systems of concepts—and that is already substantial. But whether the verbal form 'A rose is a rose' (not used in any context which might give it some special significance) is more than pure vacuity or serves to make some sort of statement, can be left to anyone's fancy to decide.

To say this is not, of course, to detract from the value of formal systems, which may be things of great beauty in themselves and great utility in their practical application. What is essential is that we should not ask them to serve in rôles for which they are obviously not meant. A formal system in itself is uninformative, and but for the possibility of such steps as go beyond what such systems can warrant—but for the synthetic *a priori*—there would be no such thing as knowledge at all. We should have at most, on the one hand, formulae or would-be formal statements, that tell us nothing; and on the other would-be incorrigible statements about present experience, which tell us nothing.

where practices such as injury, honest dealing and the like are chiefly in view. But inference may count as practice too; the use of language, the passage from one utterance to another in accordance with recognized rules, is surely a form of activity. And we can make no sense of the notion of a theory or a theoretical position in which systems of inference are not embodied; our views and the procedures that we follow are inextricably bound up together. The same holds of our commonest beliefs; even ordinary judgements of perception hardly make sense apart from our readiness to do or refrain from certain actions. A man sees a massive solid object poised before or above him, and professes to believe in what he sees: but suppose that in everything he does or attempts, in his movements, arrangements and the like, he takes no account of it, makes no attempt to avoid it—though we have no reason to believe that he desires his own destruction. In such circumstances we might hesitate as to what to say: perhaps he believes in this thing 'in a way', but in default of all appropriate behaviour we should hardly say baldly that he believes in it.

I shall not, however, urge these difficulties further. The moral to be drawn, I imagine, is that in some regions of discourse the present distinction breaks down; but elsewhere it is, no doubt, clear enough, and we may leave it to those more deeply committed to it to put to the proof how far it can be taken or pressed in detail. Practice and theory, I have said, even where they visibly stand apart, are not mutually separable or indepedent: no inference, says the Humean law, can ever cross the line that divides them. This assertion, one might claim, is worse than false: but for this one mode of inference, it would be truer to say, there would be no such things as inference at all. Our views or our procedures go together; we have no way of changing either one except by first changing the other. I shall seek to make that clearer directly. First let me repeat that this passage or step from thought to action—or its logical equivalent, the inferring of evaluative statements from factual ones—comes to be embodied, like others, in languages or systems of usage. Within these it is then 'analytic'. We infer from a description of a course of action that it would be honest to take it, and hence right. Or again, as Hare has shown, and Aristotle before him, we may draw the conclusion not in language at all but in deeds; in adopting the course of action in question. That, to be sure, cannot be a rule of the language, but it may of the 'language-game' in a wider sense.

In order to get a man to act differently we must get him to see, in some new way, those things which his action concerns; and conversely, to get him to see them differently we tell him to look at them in new ways: we shall point to this analogy or that, getting him to attend to new features. What we attempt, then, is to make him re-focus his mental vision so that the same material appears in another light. He is to adopt a certain attitude, a certain stance—which so far, I suppose, will be reckoned as a matter not of seeing but of doing. By reason of what we do, it seems, our vision changes. Even of deductive argument that same holds, indeed it holds even of formal logic. Suppose that a student is held up by a step in an argument, some particular point that he cannot grasp: we set out to make it clear to him and get him to see it perhaps, by making him put it alongside others—simpler steps but no different in principle, which he has already seen and accepted.[1]

All this as an account of techniques of instruction may be accepted. But these, I shall be told, are not examples of inferences, and hence do not tell against Hume's principle. So far, perhaps not. For one thing they concern particular cases and not general rules; and secondly inference in the narrow or strict sense, must fall within language, and the mere definition excludes the passage beyond language to action. But language-games, I have said, are wider than language: any inquiry, we shall find, is bound to involve rules of this form, 'Adopt procedures, in given cases, of such and such sorts, and accept whatever views they may reveal.' Here we pass rationally from conduct to theory; and I have already given examples of the reverse process. It only remains to speak explicitly of evaluative language, in

---

[1] This advice 'Do it differently and you'll see it differently' is valid and valuable nearly everywhere. Adopt, for instance, an aggressive instead of a retreating stance, and your opponent may not look quite so dangerous as he did before.

its relation to conduct, to arrive at inference in the narrower sense; and that I shall turn to in the next section.

## III

Yet one other topic remains to be dealt with under this head: the problem of conduct before us obliges us to raise once again and finally settle, perhaps, the issue raised at the very start, namely the character of 'moral vision'. It is in relation to practice that this problem—the problem of the object of our perception, where we see or claim to see something as wrong—has in fact chiefly been raised. I use the term 'practice' quite generally: most writers seem to assume a vast difference, even where they talk of 'procedures' or 'rules', between say, the practice, of logicians and scientists and that of anyone seen as a moral agent in the ordinary conduct of life. Differences, no doubt, exist, but it does not appear from our account that they are such as to affect the present issue. A third thing that also remains to be distinguished from both right views and right practice, is our use of evaluative language: we still have to see what is involved in *calling* any action 'right' or 'wrong'.

Of all ethical theorists the imperativists have gone furthest in treating moral utterance as a practical thing, in effect a kind of action. For a command that we receive does not tell us anything; at best we respond to it and obey. It is a way of effecting results. This view, then, is more definite than any in its exclusion of the vocabulary of perception from the theoretical language of ethics; a command is not called 'true' or 'false' and its utterance points to no factual correlate. Nothing that we might discover could be said to verify it. The doctrine, I have argued at some length, remains ultimately unworkable; indeed we may lay it down generally that we shall never make sense of discourse in terms that provide no ultimate distinction between the arbitrary and the obligatory, the freely chosen and the rationally binding. Nonetheless it has won many adherents—nor always reluctant adherents, out to make the best of necessity. It does not owe all its plausibility to the uneasiness that may very well be felt at what rival views seem to commit us to; at the reality of Platonic standards, for example. What recommends the theory more is its emphasis on the practical character of moral utterance, on its function in the direction of conduct. Such utterances are indeed more akin to action than to statements—to what are typically thought of as statements. And in that they resemble commands.

We can hardly mean to tell someone that something is right— something that he can do if he chooses—without at least an ideal presumption that he will listen to what we say and act accordingly; it would seem that that putative consequence is involved in the very notion of moral utterance. Sometimes, indeed, a man may recognize a duty, to give a reproof for example, and satisfy himself in discharging it, without the least hope of its proving effective. What is hard if not impossible to conceive is that this special case should be generalized; we cannot systematically divorce moral utterance—say, the condemnation of some action as wrong—from the thought of its practical consequences. So far, at least as regards these deontological words, (the case, we shall see, is less plain when we turn from 'right' to 'good'), we must follow the imperativists: any moral assessment, addressed to a person whom it concerns, will have something of the force of a command. Yet that is not its primary character; it derives from another still more basic. After all what is essential to morals, so far as we take our morals seriously, is rather that we act than that we speak; that we adopt a given course and not others—and adopt it because we see it as right. It will be time enough to speak of the use of moral utterance when we have seen what moral action involves; and thus we shall have completed our account of the acceptance of what we see as right views with a parallel account of right practice.

The difference in question, we must notice, need not appear in our conduct itself: we find cases where the same observable action may be done for a moral or an immoral reason, or again for no reason at all. And similarly to alter the position of two particular pieces of carved ivory may or may not be to make a move, to castle, for instance, in a game of chess. Or again the same lines might occur, and the same actor speak them, in two scenes in two different plays. But he does not speak or see himself as speaking them in the same character; he is placed differently, we may say, differently oriented in a different setting. And the action is made what it is by the whole system to which it belongs. You cannot castle if you are not playing chess nor abstain from voting where no election is in process: harder, you cannot pointedly overlook someone who shows no sign of looking at you. The description of the action reflects its setting, but our present concern is with its rightness; or rather, with the possibility of acting, like this, because one conceives it as being right. And the rightness of castling or abstaining will reflect its setting in a still more intimate way. But now as to moral performances, or again as to scientific procedures—I may be asked in what light they are to be seen or what sort of system they belong to. I can only answer by referring once more to the foregoing discussion, to the account I have outlined of the process in which the search for common views is carried forward; for here, too, one might speak of a 'system', though the word claims too much and sounds too rigid. These systems are loose and incomplete, are for ever absorbing new elements, for ever developing and imperfect: but such, of necessity, is the general body of our thought, and such are our codes of social conduct. We proceed in theoretical no less than practical things by whatever bearing we can find; we try to connect what we see, to adopt some stance we can hold, a course we can follow, and construct our speculative charts accordingly. In face of a practical choice, we ask ourselves what course would be right, and that in effect is to identify ourselves with the system that it will contribute and belong to: we seek in some given situation to realize in ourselves, in our own action, what the incomplete pattern requires. Chess, though a closed system, resembles logical argument: imagine, then, that the white king's rook, come alive, should take stock of the state of the board and, acting for itself, seek to move as White's game demands.

This, so far, is to speak of conduct itself; action will be of this kind so far as we act as moral agents. We can now go on to speak of moral language—or, rather, of evaluative language in general.

I have suggested that the notion of right conduct is the fundamental one, but we still have to see how, if so, the other derives from it, we have to ask how evaluative language is possible. Here we find a more familiar analogue that may be useful, we may return for a moment from practice to theory; for to speak of an action as 'right' is not very different, from the present point of view, from speaking of a theory as 'true'. Now it has often been observed that to call a statement true, in one sense at least, adds nothing to what has already been said; it merely reaffirms the initial statement. The two statements 'It is raining' and 'It is true that it is raining' supply us with no different information; and so far the case is plainly similar when we speak not of 'true statements' but of 'right views'—for 'right' and 'true' here are all but interchangeable. What we do is to reaffirm the views in question, or to endorse another man's affirmation. So much of theory: turning again to evaluative language, we shall find that the same account holds. We shall suppose first, what we have already found possible, that a man takes a given course of conduct which he sees as right—and because he sees it as right. Now we are to speak of a second person, not called on immediately to act, who endorses the conduct of the first: he uses language and calls it 'right'. To reaffirm a statement is, in effect, to repeat it, to make the same statement oneself. That, we said, is what a man does in calling it true, and indeed a plain repetition, or an abbreviated repetition, will often serve instead and have the same effect. Someone asserts that S is P and we answer either 'True', or else 'It is'. Suppose now that an action is in question: men in a drawing-room, perhaps, are discussing what someone did in a fight, or a gathering of spinsters is concerned with the conduct of a married friend who has left her husband: there is here no question of a literal repetition of the same action, but it may perfectly well be reaffirmed. One may go through some token repetition, as if to say, 'I should do the same myself.' Strictly that is not said but shown, which is the force of the terms 'right' and 'wrong': to give a kind of ritual demonstration of what we ourselves would do or abstain from—yet always of what we would do, not as self-seekers or merely arbitrarily, but

N

in so far as we act as moral agents. Right action is the primary notion: we conceive ourselves as conscious participants in the whole moral process or system, and as such we can act or speak appropriately. To any hearer suitably placed who sees himself likewise, who understands the concepts of right and wrong, this special ritual or token action may serve as a sort of command. For seen in this light, but not otherwise, another man's demonstration of what he takes for right conduct may reasonably influence his own. But it is still only conduct that we are concerned with—conduct that we demonstrate or reaffirm. And it is typically to practical policies, to attitudes, action and the like, that the terms 'rational' and 'irrational' are applied.

## IV

In all this I have spoken of evaluation in general, but for illustration I have mostly referred to 'right views' or 'right practices'. These, no doubt, are fair samples of evaluative language, yet it may seem that a step has been left out; that the general applicability of this view of 'right' has too easily been taken for granted. Now a systematic or exhaustive account of the various forms of evaluation would be no slight undertaking, and I do not propose to attempt it here; it may be useful all the same, if not to fill the gap, at least to indicate how it might be filled. And to this purpose in the present section, I shall, taking 'right' and 'good' as our two most general evaluative terms, say a few words of the connexions and differences between them. Indeed it is necessary to our general account, for we shall find after all that there are special problems connected with certain uses of 'good'.

I called these our most general evaluative terms: between them, perhaps, they cover the whole field, the rest representing no more than particular determinates of these two. But many philosophers have gone further; they have thought it possible to reduce our two ultimate notions to one, defining 'right' in terms of 'good' or *vice versa*. It is along these lines that a possible systematization of our various evaluative expressions has most often been sought. The

project recommends itself, no doubt, partly on account of the influence
of the *quasi* geometrical model which we have repeatedly met: the
demand that all arguments be set out, for formal occasions at least,
in accordance with certain favoured schemata. But, further, if any
sort of order was to be introduced into ethical discourse, no other
likely method suggested itself. And to reduce what seems arbitrary
to order is the business of theoretical thinking everywhere; a mere
manifold can never be acceptable. Besides so long as our evaluative
terms are thought to require the postulation of some sort of objective referents—nonsensible qualities or the like, to guarantee their
meaning—some comfort was to be had from not multiplying them
further than should prove necessary.

The terms 'right' and 'good' are admittedly pretty closely related,
and more or less plausible interdefinitions can be constructed with
sufficient pains and ingenuity; nor is the exercise without its value
in promoting an understanding of both concepts. But once we conceive evaluation in general rather as a single function, though presenting or admitting of different forms, we may no longer feel the
same pressing need to reduce ethics to order by definition. There are
more sorts of order than one; and what we have here is best seen as
a single determinable concept, differently determined in different
fields. Here, as so often, the imperativist account of evaluative
language shows us the way; for we find Hare treating both 'right'
and 'good' as prescriptive expressions, though he distinguishes different forms of prescription.

It is easy to set out the different force of these words in broad
terms. 'Right' is the more legalistic or logistic of the two notions; it
has a sort of authoritarian force and draws a line. 'Good' is, or feels,
less compulsive; and goodness admits of degree. Outside logic, we
most naturally use the terms 'right' and 'wrong' in areas that fall
under the jurisdiction of positive law or at least of a well-established
social code: in each case there are rules to appeal to. But, odd as it
may seem, the same words have a common aesthetic use too: 'the
right shade' for the curtains, 'the right word' in a poetic description
—these phrases are no less familiar. And again where we tackle

problems, especially in new fields which, as yet, we do not see our way through—where we proceed not with formulated rules but merely on the supposition or postulate that some sort of right answer may be found—our use is perhaps closer to this aesthetic one.

Broadly then, there are two sorts of context in which the word 'right' does its work. In one there are rules to refer to which are established and recognized; and here whether they are laid down for convenience, like the rules of a game or a club, or derived from the recognition of principles embodied in previous practice, is immaterial. The other sort of context is that in which 'right' has been identified as roughly synonymous with 'fitting'. This latter is the more fundamental both for morality and for theoretical inquiry, but we shall perhaps see the contrast of 'right' and 'good' in a better light if we start with the more familiar and clearer notion: our ordinary language is here more adequate to the part it is required to play. The easiest application of the term is the one that current philosophy has seized on, which presupposes the authority of rules.

The difference which we noticed above, that 'good' unlike 'right' admits of degree, is a consequence of this ordinary connexion of 'right' with rule-giving. We should like to be able to say that a rule, at least an ideal rule, allows only two possible courses, it must either be broken or obeyed. For the whole point of rule-making is to draw a line, and we wish to know exactly where we stand—within the safe circle or outside it. Now that, as I said, would be an ideal rule; it is not something we ever actually possess. Indeed a rule so formulated as to foresee and forestall all possible contingencies, all borderline cases and the like, is not even theoretically possible.[1] Nonetheless we keep up the fiction even in language we use; for we speak not of 'more or less violation of a rule' but of its 'grosser' or 'more obvious violation': as if the rule in itself, truly grasped, could leave no room for only two possibilities. And, naturally enough, we treat 'right' in the same way as we treat rules, and allow it no comparative form; but it seems that we amuse ourselves or we play games, setting up barriers first and then finding ways round them after all. For we

---

[1] Cf. Wittgenstein, *Philosophical Investigations*, i, 84–91.

make free use of phrases like 'not quite right' or 'not badly wrong' which are only disguised forms of 'less right'.

The two evaluative terms that I undertook to discuss were 'right' and 'good', for these two, I said, seem the most general; but after all there is a third to be dealt with—what amounts in effect to a third —which we cannot ignore without confusing the picture. The visible difference may be slight, but it is significant: this third expression which I wish to speak of is the phrase which we often use 'the right'. The force of 'right' by itself is strictly no more than 'not wrong'; we need rules so as to know what to avoid, we shall keep clear of pro- hibited ground. 'Right', therefore, is not properly a term of com- mendation, it only tells us what is not to be blamed; and honesty is a minimal virtue. As the world goes, no doubt, to abstain from actual wrong-doing may win some praise; and at least consistent honesty is admired, or honesty in difficult circumstances. Here as before, we shall find, the attempt to make life simple or regular, or in this case to make morality simple, by fixing a sort of Plimsoll line of duty, a level we are to watch—to sink lower, we shall know, is to expose ourselves to censure—ends largely in fiction. It may also be worth noticing in passing that 'bad' differs from 'wrong' much less than 'good' differs from 'right'; the intensive form, for instance, 'very wrong of him' is found quite natural.[1]

---

[1] 'Right' is an administrator's notion, assimilating morality to law; and the ethic of duty and desire—'middle class morality' as the dustman, Doolittle, calls it, whose greatest representative is Kant—is, so to speak, the apotheosis of administration. It meets psychological needs too: 'home', the safe ground, is marked off; duty is known *a priori*; and desire, so far as it has a part to play, appears rather as the wolf at the door, howling and hungry; that duty keeps at bay.

All this has little to do with moral reality. Desire, and its expression in action, is not something outside morality, but rather the stuff that it is to be made of, the material on which it sets to work—which is moralized in virtue of its form. We act, as we are bound to act, on desires; but still we act rightly or wrongly. Neither, for instance, to unchain aggression nor yet to be ineffectually tame; neither too sloppy nor prim; neither pharisaically rigid nor quite 'all-understanding, all-excusing'; in brief to be gentle and firm, cautious and bold, in the right way and at the right time—which Aristotle called hitting the mean—these are the real issues of moral life. General rules, of course, still have their function, but they do not mark boundary-lines; rather, they are pointers to judgement, the framework within which we take our bearings.

Now the third phrase that I have mentioned 'the right', unlike 'right' alone, has a positive force of commendation, and belongs, indeed, to a different sort of situation. 'Right' by itself serves only to pen off the sheep from the goats, but it makes no further selection among the former: but often we feel the need for expressing a more exclusive interest, our whole concern is to install a single prize-winner. We need the phrase 'the right' for all competitive situations, and these are numerous. Yet it may be asked—and the question is important—whether we do not make them seem still more numerous than they are. Certainly there are many theoretical problems where the different solutions put forward contradict each other, and it follows that they cannot both be right; but the truth is that we con-stantly use the same phrase, we ask what is 'the right view' or 'the right solution', where we have no such assurance beforehand. For we may arrive at alternative positions neither of which can be elimin-ated. The case here is the same as before; we speak of what is a kind of ideal as if it were already reality, and doubtless that is natural enough. For the sake of mere manageability we should wish to find a sole exclusive answer; and moreover truth is so often reached through the trial and elimination of error—inquiry proceeds so largely by conflict—that it is not to be wondered at, perhaps, that this sort of language seems to come of itself. Nonetheless in tackling new problems we cannot lay it down in advance that more than one possible view-point, equally good, may not be found. Indeed in recent philosophy we have heard much of the development of ways of speaking which are seen as alternative possibilities, where earlier philosophers saw theories which conflicted and could not both be right.

In all this I have been speaking of the term 'right' as presupposing the appeal to known rules; that, we saw, is what gives it its peculiar definitive force, leaving no room for relative assessments. Yet often we seek for some view-point on the assumption that principles are to be found, although as yet we are unable to formulate them; and here once again, it would seem, we naturally assume that only one such position is to be found. We speak of it in advance as 'the right one'. We may feel that it would be gratuitously optimistic to hope for more, or again we may prefer decisive and thus exclusive answers. It seems, certainly, that reason is restless until it can eliminate alternatives, and we naturally go to work on that basis. Yet here, as elsewhere, though we trust our intuitions or natural feelings, we must also be prepared to submit them to correction in the process of inquiry. And we cannot lay it down in advance that our alternatives will always prove eliminable. Indeed one can imagine a state of mind that positively preferred to range freely and choose between different ways of thinking.

Given an incomplete jig-saw puzzle or a pattern of a simple, mechanical sort, like a floral design on a cushion-cover, there is only one piece or one shape that will fill the gap. Here, certainly, alternatives are ruled out; and here, too, 'the right piece' means in the clearest sense 'the fitting piece'. We may think in much the same way of an incomplete work of art—and again of the whole process of inquiry where we seek for solutions to problems: 'the right view' is the only one that will fit, resolving existing discrepancies, conflicts not overcome within the system as it stands.[1] But it is doubtful whether this usage, general as it may be, is really justified; certainly it is no more than a romantic fancy that an unfinished poem or painting allows only one possible development, the sole right word or right brush stroke—other than which all the rest are sheerly wrong. Theoretical inquiry as well may have room for different lines of development; there may always be alternative conceptual schemes.

To sum up: 'right' operates in the context of rules, prescribing nothing definite but making quite definite exclusions; 'the right' presupposes competitive situations either in the context of rules or the larger context of rational inquiry generally, and seeks not only to make a definite exclusion but to lay down prescriptions as well. And in both cases these demands represent ideals, and sometimes plain fictions, rather than actualities—though fictions too, as lawyers assure us, have their use.

Let us turn to 'good'. Whereas 'right' presupposes rules 'good',

[1] Cf. above, pp. 139-41.

we saw in an earlier chapter, normally presupposes criteria; we may ask in virtue of what features any given object is called good. A good theory must fit the known facts, be free from unnecessary complication and so on; a good batsman will be normally expected to get a fair number of runs and defend his wicket effectively when necessary. Good apples and good automobiles have other features again, on which other philosophers have dwelt at length. Here only one qualification needs to be added, though a qualification of some importance. I spoke previously of the use of the word good as normally presupposing criteria; so that what we commend in effect is a kind of object, and any similar member of the class will be counted as good too. But uses of 'good' are to be found where this pattern of analysis no longer applies; for we commend unique objects too, such as works of art and philosophical theories. And already our study of 'the right' has brought us to the edge of the problem: it would be useless to say here that any other work, or other theory, showing identical features—features that we can catalogue or describe—would qualify for the same commendation. Indeed we may make a start along these lines, we may pick out broad features; and the method is the only one we have. And yet it remains true that we cannot say that these features alone, occurring as they may in a slightly but significantly different context, will ensure that the new object is good too; they create a presumption in its favour but no more. We may, indeed, list its merits in full, omitting no detail, so as to make it impossible that another work or another theory possessing them should fail to be equally acceptable; but that will not meet the case either, for once that is really assured, any theory answering to the description will no longer be another one but the same. In the absence of relevant differences a verdict passed in any one case applies generally: but anything aesthetically relevant is part of the notion of a work of art—just as anything logically relevant is part of the notion of a theory. For the same reason, we may notice in passing, these concepts of theory and work of art intrinsically involve evaluation, so that the 'descriptive-prescriptive' analysis can never be finally carried through.

I have described the whole process of inquiry as an attempt to focus recalcitrant theoretical material in new ways; to get men to see it differently. And in this process, so far as thought progresses, our different views or attitudes are brought into line. We meet, to be sure, with various success; and in some fields it may be the possibility of illuminating discussion, of provisional agreement at all sorts of level, rather than any firmly formed consensus, that makes evaluation significant. We can, for instance, quite intelligibly speak of a piece of philosophizing as excellent, though of a kind from which we ourselves radically dissent. But this is to digress; our concern here is with the evaluation of unique objects—for which, in the nature of the case, general criteria no longer suffice. But that really has been our theme all along; I have said that the whole task of inquiry is the search for generally acceptable points of view. 'Points of view' are unique objects in this sense: and a work of art might be thought of as the opaque image or equivalent of a point of view—the focusing in some acceptable pattern of objects or forms. The objects may be abstract or concrete; for theories, no less than canvases, may be contemplated aesthetically, and merely experienced and enjoyed.

In formulating new concepts and points of view we arrive, as we previously found, at a new classificatory system; our refocused vision shows us different things as like and unlike. It may lead us, for example, to treat certain diseases as forms of neurosis or *vice versa*; on the other hand the classification itself rests on and represents a concept, perhaps a new concept of disease, which we can only accept as unique. And again we may isolate single features, not hitherto characterized or known; with our changed focus new percepts may crystallize. Now if we wish to do more than merely gaze—perhaps even to gaze—we shall need to describe them, and therefore to apply general terms; for all descriptive terms are implicitly general. We may commend certain features of a work of art, and these, therefore, serve as our criteria of value; and criteria that serve in one instance will serve in another. Nonetheless the situation is unique: description serves here to illuminate a particular object rather than to align or class it along with others; its full force can only be felt in the presence of whatever it describes. It is, therefore, more like a magnifying-glass than a faithful representation or a picture; it shows us what we have in our hands rather than deputizing for it *in absentia*. What counts, say, as a more imaginative piece of characterization, or again a more economical or systematic theory, must in the last resort be seen and understood in terms of the work or theory before us. Yet for all that it is with general descriptions that we begin; we do not possess any other language. In seeking to establish a point of view we first appeal to criteria, to namable features that we might find elsewhere and equally commend; otherwise we should have no way to proceed and never break silence at all.

I have introduced this topic under the heading of the use of the word 'good'; and 'good', as I said, admits of degree. Yet here we have something of a paradox, for where our evaluations are really unique no difference of degree can be recognized; one such object cannot be better than another for the good reason that no other can exist. We have no use for the comparative form where no question of comparison can arise, and every unique object is incomparable. We only call *King Lear* a better or greater play than *The Cenci* (immeasurably greater, of course) in so far as we appeal to criteria that are in some measure applicable to both. But leaving aside the special case of unique objects, it is clear that the sort of features we have mentioned as criteria of merit in apples, cars and the like, all admit of degree; and so far as we find criteria for the assessment of works of art or theories the same holds. Theories may be more or less rigorous, more or less systematic and so on. And though more of a good thing is not necessarily better, it normally is so, and there need be no limit in principle. 'The more the merrier' may be a saying that is rarely meant quite literally—the most generous sociability has its limits—but at least in logic no reason appears why quantity should not be extended indefinitely. Our concern here is neither to divide sheep from goats nor to fill a single prize-winning place; what we seek is a graded order of merit. Nor are these differences, or the fact that we have occasion to use all these various modes of evaluation, anything we shall puzzle over; there is no occasion to seek to eliminate the notion of 'good' in favour of that of 'right' or *vice versa*. If we evaluate things as better or worse no doubt we must have standards to which we appeal; and a question may always be raised as to whether these standards are the right ones. But then again our standards themselves may be assessed as better or worse—or the judges whose verdict we invoke—and it does not appear that either concept is more fundamental than the other.

There are, however, more serious problems connected with the evaluation of things as good or bad; certain qualifications prove necessary if our previous account of 'right' is to be extended to cover these cases too. For we spoke of right views and right procedures: to recognize a practice as right is, other things being equal, to adopt it; the use of evaluative language appeared as a kind of hypothetical action. Now the problem we meet when we turn to 'good' is that in a large class of cases no question of action seems to be involved. Hare, indeed, connects 'good' with choices, and choosing is certainly an action. The theory may go a fair way to meet the difficulty—though perhaps what has been said stands in need of one small development: comparison will have to be treated preferentially. Let us, for simplicity's sake, express ourselves after the manner of the imperativist theory. If 'That is good' means, very roughly, 'Choose that, and that sort of thing', then 'The other is still better' will mean 'Choose the other, or any one like it, where the choice lies between it and the former.' And again 'The third is best of all' is easily interpretable along the same lines.

So far this account appears to meet our needs; yet we find in large classes of cases that this account of the word 'good' in terms of choice—if not demonstrably false—is patently strained and artificial. And at this stage we need not assume that the same word serves only one kind of purpose. Not only dinners and like things, which we may well have occasion to choose, are commonly assessed as good or bad; we commend sonnets, mediaeval buildings and the conduct of a person belonging to times and cultures extremely remote from our own. Now the simple and obvious account is that in calling them good what we do is to express our admiration.

Suppose we stand before the cathedral at Pisa and praise it in enthusiastic terms: what sort of choice is supposed to be in question or to whom are we addressing imperatives? We can hardly be telling modern architects to build buildings like the one before us; the attempt would almost certainly be disastrous. We might be telling our companions to choose Pisa rather than other places for holidays; but then again we might be speaking to a native Pisan who anyway sees the building every day. The only other interpretation I can think of is that we are concerned with the preservation of such a monument; so that where the choice is one of how public money should be spent, we urge or prescribe that this use should come high in the order of priorities. But this account would surely be fanciful; no such question need have entered our heads. Indeed our naïvety may be such that we do not even realize that old buildings stand in need of repair. And supposing that a visitor looks up and exclaims 'What a magnificent building!' it would be odd to gloss his remark with 'You mean (of course) "Let's do all we can to preserve it." '

I have said that the natural account to give here is the one that we find, not in Hare's work, but in that of his more outrageous predecessors: what we are doing is simply to express our feelings. All that I find to dissent from in the exponents of this view is the irrationalism that they seem to infer from it; but I can see no reason why that consequence should be thought to follow. Perhaps it is a residue of a psychology which divides mental happenings into two kinds, of which feelings make up one and thoughts the other; so that the expression of thought is essentially rational—or at least falls within the sphere of rationality—while the expression of feeling falls outside it. Or again the explanation may be that when irrational conduct is to be accounted for, we may refer to a man's feelings or emotions to explain it: it was anger or jealousy or the like that made him behave as he did. And here again it appears that rational and emotional behaviour are specifically different things. Yet, merely psychologically considered, it is not clear that these two things, to think an inference false and to feel a resistance to accepting it, need in any way differ.

To be sure the two usages have different functions. 'I feel' is more tentative than 'I think', though that in turn lacks the final commitment of 'I see'. Indeed where we say only that we feel something we express more than hesitation; we imply further some sort of obscurity—that our own views are not yet transparent in themselves. But it is superfluous to dwell further on these differences; the distinction that it concerns us to draw is between feelings that are merely personal or merely casual—we do not claim them as anything more—and those that submit themselves to discipline. In brief we shall wish to distinguish between a trained and an untrained sensibility: for what reasoning we feel it natural to accept (and as before I use the verb strictly psychologically) or what buildings move us to admiration, may be much changed by the process of training. And that training in turn will reflect whatever tests are appropriate in the field. We use the word 'good' to express feelings which claim implicitly to stand up to criticism; and should they not survive it after all, then we are logically obliged to withdraw our previous verdict.[1] Judgement, in other words, is trained feeling.

I have spoken at length of the process in which our initial instinctive tendencies are brought into line; the procedures that we find it natural to adopt change with reflection and experience. It is a matter of course that these overt responses will be accompanied,

[1] The account given here partly derives from Professor J. N. Findlay's article 'Morality by Convention', *Mind*, liii, 1944, pp. 142–69. Cf. further below, pp. 208 ff. The minute or meticulous reader of these pages may further have noticed the vocabulary that I have adopted when questions of this sort arose: I have spoken of our feeling the force of a given logical demand or again feeling the discrepancy implied in two conjoined statements and the like.

One other problem that deserves a word here is that of acts of supererogation—which we admire and accordingly describe as good. That judgement can be universalized of course. What is good for one man is good for another similarly placed. But the action is not 'right'; there is no obligation to do it, and hence there can be no question of universalizing the judgement, 'I ought to do it'. Indeed the agent may believe and say that he ought to do it; he may even treat that as a non-universalized obligation—which is a common piece of special pleading—but he will be wrong. The best way, for instance, with self-punitive or conscience-driven people (as with those whose conscience is sluggish) is to show that they do not really regard their own judgements as applying universally.

barring special contingencies, by appropriate feelings; and if we postulate the possibility of reaching agreement as to the one we shall naturally say the same of the other. Intuition, on the psychological side, is feeling too; and in common speech the terms are often synonymous. There appears no reason, then, why the word 'good' should not be used to express feelings and yet come within the compass of argument. For the rest, it is plain that the expression of feeling admits of degree.

This account of the use of the word 'good' comes near to one definition sometimes favoured, namely, that it serves to express 'right satisfaction'. If we are to follow the practice of logicians, making our great aim the elimination of undefined terms, this way seems as promising as another: and very likely an account in terms of right choices or right commendation might be made workable too. For there is no difficulty in supplying rules that allow for degrees of commendation; we have already noticed the saying 'the more the merrier' which clearly might be taken as a rule. But conversely some more or less plausible definition of 'right'—or even, what is harder, of 'the right'—may be possible, and here we shall take 'good' as undefined. Let us lay it down that among a given class of objects only one can be good, and further that the goodness of any one entails that all the rest are positively and equally bad: this is perhaps pretty much what we mean when we speak of 'the right one'. But I shall leave the working-out of these possibilities to those who have a special taste for such logistic exercises.

# Morality and the Form of Moral Concepts

I MEAN at this point to take leave of the larger problems of axiology and concentrate on a more specific field of thought; I began with the concept of intuition as moral philosophers have used it, and it is to moral philosophy that I wish to return. Indeed what follows may be thought of rather as an extended appendix; yet our account so far has been largely general and something by way of a rather more concrete application may fairly be asked for. I shall attempt, then, to supply the deficiency. In accordance with our general position what we shall expect to find, here as in other fields, will be the emergence of certain tendencies, of certain broad tests and procedures: these together will serve to define the province of morals, and to define it progressively as they crystallize—and again, applied to particular problems, to determine the detail of moral judgement. This marks out our line of inquiry; yet neither this department of thought nor any other is differentiated solely in terms of the procedures appropriate to it. Morality has its own character apart from that—its institutional and social character especially—which we shall do well to take notice of. Otherwise any charting of moral argument may seem something of a theorist's exercise, lacking an adequate background or sound basis.

Conscience, we are often told, is a social product; what a man finds in his conscience, the vetoes and laws that it issues, represent nothing else than the code of the society to which he belongs. It is plain that this account is largely true; it is true, at least, that each man's morality, first if not last, is stocked, so to speak, from the common pool. But it is a truth whose bearings or background have been consistently missed or misconceived. Whatever the significance of the thesis it is certainly no *differentia* of moral judgement; for the judgement of a scientist or a lawyer will need to be described in the same terms, or substantially the same. It, too, is formed in a tradition, a school of thought, where men have co-operated in inquiry; and where a scholar with his trained mind makes assured discriminations he sees with his predecessors' eyes. All judgement is a social product; much as we sometimes say that it is ideally no private mind but the law that speaks through the mouth of a judge, so it is science that speaks in the mature judgements of scientists. Language itself, the medium in which our thinking is cast and through which it operates, is a part of the life of a community; we see the world in the light of these concepts which our culture has framed and focused. Indeed for a child to learn a language and come to work with it is, more than anything else, what assimilates him to his community and makes him part of it; he grows into it and lives in its life.

Single individuals, no doubt, may also oppose the tradition, they may stand out against the orthodox body. But that is no exception to the general rule; properly understood, it confirms it. For there are sorts of criticism that we are bound to take notice of and others which we can afford to ignore; we are entitled to some summary judgements. And if such sayings sound harshly dogmatic, I leave the putative open-minded objector to go through the pages of *Old Moore's Almanac* from crystal-gazing to astrology, to pills, in hope of finding a grain of pure ore among the rubble. There is, however, informed criticism too—criticism that comes from within a given body of theory or practice. For thought is never a static thing or a lifeless organism; no system of thought at any given time is wholly self-consistent or rigid. But if not, the system in its own working opposes or criticizes itself, and also grows and recreates itself in the process. In the opposing views of scientists or moralists, men educated and trained in ways of thought, we find the vitality of a tradition; what we have here are not merely the voices of individuals taking their stand on arbitrary preferences for this view or that— if that were all there would be little need to listen to them—but rather the working out of the general process, the movement of inquiry itself.

Morality is a public, social thing, reflected in the minds of individuals. In reality the process has two sides to it: the public code that makes and moulds the private conscience is remade and moulded by it in turn. We find some philosophers, born rebels perhaps, or temperamental outsiders, who can see no picture here but a single set battle-piece; they see one man's conscience against the Leviathan —against the tyrant custom and the giant authority, Jack the individual who stands alone. Others go so far the other way as almost to submerge us in the social organism. But in the real reciprocity of the process, public code and private conscience flow together: each springs from and contributes to the other, channels it and is channelled. Both alike are redirected and enlarged. Every tradition, it is true, will also have its tendency to freeze and harden; mere withdrawal or self-fortification is the first natural reaction to disturbing experience, equally in an individual or a group. And all criticism is disturbing at first. Where custom is reinforced by armed authority, so that dissidents may easily be silenced, the tendency, and the temptation, is doubly strong. At the same time we must say this on the other side: an individual conscience that showed itself in no way responsive to general feeling—that felt no challenge, no need for any re-scrutiny, in face of universal opposition—would have no great claim to be heard either. We owe to the Protestant tradition, no doubt, that respect in which private conscience is held in Britain, and so far as social practices go we have reason to be grateful to it; if, however, philosophers draw the moral that the utterances of any one man's conscience have, and must always have, an equal logical status with another's, it cannot be wondered at that they sometimes find ethics irrational.

This social source or matrix of judgement is, we find, nothing special to morals. But there remains a sense in which it is true that morality is social, say, in contradistinction from the sciences. Physical science, for instance, though no doubt it grows out of the activities of special groups, has material which it works on which lies outside them; it investigates the phenomena of nature. Now moral judgement is not only formed and moulded by the operation of a given social system, it must also work primarily within it; it resembles, say, the judgement of a cricketer, used inside the system

o

that produced it: there is no further material beyond. A team-player, too, will have his rôle, he is a slip-fielder, an opening batsman or a captain; and his judgement will show itself, where it exists, in a better specific performance. Similarly a moral or a social code, the customs and institutions of a society, serve to organize individuals into a system, reshaping their original desires—a system itself being nothing but the form of material thus shaped and organized. For we can at least abstractly conceive of the primary material of human nature, which, seeking expression in social forms, is also remoulded in the process. To fill a rôle or find a place in such a system, to recognize and act as it requires, is, in the root sense, to do one's duty—a duty that can only exist because the system has assigned rôles to different actors. A man only knows what is demanded of him because he has been educated in a society organized in accordance with a certain code; therefore the demands of the code, and hence of the whole social body, as passed on by parents and other teachers, make themselves heard privately in his thoughts.

These notions are plainly correlative. A moral code is a system of relations which harmonizes the activities of individuals: a moral conscience expresses the mental attitudes, the educated mind of a person that this system has formed. And where we find one man's conscience in conflict with another's the system itself has partially failed; for it must either be discordant in itself or at least the material has proved recalcitrant. But this is to talk quite abstractly: no social conditions are static, nor is all human nature ever harmonized. Rather, what we may look for from conflict is the development and adjustment of imperfect codes.

Such talk of rôles within a system may sound feudal or archaic, perhaps: do we still live in a society, I may be asked, where the various orders of men—monks and merchants, villeins and knights —had each their fixed place assigned them, with duties belonging to each? Now as to social differences, the egalitarian trend of modern western society is plain enough; and in other ways something similar may hold. One man in our time must play many parts, and often in swift alternation. The whole tenor of his life, his right and duties, will no longer be bound up with a status—'status' being much more than our 'profession'. Yet there are still different parts to be played. We broadly take it for granted that we are all equally, what the French revolutionaries called themselves, 'men and citizens'. Nonetheless we still act in more specialized rôles as particular occasions arise. The obligations that we recognize are to a far larger extent institutional than many philosophers seem to allow. Let us take, for example, Sidgwick's principle that a man ought not to prefer his own lesser good to the greater good of another, that 'each one is morally bound to regard the good of any other individual as much as his own'.[1] Seen as basic in some sense or regulative, that this principle expresses something valid—that I shall not deny. Nonetheless it has to be interpreted, like an artistic theme worked out in different media, through the institutions of some given society. Westermarck had no difficulty in finding counter-examples; a business man in an open economy or a candidate in a competitive examination who failed to put his rival's greater good before his own, would hardly be blamed for it.[2] And Sidgwick himself allows that, if it is to be effective, a man's benevolence must be canalized, so that his family and his friends have first claim on him. Generalizations apart, what anyone ought to do here and now will always reflect the social nexus and the special relations in which he finds himself: commercial dealings or marriage, parenthood or friendship, all regulated by custom or law, decide what is allowable or wrong.[3] Again where the same duties reappear—or what seem at a glance to be the same duties—in widely different societies, much room for interpretation may remain.[4] Murder, perhaps, is generally condemned; yet what killings count as murder, and of whom, is by

---

[1] *Methods of Ethics*, seventh edition, p. 382.

[2] E. Westermarck, *Ethical Relativity*, 1932, p. 13.

[3] It is singular that in the work of Ross, whose ethical system is centred on his short list of self-evident *prima facie* duties—applicable to all men universally—we also find these relations insisted on. Cf. *The Right and the Good*, p. 19. The emphasis is excellent but not easy to square with the rest.

[4] The point has been forcibly made by Professor Macbeath, whose work will be further dealt with below. See his *Experiments in Living*, pp. 73-6 and 100.

no means so easily decided. Infanticide, private revenges, the killing of enemies in war or of robbers or assailants in self-defence, duelling, suicide, euthanasia and judicial execution—all these have been established or excused. The hangman's profession, like the soldier's, forms part of a working institution; a mere list of duties that ignores it will not give much guidance to moral judgement.

The perspective that now seems to emerge must, at first glance, cast doubt on the whole project that we have embarked on: it would seem that there can be no general forms of moral thinking. We shall find as many codes as there are communities—as many as there are variable ways of organizing men or moulding nature into some tolerably harmonious way of life. I have spoken of tendencies appearing in the development of moral concepts: but it seems that each system, working in its separate material, will have its own rubs or points of tension; that the several developing patterns, each one solving its own problems, will only get further apart. We should no more expect a dozen unfinished canvasses, with a dozen artists at work, striving to bring into a unified vision any recalcitrant matter that still stands out, to get more and more like one another as they progress. The artist may still have his special skill, just as a cricketer or a wrestler has his skill; evaluation might perhaps still be possible —it is not wholly clear. But if so, it would only be possible within the context of the individual picture or game.

This approach to ethical problems has been persuasively developed by Professor Macbeath. The varieties of moral systems are, in his view, so many 'experiments in living'—experiments on which different societies embark. The direction of moral effort will reflect the way of life of a community, development is always determined by a particular vision and ideal. Each society, according to Macbeath, has its own vision of the good life. Two things, however, remain constant, and these form the essence of morals: the first is the drive towards the satisfaction of human needs—though the patterns in which they fulfil themselves are very various—and the other a general principle of justice. Macbeath sees this principle, I believe rightly, as having a status wholly different from that of particular moral principles, say, those, of veracity or honesty. Rather, we have here the general form of morality itself: persons who engage in this activity, in the attempt to live or find a way of life in common, commit themselves to what the enterprise involves. Each, then, must recognize his neighbour as equally involved with himself—as a person who makes claims no less than he does. People are ends-in-themselves; and a moral code is any sort of system in which the ends of different people are harmonized. This account, though it gives a fixed definition to these two basic ethical concepts, is far from excluding development. Moral progress expresses two things: on the one hand our understanding of human nature, of what is involved in a personality, and hence in the satisfaction of human needs, is progressively deepened and enlarged; and secondly we progressively extend our notion of the society or the group. All men may at last be included within our community of moral persons; and ideally the whole of human nature will be what our system seeks to satisfy.[1]

An account such as this, at once philosophical and realistic, has much to recommend it to a serious student of morals. It shows us a general point of view, a pattern that is quite abstract and general, which leaves room at the same time for what is concrete, and does justice to the complexities of the subject-matter—to the actual struggling process of moral life. Hence one turns from other recent systems, characteristic artifacts, fine products of logical and conceptual analysis, to a work such as this—or to Bradley's great work on morals—with a strong sense of firm ground regained, and open air. Nonetheless there are difficulties that we must face.

I am far from denying or doubting that the satisfaction of human needs in accordance with some principle of equality or justice is essential to our notion of morality; that here we find a large part of its form, in so far as we can speak of its form, as distinct from its variable content. But while it may be a part it is not the whole of it; after all this term 'personality' covers too much, and that too loosely. We may compare types of persons with different needs and we can

[1] Op. cit., pp. 52 ff., 101-2, 435-6 and *passim*.

also compare societies and moral systems and the type of person that they tend to produce. That will be one standard that we judge them by. The truth is, surely, that this common human nature which, prior to any social conditioning, is to be more or less fully satisfied, is hardly more than a convenient fiction. Again Macbeath himself speaks of 'comprehensiveness' among the criteria by which the merits of different systems must be assessed: the ideal that societies set up, that they endeavour to live by, may, he writes, be more or less enlightened, richer or narrower.[1] But it is not clear how such an appeal to richness as a criterion for moral systems can follow from the principles that he has laid down. Personalities, indeed, are rich and poor, and different societies encourage the one sort of person or the other. A contented pig, or a man who resembles one, has presumably satisfied his needs better—shall we say, to vary Mill's example, (for Socrates seems to have been a serene person)—than a restless or angry intellectual. On the other hand I must confess that these arguments draw on a part of ethics that seems harder to deal with than any other; I shall shortly return to it and say more, but I cannot pretend to be very well pleased with my own account.

In spite of these difficulties, and others, Macbeath's position shows us a broad approach: our concern is with something like a general form, and the ultimate uniqueness of different systems does entirely exclude the appeal to formal principles. Even though we should go to the extreme of taking each code as a thing by itself— as a unique working-out of the general problem—on Macbeath's own showing at least two universally applicable tests still remain: first, a general principle of justice; and, secondly, the adequacy of the view of human nature which the system implies. Now once we acknowledge these criteria there seems to be no *a priori* reason why there should not be others as well. The different sciences work in different ways on materials that vary enormously—geology and neurology and physics cannot have much common ground—yet the demand for the publicity of data, the testing of theories by experiment and the exclusion of *ad hoc* hypotheses, are applicable to all

[1] Op. cit., p. 345.

of them. Even the other cases that we took—those of different sportsmen skilled in different games or of works of art variously taking shape—though these might seem extreme examples, do not really illustrate the impossibility of the appeal to general rules. In art we shall certainly find the hardest case; yet the fact is that we constantly compare works of art and make comparative assessments of their merits. We give general descriptions and appeal to principles. Rather, the difference, which I touched on before, seems to be this, that a description of a work of art—where the descriptive terms are also evaluative—can only be properly appreciated alongside the object that it describes. It cannot be used in abstraction as we use most descriptions of other sorts. Such a description, in the last resort, aims at showing us the unique work in a new way; it seeks to establish a mode of vision.

But what we are touching on here is in fact another facet of the larger problem, which we have met already, of the relation of abstract and concrete, of general tests and the objects to which they apply. Where the objects, like works of art, are ultimately unique, abstractions tell us little by themselves: and the same holds of conceptual innovation, theories and points of view. Certainly we shall still need general terms; we shall speak of 'rigor', 'coherence' or 'precision'. But their meaning is not fully established, not something we fully assimilate, until the material itself comes into view. Again one may possess either side of knowledge without the other. A late scholar may learn what prose is, never having known the word; and one might learn, say, what humility is, though one had been using the word all one's life. Illustrations such as this, perhaps, are not common in methodological discussion, discussion of such concepts as coherence or economy, for instance; the text-books suggest nothing of the sort. If so, I can say only this, that it is pity. They might prove illuminating. For suppose we claim to have replaced a less by a more coherent account of some theoretical concept; perception, freedom or what you will. The old account, we say, contains inconsistencies: in saying so we know what we mean; we could make the complaint good. The logical grammar of one term permits these and these operations, while another permits these and these; and the two sets of operations conflict. Later we find a new view; we introduce concepts and ways of speaking, and therewith the conflict disappears. It disappears, that is to say, for those who can be brought to perceive and accept the possibility of a different view-point and new sorts of logical operation, a pattern not recognized before. 'There', we may now say, ostensively defining it, producing the genuine article for the first time, 'there is coherence indeed!'

The institutions of different societies, like the logical grammar of words, form, as it were, a concrete medium; our general tests do not fail to apply, but to apply them we must know the special field. For what changes from one society to another will be the nexus of social relations—the ties of kindred, say, or the ties binding vassals and their lords—which give rise to particular obligations. But notions such as honesty or charity are more fundamental than that. In the abstract they may mean very little; for we cannot tell what we must call honest dealing until we know what is expected of a man. And that will depend on local custom: or if a diplomat or a salesman is strictly honest, or a magistrate wonderfully charitable, it may not be quite in the usual sense. It does not follow that these general notions are merely empty; when we compare one society to another, or when we ask as legislators—or at least as newspaper-readers—what sort of society we would wish for, our appeal will be to principles such as these. Burke compared what he called the primitive rights of men to rays of light entering a dense medium, which, he said, by the law of nature are refracted from their straight line.[1] So, too, the general principles of morality, though they can appear only through the medium of local custom, yet retain a real tendency of their own. Each society may have its vision of the good life, just as each philosopher has of good logic; yet we may still look for modes of procedure which reflection may progressively establish, for which we claim general application.

Even so there are reservations to bear in mind. The common distinction between form and content, useful as it is, is not to be

[1] *Reflections on the Revolution in France*: Works of Edmund Burke, 1834, i, p. 404.

thought of as absolute or precise. Contrary to what seems to be the general view, there is no way of studying moral concepts, or the patterns or roles of moral argument, which does not commit us to substantial conclusions, in some measure, at least. For the concrete moral views that we adopt follow solely from this, the progressive application of these rules. Further we must not expect too much: here, as in logic or the philosophy of science, we shall find a few very general principles or procedures that, in their concrete application, cover a vast complexity of ground. We should be wrong to mistake abstract knowledge of rules or principles for the judgement that we shall need to apply it, and equally wrong to reject them as vacuous merely because they are abstractions. If that were a legitimate objection there could be no such thing as thinking at all; for all thought, presumably, is abstract.

## II

I have spoken in the previous section of an ethical theory which takes the satisfaction of needs or desires, along with some principle of justice, as constituting the whole form of morality. Certainly both these things seem to be fundamental: that all actual moral argument appeals to consequences, to effects on human happiness or well-being, is the claim of utilitarians from Hutcheson on. We find it in Bentham, in Sidgwick (worked out by him, as one would expect, more fully and carefully than by anyone else) and in the ethical work of Professor Toulmin. Indeed the full claim—to which, I believe, all these writers subscribe—is that this is the sole ultimate appeal; but this there are familiar grounds for doubting. And Ross's treatment of *prima facie* duties may be taken as an answer to Sidgwick's case, which is probably the strongest that can be made out. But it is certainly one test that we always use; in a sense, perhaps, the first or most fundamental.

The problem, however, is complex: there is egoistic as well as universalistic hedonism to take account of. The utilitarian appeal is part of prudence, of the rational regard for one's own welfare, apart from the consideration of others. Now I do not pretend to offer a deductive demonstration of the necessity of regarding either one's own welfare or other people's—a demonstration, I suppose, that would have to be drawn from some premiss more obvious still. But as to the former, at least, when a man tells us he does something because he likes to do it, simply because it gives him satisfaction, it is hard to see more could be sought; what sense could be made of the suggestion that some further reason should be found. In saying so I do not mean to make it a tautology or a rule of language that one likes doing whatever one does, that one necessarily satisfies one's paramount desire; at least in the ordinary sense there are things that men do and yet dislike. I suggest only this, that if we give reasons for action, if we are to enter into such a discussion and treat it as legitimate, we cannot begin by rejecting a reason of this sort: one that all men find more obvious, more natural to give and accept than any other. On such principles, as I have said with perhaps wearisome repetitiveness, no inquiry is to be conducted at all.

Supposing, then, we find in this satisfaction a good reason for doing what produces it; next, still merely as prudent creatures, not yet as moral ones, we may compare one course of action with another. For we find that there may be a discrepancy between acting on and satisfying a desire, and that one may conflict with another; and this conflict, giving rise to reflection, must lead us to seek some general scheme for regulating our conduct. It cannot be rational to pursue conflicting ends: and here our only principle can be that of maximizing our satisfaction on the whole. Some such course might be said to be implied in the very notion of giving reasons for conduct; for until we are conscious of a possible question, of alternative ways open, we shall not reflect at all but merely act. And if the prospect of satisfaction serves as a reason for doing particular things, then a tendency to greater general satisfaction is a reason for preferring a general plan. Here we first have a practical use for the word 'good'. It is true, in some primitive sense, that the object of a man's desire or appetite will be what he for his part calls 'good'.[1] But until we can distinguish those desires that submit to and stand the test of

---

[1] Cf. Hobbes, *Leviathan*, Everyman Edition, p. 24.

reflection we can hardly think of 'good' as a word having meaning; it is merely an expressive noise like a grunt. To call a thing good is to make a claim for it, one which we believe true, but which might still prove false; for there is no claim where there is no room for error. And plainly that possibility arises once future satisfaction is in view, and the test is a simple empirical one. Later on it is doubtless less straightforward; and yet in some sense it remains true that the utilitarian appeal is fundamental. We cannot ask why a man does what he likes doing and expect an illuminating answer; this we have already seen. But take any other case: say, where he does something because he dislikes it—as drinking vinegar, frequenting brothels or taking showers—or again because he thinks it wrong or right. Here it is sensible to ask. We have entered the region of arguments; and even if new values should be found, where we rely on intuition in the end, we shall still argue, still try to get people to see them. And again, though there may perhaps be individuals who dislike everything that they do, that is an attitude that cannot either logically or psychologically be primitive.

Utilitarian considerations, as we see, already appear in rational prudence; but once we recognize a principle of justice we go beyond prudence to morality. But this principle has its counterpart already within the system of self-regarding calculations: in so far as we calculate at all we shall give equal weight to equal satisfactions where or whenever they occur. And that is not merely to pursue satisfactions but to think of them as good, to allow them a claim. The next step is to recognize another person's feelings or satisfactions as having an equal claim with one's own. Now to consider the interests of other people is to take up a new point of view: here, as elsewhere, inasmuch as it is genuinely new, there can be no deductive argument to prove it necessary. Yet we find that the whole process of thought at its highest levels no less than its lowest, presupposes the possibility of growing judgement, of bringing people to see things in new ways—and, further, to agree on what they see. We suppose that the new view, once it is found, will prove satisfactory or convincing; or again where it satisfies one man and fails to satisfy another, we shall feel the need to remove or at least, failing that, to explain the difference. If logic, as it is commonly understood, has little to say of these things then it can say little about judgement or inquiry; for all inquiry, as we have seen, presupposes that, with reflection, divergent views may be brought into line.

In face of any ordinary instance of moral blindness, at whatever level we meet it, in little children or in adult racial persecutors, there is one appeal that we all naturally make: we ask, 'How would you feel in his shoes?' It is the most fundamental of all moral arguments: a person who can never enter into another's feelings is no more capable of moral reflection than someone, for instance, incapable of grasping or applying a new model, a new scientific point of view, would be able to make progress in the sciences. It is, further, an imaginative appeal, which we respond to in various degrees; we can enter more or less deeply into other people's feelings and views. So, too, with philosophers skilled at refuting rival systems, having learnt them like the rules of a game: serious criticism begins when we make the initial experiment of seeing the world, as it were, through new glasses; of trying to use, to work and think with another system of concepts than our own. But it is, perhaps, an experiment that many philosophers never make at all. This much is certain in general, that man would never be a rational animal if he were not first an imaginative one.

If, then, we can imagine the feelings of others, and further, we treat satisfaction as a reason for doing whatever yields it; then justice, as soon as we come to recognize it, requires us to take account of other people's satisfaction no less than our own. In this account of the advance from egosim to altruism I do not, of course, aim at reconstructing any actual psychological history. Some such general tendency may be found; but for our purposes it is enough that in some measure other-regarding as well as self-regarding impulses appear before reflection sets to work, or morality arises. Feelings of this sort are presupposed in the basic appeal that I have spoken of; they must already be present if a child is to identify himself with another—say, an injured party. What we shall expect, gradually emerging at least, is the assertion of principle over impulse: for out of this appeal there develops a new habit of regarding others' feelings, no longer entirely dependent on the sympathetic promptings of the moment. Similarly a scientist acquires the habit of referring his theories to the facts and especially to such facts as prove recalcitrant—which is unlikely to be his natural impulse in the first place.

Morality, according to Piaget—where it does not derive from authority—originates in reciprocal dealings.[1] There may be more truth in the ancient fiction of a first contract than we generally allow. 'I will so long as you do', might be a mere expression of self-seeking, but already it trembles on the balance; and once we add, 'I am not obliged to, because you didn't', then moral concepts have emerged. Certainly the full-blown notion of a contract already presupposes morality, but in another sense it may also create it. I may remark here in passing that Piaget's view on this matter seems very close to those that I wish to advocate. The concepts involved in distributive justice are, according to him, *a priori* to this extent, that they represent a norm

'towards which reason cannot help but tend as it is gradually purified and refined. For reciprocity imposes itself on practical reason as logical principles impose themselves morally on theoretical reason'.[2]

But the notion of justice is more complex; often, along with certain other terms, as 'impartiality' and 'equality', it is made to serve in several rôles at once. A great part of justice is nothing other than that implicit universality of moral judgement which has figured so largely in recent discussion—a requirement which, we saw earlier, progressively emerges with reflection.[3] 'Reason cannot help but tend' to the recognition of this basic demand—that where differences are made differences should be shown: that having passed one verdict on some one present case we must justify ourselves in judging another differently. And to justify ourselves is to point to a relevant

---

[1] Cf. J. Piaget, *The Moral Judgement of the Child*, London, 1932, pp. 275 ff.
[2] Ibid., p. 316.          [3] Cf. above, pp. 111 ff.

dissimilarity between the two cases. Yet, as Macbeath has pointed out, this principle of justice has a special status; it is not peculiar to morals or even to axiology. The casual principle, too, in its sphere, serves to formulate or represent the same inherent demand of rationality. Indeed it seems that some principle such as this, however imperfectly applied or grasped, is implicitly involved in all thinking: namely, that where different conclusions are drawn or different procedures adopted, factual differences must be cited to justify them. No doubt there is a trivial sense in which two non-identical cases can always be spoken of as 'different'; our concern here is with relevant differences. What we see or count as different cases represents a classificatory system, a system of concepts and classes; and that in turn will reflect our way of regarding the material —what 'strike us as analogies' in Wittgenstein's phrase. To arrive at such a common point of view is the whole project of collective inquiry.

That, then, is one sense of the term 'justice'. I shall not seek to deal with retributive justice—though there remains one further use of the term that will occupy me directly. But let us notice first that impartiality, in effect, is no more than the same notion used in special circumstances. To commend a man as impartial, we shall find, is to commend him for applying this principle, that like cases should be dealt with in like manner—for applying it, however, in circumstances where natural impulse alone, apart from all principle, might well have prompted him to do otherwise. Every man has his whims and his preferences which are ordinarily harmless; it is only on special occasions that their repression becomes an urgent matter. And again parents, potentates and judges have so often been subject to temptation, where bribery, favouritism, nepotism and a dozen other claims clamour to be heard, that merely not to make arbitrary exceptions is felt to deserve a name to itself. Perfect justice for the same reason is sometimes felt to be slightly inhuman, for all these are very human weaknesses. And besides, the law that a judge has to administer is unlikely to be a thing beyond criticism, and may be inhumane in the extreme; and yet a just judge, in this present sense, will merely enforce it as it stands. Later, indeed, the more sophisticated notion of equity or mitigation arises, and the case may be considerably altered.

So far we say, then, that any law can be administered justly—which is merely not to make arbitrary exceptions. And here we have one use of the word; but of course the law itself may be unjust. A rule of conduct that is grossly unfair may nonetheless be impartially applied; the demand for universality is admitted. A man may, for instance, distinguish human beings for the purposes of moral judgement, as white and coloured, or as clansmen and the rest, and apply the rule perfectly universally. But if we achieve another and better outlook, bringing with it another classification, what differences seem relevant will change too. But now what we call a just law will be nothing but the notion of an ideal applied in the particular context; the two notions 'right' and 'justice' coalesce, and often, indeed, the two terms are interchangeable. We postulate a point of view to be arrived at, to emerge from the process of inquiry, on which rational men might generally agree. But justice now, like the older notion 'righteousness', is no longer being treated as a separate principle: it is equated with morality as a whole—or perhaps we should say with morality as somewhat legalistically conceived.

I have spoken so far of the demands of utilitarianism and the demands of justice. Utilitarianism, egoistic or universalistic, has always been represented by its adherents as a pre-eminently rational moral system. In some measure the claim may be legitimate: we normally seek to satisfy our impulses and that demands no special justification, but with a rule that forbids it the case is different. Some further account, we feel, is called for here. In face of this sort of prohibition 'Why shouldn't I?' is the inevitable question. The answers may be complex and various—satisfaction is not the only value that we appeal to in justifying rules—but the form of challenge is fundamental in moral criticism. And where it is pressed home and never met, where we ask 'What good does it do?' and get no answer, the rule in question will presently lose its hold.

It may be useful to pause here to pull together the threads of a rather rambling exposition. I have spoken first of merely prudential reasoning; where a man is asked a reason for his conduct, the basic reason, the simplest that he can give, is that he likes one thing or dislikes another. And here what we take as our starting-point is merely what everyone finds obvious. Supposing that some moral philosopher fails—or professes to fail—to see or feel the force of this answer, then, certainly, we shall be hard put to it to make it plainer; but he may find it still harder, perhaps, to show how there can be any account of practical principles on those terms. From the satisfaction of these particular desires we proceed, following the natural course of reflection, to the greatest satisfaction on the whole; and again, from our own satisfaction we go on to take account of other people's. This, like any advance to a new point of view in morals or elsewhere, presupposes imaginative powers, and here sympathetic imagination. Mere social feelings prompt us to care about other people's suffering or well-being; but, the issue being once presented, a further principle, that of justice, makes us go further and recognize a rule. This in turn is a particular application of a more general principle of thought and action involved in the very notion of rationality: here, too, there arises the demand that moral estimates and verdicts should be universal—a demand that we apply with increasing rigor as our judgement develops or matures.

In these simple rules or procedures we have at least the foundation of moral argument. Professor Findlay in a noteworthy article, which tackles the question directly from this point of view, has covered most of this ground; however he has also more to add.[1] Findlay is one of the few moral philosophers, as distinct from psychologists and sociologists, to have recognized progress or direction in moral thought. Further he lays down a distinction between what he calls 'developed' ethical responses and those that are 'undeveloped' or 'distorted'.

'Such a distinction (he writes), is valuable because there has, in fact, been a definite line along which the attitudes that we call "ethical" have

[1] See 'Morality by Convention', *Mind*, liii, 1944, pp. 142–69. Cf. also *The Structure of the Kingdom of Ends*, British Academy, 1957.

developed, as life has grown progressively more secure and easy, and as men have had more time to ponder over moral questions. . . . We may sufficiently suggest the kind of movement we are thinking of if we say, somewhat banally, that it leads from arbitrary taboo and tribalism to the reasoned pursuit of what is genuinely best for everyone. It is, in fact, the kind of movement that occurs in every field, as soon as men become conscious of the strangeness of including certain objects or phenomena in a class, although they differ widely from the majority of its members, and of excluding other objects or phenomena although they very much resemble the majority of its members. In all such cases reflective thought tends readily to *drop* the former from the class in question, and to *extend* the boundaries of the class until it includes the latter.'[1]

This development that Findlay speaks of is not merely histroical but natural; the usage that he seeks to distinguish is to recommend itself to 'reasonably reflective people'.[2] At this stage there is no need to dwell on my sympathy with this general approach; I differ only with the conventionalist terms in which it is cast.[3] To prefer the formed preferences of reflective people would seem to me as arbitrary and irrational as any of the prohibitions or taboos that Findlay relegates to the nonage of morality, if it were not that we suppose that reflection is likely to bring us nearer to the truth. That apart, we might rather appeal to numbers, and cruder and more garish moral systems will then be more likely to gain acceptance.

This is, however, to digress, for we have not yet done with the tests of developed judgement; besides those I have spoken of Findlay adds others. First, here as elsewhere, we expect to find in well-developed judgement a close concern for the facts of the case; in morality no less than science judgement must submit to the findings of careful and critical observation. But further—a point that I have touched on already but not developed—morality

---

[1] Ibid., p. 151.  [2] Ibid., p. 152.

[3] Apart from the title and many passing references, we are told explicitly, of the axioms of utilitarianism, that 'we simply should not *call* any set of feelings "ethical" in which they were not followed and approved'. (Original italics.) And he repudiates the notion of a 'super-normal intuition' as a source of moral knowledge. Ibid., p. 161.

P

especially requires a kind of imaginative capacity; the facts are not only to be cognized, not only known, they are to be made real or brought home to the imagination. For what moral issues involve is primarily the feelings of people; hence the extent to which we share or enter into them, feel them and make them vivid, will play a large part in deciding what judgement we make.[1] Differences of this sort, I have suggested, appear in theoretical discussion too, and are, indeed, far more deeply involved in it than is generally allowed. The difference between bare intellectual assent to a possible view and imaginative identification, entering into it, is a great and a crucial one: and all progress in inquiry in its deeper or wider bearings depends on this capacity, on our power of seeing different possibilities and taking them seriously, of adopting new points of view. Yet broadly the distinction holds: that we imagine others' feelings and enter into their views, into those of every person involved, both the few and the many—the single delinquent, let us say, and the anonymous, remoter victims of his wrong-doing—this is still typically the demand of morality and moral reflection.

Findlay draws attention to one other important mark of ethical attitudes; it is that they progressively concern themselves with inward as against external things. Sensitivity to motive and intention distinguishes a developed morality. It is only, he writes '*to the extent* that agents know what they are doing, that we should say that we are *ethically* affected by them: whatever they may do unwittingly, even if it happens to be a part or a consequence of some conscious action, can never be a source of *ethical* emotion'.[2] Though he later observes, justly enough, that we might not withdraw the name 'ethical' altogether, but would rather speak of an 'undeveloped' or 'distorted' moral sense.[3] The same tendency towards the 'internalization and individualization of conscience' that appears with progressive moral development has been noted by Professor Ginsberg and others.[4]

[1] Ibid., p. 158.　　　　　　　　　　[2] Ibid., p. 153.
[3] Ibid., p. 154.
[4] See his *Moral Progress*, Frazer Lecture, 1944, p. 23.

The great value of this distinction between more or less developed moral systems is something on which I have already dwelt; for without it a philosopher can do nothing better than draw an arbitrary line—either excluding what is plainly moral in some sense, or else putting all morality, crude or mature, into a single, comprehensive locker. What we shall need, however, is not only to distinguish the different forms but also to bring them into relation; we may do so by means of this notion of different degrees of development. So far Findlay's account chimes perfectly with ours; but at one point I find myself in sharp disagreement with it. He finds in morality in general what he calls an authoritarian spirit—something that it never wholly outgrows: for we demand the acceptance of our views; we expect other people to conform to them. And where this acceptance fails,

> 'we make our appeal above the unreflective heads of "present company" to "the great company of reflective persons" wherever they may be situated in space or time'.[1]

I find this account pleasant, but puzzling too; it is, perhaps, hard to make it consistent with what has gone before. To expect and to demand of other people that they should agree with our views are two different things, and not only different but incompatible: if our expectations are justified, it would seem that the demand is superfluous. Otherwise, that is, if they disagree, they are simply false. Conflicting tests cannot define the same attitude: moreover it was made a matter of definition that any attitude to be counted as 'ethical' should submit to the test of reflection—including, as such a test must, sensitivity to the reactions of other reflective people. It is hard to see how it can be marked at the same time by its rejecting the results of just that test. Alternatively if, as rational people, we stand by our belief that posterity will vindicate our out-numbered right, as against what Findlay calls 'present company', we must have grounds that we can offer for saying so: and good grounds must be such, at least in principle, as can hope to gain general acceptance. Findlay's whole account apart from this one passage—here in line

[1] Ibid., p. 160.

with that of Piaget, of Flugel and others—suggests a morality passing from intolerance to criticism, from authoritarian to egalitarian; this present doctrine seems something of an anachronism. Or, if not, it means no more than this: that in morals or elsewhere when we call a given view 'right' we are committed to rejecting others inconsistent with it; to contradicting anyone who calls it 'wrong'.

Findlay's general account may be taken as representative of the trends that have been found in the development of moral thinking. I have neither space nor competence to attempt any general survey of the literature of the subject, but it may be useful briefly to mention the work of one or two other writers. Piaget's account in the work already quoted, and Flugel's in *Man, Morals and Society*, indicate the same general tendencies. And I have also named Ginsberg who, in his discussion of moral progress emphasizes, as Findlay does, the increasing internalization of conscience. He stresses, too, the progressive rationalization of moral codes, which follows from criticism and reflection. Another tendency which he dwells on is that towards increasing comprehensiveness: thus 'all men'—not merely the group—is the constant theme of the great ethical teachers.[1] And this is, in turn, the natural consequence of that exercise of sympathetic imagination to which Findlay—with a glance back to Adam Smith—assigns so large a place in moral reflection. Morality, which begins in the recognition of reciprocal rights, is bound up in the first place with the group. Group sentiment accompanies and upholds it; the appeal to the service of the community is the first great objective that we can set before ourselves to rise above personal interest. It serves in place of the appeal to abstract right. Yet there is in morality a dual tendency: once established, at first within the group, its own law demands its extension; the very tests that we apply lead us forward—though the process, as we know, may be hard and slow.

In this connexion we may perhaps add, to those already mentioned, the name of Freud. What Freud originally saw in morality

[1] Ibid., pp. 19–21. Findlay also makes this point, and shows it as following from the other tendencies he has noticed. Loc. cit., pp. 161–2.

was primarily the embodiment of social forces; morality represented tradition, working through parental authority—the graven image of hereditary law.[1] Now what such a picture shows is surely true; it is true on its positive side. That need not be disputed. But a tradition, we have seen, need not be static—whatever tendency it also retains towards primitive inertia or stasis. A living tradition is one which instructs those who inherit it to think and experiment; and hence we find Freud himself, moved forward by the inherent direction of the technique that he himself had created, finally enunciating the slogan 'Where id was', (which also means 'where super-ego was') 'there ego shall be'.[2] But what is this concept of the ego, or what rôle is it called on to play? The notion can hardly belong to the causal or the mechanical psychological system that Freud had originally conceived. It may first have represented no more than part of the organism in touch with its external environment, mediating between that and the rest. In these terms it is first introduced, but it comes in time, perhaps, to mean something very different.

Suppose we look closer at this mediation, and ask between what parties it is to mediate, or to what end. Broadly speaking, instinctive needs, seeking satisfaction, are set against the world as it is—as experience and thought find it to be—which determines how satisfaction is to be got. We may respond to it realistically or otherwise; we are said to respond unrealistically where we respond to it, not as it is, but as our own phantasy has made it seem. A burnt child afterwards fears fire, naturally and realistically enough; a neurotic adult, tied unconsciously to early phantasies, fears—or behaves as if he feared—certain objects that do not in fact burn. Suppose now that these fears are removed: made conscious of his own real desires, and coming to see things as they are, he seeks satisfaction where it is obtainable. Now he is responding realistically again, and we attribute the response, no longer to the super-ego or id, but to the ego.

This is an attractively simple picture; its application seems simple too, so long as we think chiefly of a more or less animal organism

---

[1] Cf. e.g. *The Ego and the Id*, p. 47.
[2] *New Introductory Lecture on Psycho-Analysis*, p. 106.

seeking straightforward sensual satisfactions. But suppose now that the altered responses are those or an artist or a teacher; or again, more humdrum still, of a husband in his dealings with his family, or perhaps with his employers or his friends. First, it is normally held that psychological hedonism was refuted over two hundred years ago; a normal man seeks love, power, useful employment, the well-being of other people or realization of abstract causes; but not simply or primarily satisfaction. And if a more realistic response is not necessarily a more satisfying one, we shall have to look somewhere else for a standard. Standards are not far to seek: a man acts within a social context, conforming or failing to conform to an elaborate system of social rules. Suppose after all that satisfaction is our sole object; the shortest way to get it, if we like acceptance and approval, will very likely be conformity. And that is, as far as it goes, an excellent reason for conforming. Let us give it all weight: yet I suppose that no mature person conducts his life solely, or even primarily, on the consideration of such grounds as this; and it can hardly be the aim of analysis to reduce men to the state of their moral infancy. But even if it were, the thing is impossible, unless other criteria operate first. Let us return to our previous example: the teacher or the artist, made conscious of his own desires and fears, finds his real powers newly released—a change that we shall call an improvement. There are, of course, standards to appeal to. We start, as we are bound to start, from those that are generally accepted; so that we know what to call a release rather than a suppression of a man's gifts. If other people presently observe and appreciate the change, their praise and any satisfaction that it brings, would be a further reason for preferring it. But meanwhile the artist is doing better work; the teacher is meeting his pupils, perhaps, with a new friendliness and warmth, or with a new authority; and that is the immediate satisfaction. The work is more satisfying because it is better, not 'realistic' because it is satisfying. Suppose, to take another example, that we have to deal with certain feelings of guilt. No analyst would get far in his work, surely, who could not recognize and respect, let us say, remorse for some wrong really done, as distinct from—though perhaps reinforcing—the self-accusation of morbid phantasy.

The upshot appears to be this: once we leave primitive situations behind us, what we mean by a realistic response is simply a right or a good one. We attribute behaviour to the ego—and the notion seems to be an irreducibly evaluative one—in so far as the agent's moral consciousness approaches autonomy and maturity.[1]

I have spoken of a general tendency of moral reflection which brings divergent views into conformity. We may see how the different demands—the tests which moral feelings or judgements, if they are to sustain their claims, must subject themselves to—reinforce and grow out of one another. Reason everywhere eliminates what is arbitrary; it demands that where procedures differ a ground for the difference should be shown. And that demand appears in morality

---

[1] I am tempted to add a few suggestions on the working of psycho-analysis itself, since it is after all a special case of the sort of general process that we have been concerned with; here too, though in a particular way, new attitudes come with a new vision. Mr. A. C. MacIntyre in his monograph *The Unconscious* (London, 1958) has suggested that the process is essentially one of redescription; and after all it is no novel discovery that people may tend to behave differently when their own behaviour is described to them in new ways. The discovery is the extent of such changes—provided that the description is one of a certain kind, and given under certain favourable circumstances. But even here what we find is not wholly new; we already know the kind of difference that matters.

For such a description to be efficacious it must, first, be cast in concrete terms and not abstract; it must be so cast as to bring the matter home to the person whom it concerns. But again it must be such that he can accept it: too vivid a concrete description, offered in circumstances where it most obviously applies, may be effective indeed—but it may have just the opposite effect to what we desire. We seek, as it were, to get as near as possible to reality, and yet retain the security of mere ideal experiment. Now the real situation is supplied by the transference; the redescription that analysis provides is as concrete as possible, and is a description of present goings-on. At the same time the situation is such that the description can be accepted—in a relationship sealed off, so to speak—where offered elsewhere it would be too much to accept, too violent or unmanageable. And one hears of certain forms of therapeutic practice which rightly start by emphasizing that all analysis rests on a human relationship, and end by a relationship so human that the counter-transference virtually swamps the transference. Here no doubt the material is all present, but none of it usable. That would illustrate one half, without the other, of the union-in-difference, the more-than-usual compresence of opposing factors, that analysis represents.

as the basic principle of justice which requires equal treatment of human agents. Secondly what we require wholly generally is to remove differences of attitude and feeling, to bring divergent views into line. These requirements so far are, as I say, not specific to any one department. But next, where satisfaction to be found is taken as a reason for doing something, we enter the field of prudence, if not yet of morals. But pre-moral feelings already prompt us to consider the satisfactions and pains of those near us; and the principle of justice, applied to this material, serves to extend our pursuit of satisfaction to include other people as well as ourselves. Here we have the first and barest form of that other essential mark of moral reflection; the use of sympathetic imagination to enter into other people's experience. This in turn, progressively deepened, and joined with the principle of justice, will lead to the development of our code in at least two important directions. It will lead first to the enlargement of the group that any moral system takes cognizance of—for outsiders have feelings and interest too—and again, within that group itself, to an increasing concern with purpose and motive. One first natural prompting in case of injury may always be to discharge our angry feelings on the person we think of as its cause: the later habit of entering into the situation from other points of view than our own, may lead us to restrain ourselves in certain cases. We restrain ourselves where we see that the action was done in ignorance, or that the damage that followed was accidental. And in general, where mere justice requires nothing more than that we impartially apply whatever code of conduct we find, a more searching application of the same principle—a deeper view of what constitute different classes of people or of what human action involves—will progressively humanize and refine the code itself.

I shall only add a few final remarks. These procedures, progressively applied, will tend to bring moral judgement into conformity; ideally we postulate complete agreement as the point towards which inquiry in general directs its course. But we regulate expectations by experience too, and experience teaches us that there are limits to the agreement that we can realistically hope for. We find that in scientific and in historical studies, and certainly we find it in morals. One might, indeed, construct some kind of scale, with mathematics —at least large parts if not the whole of mathematics—forming one end, and aesthetics, perhaps, at the other. Beyond that we may pass over from the region of rational inquiry into that of mere taste. But I fear that philosophy itself would come, along with art, near the lower end. Now I have argued earlier that we regulate ideals by actualities; where all agreement breaks up we abandon the very notion of a solution—of any right answer to be found. But elsewhere we need not run to either extreme; and indeed the concept of a scale is too simple, for there are different ways as well as different degrees in which these things are measurable. Limits remain nonetheless beyond which we cannot rationally hope to find answers in morals, or indeed speak of views or answers at all; but that, one is bound to remark, would seem a poor reason for not persevering in the search, or standing by defensible views where and in so far as we possess them. Here, no doubt, a misuse of the correspondence theory of truth has done much to enforce the feeling that 'objectivity' must be a matter of all or nothing; and again this philosophical theory certainly represents a way of thinking that is pre-theoretical too. It represents a picture or an assumption on which our minds naturally seize. Now it seems that if objects or facts, corresponding to the statements that we make, are what must guarantee their objective status, no half-way position is conceivable: objects do not exist more or less. Given this picture of objectivity, it cannot admit of degree; but let us think rather in terms of attainable agreement, and the conclusion we reach may be different.

Let me lastly observe that the present section and what I have said here, is meant as not retracting but only as balancing what I have said earlier in the chapter. We possess general criteria and general rules; nonetheless it is in concrete situations within the institutions of a given moral code—as soldiers or solicitors, as parents or husbands—that we must act and judge.

## III

My purpose here does not extend to a treatment of the content of morality; there are, however, certain concrete issues, aspects of moral life which call for some account—those, namely, which the principles so far outlined may seem not to cover. I am sure, besides, that these are issues that deserve more attention than they get: though as to the first that I mean to speak of, I can do little more than point to the problem. My hope is that other writers may throw more light on it.

Pleasure, certain cultural values, and virtues such as honesty and charity: these—for moral philosophers who still think it worthwhile to discuss such things—form the chief species of good, or of objects desirable in themselves. But let us consider a man's life leaving aside the fulfilment of common social duties, and culture as well; for relatively few men possess or desire much culture or feel themselves deficient without it. Yet if what remains, these being subtracted, is all that philosophers seem to recognize, that is the pursuit of pleasure or satisfaction, this would, I suggest, leave them with some sense of deficiency. If by hypothesis we deprive people of any further end beside this, we are then virtually obliged to conceive them as seeking or making others for themselves. Some sort of purpose or *raison d'être*, some illusion or cause to devote themselves to, around which they may think their lives—here is surely as deep and general a need as any beyond what sheer biology determines. Even another person's happiness seems to form a sort of focus in a different way from our own, as a mother may live for her children: it is somehow felt as a significant object, as the other is not. Yet after all, a man's own future happiness, serving as a goal or a mark which hope can fix on, towards which his activities are systematically bent, plays the same sort of part in some lives: and no doubt an envisaged future state of affairs is the most natural co-ordinating point around which the present is organized. Yet we are not to think of his present doings and plannings simply as means, deriving their whole significance retroactively, valuable only because of the value of the end that they promote. Rather the reverse is true; men, we know, set up goals artificially, things quite indifferent in themselves, as the locating of an inflated ball between two posts, only to give meaning and interest to their pursuit. A single action that forms part of a pattern, like a gesture in discourse or a movement that is part of a dance, acquires a new quality and value.

Games, it seems, like languages, are meaningful things: and no doubt modern philosophers need not be told that languages, in significant ways, are comparable to games. Now what people look for in games, and in their own lives generally—some sort of direction or goal, or at least some co-ordinating pattern—is something that they also seek in nature as a whole; and this search is called metaphysics. We do not necessarily find what we seek for; yet whatever doubt a long story of controversy—some would maintain of recurrent failure—may throw on the whole enterprise, there can be none that the initial demand remains. We send young people to college to have it weeded out, and then they grow into philosophers; but it is there both in the simple and the sophisticated.

Nor is its presence anomalous. In all things we seek system and order, and we press the demand as far as we find that it will go. We must also suffer the tuition of experience and possibly are sometimes slow to learn. But the grand charge lodged in the indictment of metaphysics, that, namely, of lacking meaning, will seem a strange one once we see it as pre-eminently an attempt to find meaning—beyond local and limited things. Indeed the attempt may fail; but to condemn the very project beforehand for not having already what it sets out to get, is surely hard. On the other hand the demand that the metaphysician 'give his statements meaning' is legitimate enough: provided always that it is not merely a sophisticated kind of obtuseness, a refusal to learn a new language or to understand the meaning that has, perhaps, already been given them.

We are digressing, I fear, but not so far from our real business as it may seem. Our suggestion is that ordinary people not only seek satisfaction in their lives, but further that they set a special value on what they find meaningful, and call worthwhile. A language, like a game, as I have said, is a system or pattern of activities, which in part take their character from the whole; a word is meaningful as belonging to such a system. When Wittgenstein spoke, as he so often did, of the 'use' of words, when he compared them to tools, he was evidently not concerned with their utility; he was not offering what one might call a pragmatic justification for linguistic practices, in terms of the ends that they subserve. The picture he drew was of a system in which various elements play a part, and as playing such a part they have meaning. The word gets its force as a word from the pattern that it forms part of; this, joining it with others, gives it its character: and that, perhaps, is much how ordinary people feel about the day-by-day pushing forward of their lives—which they would never willingly think of as meaningless.

It is in these terms we shall best understand the special value set on intellectual culture, on science, metaphysics and art. The bald statement that knowledge is valuable, endorsed by appeal to intuition, will perhaps carry little conviction; besides we do not want to know the number of blades of grass in Hyde Park. Rather, as Ross observes, what we value is explanation; we seek to understand, to make sense of things, and this is to bring what seems at first arbitrary or anarchic into intelligible interconnexion. Things materially near and impinging, first set human faculties to work; early thought builds next the ground, it arises in immediate needs. Yet later it comes to build for its own sake: as in games we set ourselves arbitrary goals, objects themselves indifferent, so speculation goes in search of new problems to find material on which to exercise its powers, say, in remote regions of history or prehistory. It is also true, as we know, that men may partly fear what they seek; and amidst those strange seas of thought that the poet speaks of there is many a snug corner of scholarship, a cabin or a bachelor's retreat, fixed with everything requisite to a voyage—to last us until we reach port.

It is certain that we get satisfaction in what we find meaningful, and that alone would account for our valuing it; yet we seem to value it beyond that satisfaction—or better, in Mill's language, to find in it a different quality of satisfaction. Inasmuch as we have new criteria here we are not to look for deductive arguments to derive them from the old. Yet it would be satisfactory, if what I have said is true, to show these views as lying in the natural line of moral development or to make them intelligible in their setting. And how that is to be done is less clear to me.

A creature, if we can imagine such a creature, who literally took no thought for the morrow, evidently could not even pursue for himself the maximum satisfaction. Only in our reflection on the past and preparation for the possible future are we people at all; and only people can pursue moral ends. The problems that we are coasting on here have a large hinterland behind them, which I do not intend to explore. But we must remark, at least, that what we have said— that only as persons can we pursue moral ends—will not serve by itself to prove personality valuable. The necessary condition of morality need not itself be a moral object. And again what Bradley tells us may be true enough, that a fully developed mind or personality will only find itself, or find satisfaction, in some system of co-ordinated ends; that a fragmentary life of odds and ends, even of successive passing pleasures, would leave in it a deep discontent. Here, however, our sole criterion is still at bottom the utilitarian one; our reason for preferring what is meaningful will be that it is really more satisfying. Bradley apparently holds further that, since what we always seek is self-satisfaction—or the satisfaction of a realized self, of a fully developed personality—the satisfaction that such realization brings must also be the greatest. If so, we should need no special account of the value that we set on meaning; the value that we set on satisfaction would suffice to cover it. Suppose that in general it is so: we still could not lay it down as a law. Where hoggish satisfactions engross and fill up a consciousness which slouches from one to the next, never lifting its sight to look beyond, the satisfaction may be very great after all: if so, must we infer that we should rationally recommend it? Thought and reflection, more-over, which deepen the meaning of experience and add a new glaze, colouring it with a reference to other things, may also take the edge off its immediacy. And, indeed, the experience of childhood is usually thought the more vivid.

This much seems clear, that such a state of satisfied consciousness as we have imagined, at least if we take it to an extreme, could not be one that a rational being could choose for himself, unless he chose not to be; for it would no longer be himself, or any person, that would drift through this opiate dream, this continuum of meaningless pleasure. For the rest, the best I can say is that this demand for meaning in things generally, and in one's own activities in particular, is one that is virtually universal once a certain mental level is reached; and the search for a coherent point of view in any field, that will serve to reduce what seemed arbitrary to order, must everywhere express a need of rational people. It is part of what is involved in rationality. But these are questions, if only moral philosophers could be brought to discuss them, on which new light would certainly be welcome.

We have spoken of several aspects of morals at least in broad terms. Honesty, which represents our common social code, the pursuit and promotion of well-being, the worth and the meaningfulness of a man's life—these are the chief aims and standards which men have adopted or set themselves. But there remains one other that has been held in equal or greater esteem, namely the notion of honour; and honour requires our attention, for the same reason that meaning required our attention, that our previous principles do not appear to cover it. But in this case, I believe, further reflection may do more to reduce the discrepancy.

We often find that the name for the pre-eminent species of a genus is also used to cover the genus itself: and the word 'honour' has sometimes meant little less than virtue or moral worth. But why it has dropped out of use so entirely and silently—though surviving in talk of national as distinct from personal dealings and in the one living phrase 'professional honour'—is a question that might well repay inquiry; which, however, I must leave on one side. At all events philosophical truth is not confined to the twentieth century and we ought to notice so important a concept.

The term, as I say, has often been comprehensively used; but virtue itself can of course be differently conceived. And those who have spoken less often of virtue and more of honour have doubtless thought of it primarily from the point of view of a man's standing among men, of his holding up his head among his fellows. And 'honours'—the plural form having a more limited sense—are the badges of royal or public esteem. Indeed the two notions can be split apart, yielding Iago's invidious paradox,

> 'Her honour is an essence that's not seen,
> They have it very oft that have it not . . .'

Secondly honour, along with its general equation with virtue, relates to certain particular virtues, indeed to the prime virtue, as it was commonly regarded, properly belonging to the two sexes: in men, courage, with a proper sense of the respect due from others, and in women, chastity. These, in more military and chivalrous times, were taken as the cruces of virtue—and their connexion with reputation is clear enough. A woman publicly known to be unchaste, or a man who bore public indignities, could not hope to be paid further respect; and since we find that in ordinary people the great brace of morality is the thought of their neighbours and their neighbours' views, that has to be reckoned with. Someone openly branded, hooted at or ostracized by self-respecting people, will need more than usual cohesion of moral texture if he is to listen to the edicts of his conscience with quite the same deference as formerly. Only let his wrong-doings be unknown to the world and then in general his standards may hold up; but a man broken in self-respect, which in most of us requires the respect of others, cannot have much further real chance.

These facts, no doubt, underlie and go a long way towards justifying the older sort of attitude to honour; and indeed it appears that the notion still survives expressed in this weaker term 'self-respect'. The peculiarity of the old view might seem to be that it not only permits but requires of us the lively resentment of affronts; a man is to stand on his prerogatives and exact what is properly due to him. It is, no doubt, still the same notion at work: one who can be imposed on or neglected will lose status in the eyes of other people, and presently, therefore, in his own. What differs is rather the social code, and the number of openings that it gives for a man who stands nicely on his honour. The elaboration of etiquette in the seventeenth century, with all its gradations of rank and complex rules of precedence and procedure, must vastly have enriched a man's chances of giving and taking offence. Yet it is true that our standards have changed too, and honour counts much less than it did; nowadays when we assert personal rights we often do it with something like apology, or at least it is no longer a matter of life and death—as it might have been when duelling was still in use.

Another eminent code, less often put in practice, positively enjoins the sufferance of affronts and makes a virtue of meekness. The more usual view, I suppose, is that one is entitled but not obliged to resent ill-usage; and yet there is a limit to that too. The ethic of honour may have more hold on us than we recognize, for certainly there is a point at which we think it blameworthy that a man tamely lets himself be imposed on—he has after all a duty to himself. Now of all this there is much that might be said: first as to the more exaggerated claims of honour, it seems that even in its heyday there were scoffers, and scoffers not so close to mere cynicism as Falstaff. For the rest, in so far as honour is equated with other particular virtues or with virtue generally, it presents no new problem of its own. But in the generality of men the visible evidence of due regard from others is necessary to uphold their self-respect, which in turn is the mainstay of other standards. The question is how far such demands are to be pressed; and that must vary greatly from one society to another, for what in fact will lower men in their fellows' eyes varies no less. It is true that our own society bears witness that the exacting demand of the seventeenth century can be given up without an obvious decline either of courage in face of emergency or of general honesty in social dealings. But whether this code of conduct would prove equally workable in other societies, not so pacific or well-policed as ours, is something that cannot be shown.

Self-defence, with the defence of one's prerogatives, has always been regarded as a right: but to guard one's honour, for those who have thought in terms of honour, has been a duty—though a self-regarding duty, no doubt, like the duty not to let good faculties rust. Partly reasonable as the view may prove, perhaps it is partly based in confusion too. Thomas Browne speaks of honour as 'an external adjunct, in the honourer rather than the person honoured'.[1] Now that is simply to identify honour and reputation, which can hardly be right on any terms. But perhaps a confused half-identification contributed something to the older ethic; so that 'honour', which also meant virtue, was thought of as a *quasi* substantial thing, which it became one's duty to keep and guard—a possession, as a woman's honour, in the once-trite image, was said to be the jewel of her dowry. And as to meekness, again, that may have its limits and dangers too. To let other people impose too much is surely to do them no real service; and any man not very sure that he is genuinely a saint does himself no good in submitting to it. This, then, establishes a duty for most people; for we must be content to act within our own characters, even though we recognize other and higher possibilities. But in general the claims of honour, it seems, admit of reflective examination and assessment along such lines as these; they do not require us to go beyond those tests and principles that we have already taken account of—but there remain certain large qualifications that we must not conclude without noticing.

Though it is true that a man is sometimes blamed for meekly enduring too much, the case remains very different here, where one's own wrongs are in question, from those that concern someone else's. Within limits, at least, we allow that it is for the wronged party himself to decide, and in general we may waive our own rights; a thing which no one else can do for us. Here we touch on further and fundamental problems which would certainly require deeper study if what I had set out to offer here were a general treatment of moral philosophy. At the very centre of our moral attitudes we find this notion of a person, with all the special consequences that it

[1] *Religio Medici*, xxxv.

involves where relations between people are at issue. For the notion of rights that one is free to waive or enforce, of choice, responsibility or forgiveness—which lies with the wronged person and no one else—all turn on this same central concept: a concept on which, we may hope, philosophical study will hereafter have more light to throw. But for the present inquiry I must leave it here; I would go on to write more of these problems if I believed that I understood them better.

# Index